Encounter
the
Enlightened

D0369903

Encounter
the
Enlightened

Sadhguru, a profound Mystic of our times

Conversations with the Master

wisdom
tree

encounter the ENLIGHTENED

ISBN 81-86685-60-X

© 2003 Isha Foundation

First Edition: Isha Fest, September 2001
Second Edition: July 2003
Reprint: July 2005

Cover design, typesetting, book layout and
compilation done by: **The Archives of Isha Yoga Center**

Published by:
Wisdom Tree
4779/23, Ansari Road,
Darya Ganj, New Delhi 110 002
Tel : 23247966/67/68

Printed at:
Print Perfect
New Delhi 110 064

Contents

Introduction

Since offering myself in service to Sadhguru Jaggi Vasudev and Isha Foundation several years ago, I have witnessed the transformation of thousands of people in audiences as varied as humanity itself. Whether in the company of the world's most prominent spiritual leaders at the United Nations, eighty million saints and pilgrims at the Maha Kumbha Mela, or surrounded by prisoners on death row, the Master has an ability to arouse passion for truth and an illuminating power that amplifies our hidden Divinity.

As he tirelessly teaches the fundamental elements of inner peace and harmony, which are requirements to deeper inner discovery, I have followed in his footsteps as a volunteer assistant. I am always mindful of what his energy contributes to every being he meets and how he changes the world through his interactions with it moment to moment. His presence makes deep impressions on all who see him. Even in the West, where Gurus and spiritual Masters are not part of our culture, every head turns as he passes. People, unaware of who he is, are compelled to approach him and seek his blessing. Small children call him "holy man" and relate his wondrous presence to their innocent understanding of omnipotence - Santa! Many compare him to Jesus due to his beautiful demeanor, but always people want to know more about him. The Master's presence inevitably raises questions: "Who is this person, what does he teach and how can I learn more?"

As my involvement with Sadhguru expands, I am filled with love, gratitude, joy and the companionship of hundreds of thousands of the people who are also drawn to him. As the intensity and momentum of his presence continues to grow around the world, I feel an awed excitement as I watch the powerful impact he makes on our world. Yet in amusement, I reflect back on my initial encounter with the enlightened.

When I first met Sadhguru, I wasn't even sure he could speak English, and I didn't care. The energy transmitted by him coursed through my body, making every hair stand erect. Then he spoke. Simply, directly, with uncanny logic that can't be denied, yet with words that seemed to portray a deeper meaning that penetrated my heart and soul.

For years I had ached for a spiritual guide, and with painful intensity I prayed for a living Master from the East - one who knew Truth. In 1997 those prayers manifested when Sadhguru made his first U.S.A. visit to Nashville, Tennessee. Shocking he was, to a Westerner who had ingested a lifetime of solace disguised as spirituality. Yet despite my lack of prior exposure to, or intellectual understanding of the Eastern esoteric sciences and yoga, his every word resonated within me. I knew it was Truth. He disarmed me with his honesty and straight talk, burning through the cultural conditioning and resistance that separated me from Truth. His presence was like fresh water dropping on a parched spirit. He transformed me with his patience and grace and I feel an urgency to help make this opportunity available to others.

But how does one share an experience of Truth? Sadhguru says the unbounded is always there for all who can embrace it; yet like me, most of us take a series of small steps to approach the threshold of Truth. We need a Master to lead us through the process of identifying what we are not, in order to move into something greater. Using books and language for the purpose of dissolving into the formless Divine appears to be a contradiction. But when you have found water in a desert full of thirsty people, you must shout, "There is water here!"

Therefore, despite the limitations of using printed language to share this being we experience as Sadhguru, it is worth the risk. His knowing glance, the inflection of his voice, his wonderful humor, infectious laughter and his powerful physical presence will be absent from these pages. But the mystery and grace of such a Divine Being can never be limited. It is the hope of countless disciples and Isha Foundation volunteers that this simple introduction to Sadhguru will ignite a flame of passionate inquiry within all who read his words.

Linda Wright-Wooten
Nashville, Tennessee USA

Foreword

Sadhguru, a very rare being, who dares not to conform to the accepted ambiguous norms just because the majority or the so-called spiritual dictum conforms to it. His teachings are but an outpouring of his inner being, which has risen from inner awakening and not derived from textual scriptures. He is one who cares little for scholarly views and who embraces Truth and stands by it. No one single description can provide an accurate picture of this realized being whose teachings are simple and pristine. What can happen in this person's presence, his energy field, is difficult to perceive for those who are confined to just their sense perceptions.

From eons of spoon-feeding by elders, society, and religion, most people have become insensitive to tasting life firsthand. Fear of ostracism by society if their authority, their rituals and their dogmas are rejected, the fear of standing alone, and the fear of having the respectability tag stripped off has bound humanity today in many ways. An individual reared in today's reality, never seems to know when or where he got his opinions, nor does he seem to care as long as they are approved of.

I happen to be a product reared in this scenario who could never belong but somehow made my life pretty comfortable, just feeling a little stifled at times. Eventually, I thought my life was complete. Then, very accidentally, I came across this devastatingly frank, unstudied and simple being, devoid of stiffness and restraint. An out and out skeptic, I just went as an observer to hear him talk. Only then did I become aware of another dimension of life to which I was totally oblivious, and ended up certain that if anyone could succeed in waking me up from my slumber, it was he. The peeling of the shrouds of ignorance and conditioning began. In thirst of seeking the Ultimate, the conditions and conditioners lost their grip - a natural outcome this was and did not happen in reaction, but through intelligence and awareness. The catalyst in him triggered the dormant questions in me that I didn't even know existed, "Where have I come from? Where do I go hence?" The path I set on was not always smooth. I stumbled with confusions that arose in life within and without. He was always there, if not in person, then otherwise, working through many levels.

A Sathsang or even just a casual talk by Sadhguru can progress into something much more than just casual and tends to get under people's skin, as at times the comments are scathing, more than brutal, but then the end is achieved. One is awakened from slumber. Many people who come merely out of curiosity to his talks, leave mesmerized, disturbed, awed, in love, angry and they always come back for more. Nobody has ever fueled their emotions, their energies and their lives in this manner. Requests and more requests kept pouring in to publish the talks, always duly negated by Sadhguru. When requests in turn became demands, a few of us forced out an "okay," a "go-ahead" nod from the Master.

The most unforgettable times with the Master were spent during a lengthy Wholeness Program when much of the Master's initial work went unrecorded during the formative years of the ashram. This work was definitely not wasted upon us. He would speak to a small group of us, about thirty to thirty-five, sitting under the "leaning tree", sitting on the sand heaps under the starlit sky, standing under the blazing sun in the middle of a ball game, or while walking in a light drizzle or the pouring rain. For the first time, rare glimpses of why this birth for him, the significance of his coming back again to be amidst us, and why the Dhyanalinga, were revealed, some in words and some in silence.

Though he appears very unassuming, we have witnessed a very tough critic restlessly urging us to examine not only our actions, but our very thought processes. The distortion of the mind - its delusions and chaos - was able to be examined thoroughly. The immense patience and unbounded compassion in him always very discreetly guarded and guided the most intimate of our emotions and outbursts. His presence brought out the very best and the very worst in us - many times against our will. He has witnessed our growing up and accepted all the contradictions. At times an intense gaze, a pat on the shoulder, a knock on the head and one is freed not just from the mind's confusions, but, if willing, even from the web of the karmic structure itself.

No single angle provides a complete picture of Sadhguru. Once I was traveling through the Western Ghats with him, when he decided to stop at a forest guesthouse close to the Subramanya temple at the foothills of the Kumara Parvatha. He suggested we visit the temple shrine, a very powerful place.

He asked me to have a shower first, but I was in one of those defiant moods, not ready to take orders from him or anybody, and shot back saying, "I am very clean and even then cleanliness is of the inside and not the outside." Saying this, I plunked myself on the riverbank, refusing to budge. Suddenly, one side of my kurta felt damp and before I realized what had happened, I saw a dog walking away after relieving himself on me! I ran inside to the shower. As I walked towards the car very sheepishly, he cast one glance at me and said, "Now you are ready." When pride arises and before it swells and coagulates, he is always there to pierce it with one glance. Ignorance is driven away at maniac speed!

Another time, when a group from the U.S.A. was inquiring whether he was a vegetarian or not before they would enroll themselves for an in-house program at the ashram, in all earnestness he replied, "Please inform them, I thrive on human kidneys." and after seeing the startled look on the bhramhachari's face, he laughed uproariously.

The difficult choice for us was how to choose what we were going to print. His words kept lingering in my head, "Silence is the way." Where do we start? Volumes and volumes of transcribed discourses and question and answers and much more than that are stored in the archives still unprocessed. How do we go about it? Bhramhacharini Indira was more than eager to supply us with any amount of material that was required from the archives. She is always excited about bringing out anything on Sadhguru that can go public - visuals, audio and now a book!

Swami Devasatva and Rajasekar took on supervising the printing process and were always on the lookout for the missing commas and the forgotten exclamation marks and Swami Nisarga - forever there to see that the excitement doesn't go out of bounds, asks, "What? A book? Don't we all have enough work on our hands?" and adds, "Why don't we tend to the papaya trees instead? We can at least eat the fruit!" And finally succumbing to, "Okay, at least don't choose any controversial questions." And Linda in Nashville was always there with her computer to comply with our numerous requests for proofreading, however unfair and unreasonable. How can I name all those people who came forward with total enthusiasm to make this book happen? This book would not have been possible but for that unsuspecting questioner, who, staking his ignorance, elicited the Master's words of wisdom which at times fell on the questioner as thunderbolts.

After choosing a minuscule portion of Sadhguru's work for printing, the most difficult task we faced was how would a discourse or an answer, spoken to a certain person, in a certain context, translate itself into print? How can an outpouring of energies with just that wisp of a smile, a burst of laughter, a tear that escapes from the damp eyes, or a gesture of the hand and the tone of the voice, convey the subtler nuances, the space and the silence between the spoken words? Can justice be done to our Master's spoken words in the print media? The incredible diversity that he is, can one grasp him as a person, let alone grasp the intricacies or the fabric he is manifested through? Can he be comprehended by reading this book? Maybe not. But then let those who have never seen him or heard him have at least a glimpse of the possibility that he is. This is an invitation to go beyond words.

Bharathi

Note to the Reader

Dear Reader,

The following book is an unedited version of dialogues spoken by Sadhguru Jaggi Vasudev to audiences in various settings. The Master addresses each specific group with a particular intention and approach that will best unfold an inner understanding. While the energy of the Master's spoken word can guide the mind to more effectively embrace the intended message, this guidance is restricted in printed text. For this reason, we never planned to use these dialogues to constitute a book.

But the longing for truth in an age imprisoned within the confines of materialism and dogma, begs for useful tools to transform us and awaken the eternal essence dormant within us. We therefore offer this material to you with the suggestion that you vicariously become a member of the audience being addressed in order to create the necessary mental environment necessary to receive the rare gift being offered.

At the heart of the material in this book is what Sadhguru refers to as, "my tricks to awaken you," a key to transcend the mental conditioning of the three-dimensional world and glimpse the Divine that we are.

Namasthe

me and ME

The impish me
And the absolute ME

Many think is a contradiction
but a perfect complement

my love, my joy, my laughter and my play
but a facade to cover the absolute stillness that I am

my words and my songs, my smiles and my mirth
are but a ploy to entrap you in my limitless void

Both men and Gods were made in this void
O' Beloved if you dare, come—Dissolve.

– Sadhguru

Grace

Ever since the Dhyanalinga temple was built, the parikrama has been a favorite spot for that occasional Sathsang with the Master. The darkness of the starlit night, broken only by the diffused lighting of the temple, the impromptu drumbeats by the inmates formed an ethereal setting for receiving the Grace of the Master...

The nature of the mind is always to accumulate. When it is gross, it wants to accumulate things; when it becomes a little more evolved, it wants to accumulate knowledge. When emotion becomes dominant, it wants to accumulate people; the basic nature is, it wants to accumulate. Mind is a gatherer, always wanting to gather something. When a person starts thinking or believing that he is on a spiritual path, then his mind starts accumulating so-called spiritual wisdom. Maybe it starts gathering the Guru's words, but whatever it gathers, until one goes beyond the need to accumulate – whether it is food or things or people or knowledge or wisdom – it does not matter what you accumulate the need to accumulate means there is an insufficiency. This insufficiency, the feeling of being insufficient has entered into this unbounded being only because somewhere you got identified with limited things that you are not.

If one brings sufficient awareness, and above all a constant sadhana, a practice into his life, slowly the vessel becomes totally empty. Awareness empties the vessel. Sadhana cleanses the vessel. When these two aspects are sustained, when awareness and sadhana are sustained for a sufficiently long period, then your vessel becomes empty. Only when this emptiness arises, Grace descends upon you. Without Grace nobody really gets anywhere. If you need to experience Grace, you have to become empty, your vessel has to become totally empty. If you are living with a Guru just to gather his words, your life will be more wasteful than the ant that gathers food for the winter or rainy season.

If you do not experience the Grace, if you do not make yourself receptive to the Grace, if you do not empty yourself in order to bear the Grace, then the spiritual path is something that needs to be pursued for many, many lifetimes. But if you become empty enough for the Grace to descend, then the Ultimate Nature is not far away. It is here to be experienced. It is here to be realized. It is going beyond all dimensions of existence into the exalted state. It is not tomorrow, not another lifetime. It becomes a living reality.

This whole attitude that wherever you go, you must gather as much as you can, has come into you. One basic culprit has been your education. It always taught you how to gather more and more things. It taught you more and more systematic methods of gathering as much as you can. With this gathering you can make a living. With this gathering, maybe you can enhance the physical quality of life around you to some extent; but this gathering – it does not matter how much you gather, whether what you gather in your mind is local gossip or scientific knowledge or so-called spiritual wisdom – is incapable of liberating you. It is incapable of even taking you an inch closer to Ultimate Nature than where you are right now. To bring the necessary awareness and to constantly cleanse your vessel, it requires sadhana or inner work. There is really no substitute for this.

If you want to jump, if you want to jump the line and you do not want to go through the struggle of being aware, then one must be so innocent that one can simply, absolutely surrender oneself. Surrendering is not something that you *do*. Surrendering is something that happens when *you are not*. When you lose all will, when you have no will of your own, when you have become absolutely willing that there is nothing in you that you call *yourself*, then Grace descends upon you.

But I would always insist: stick to the path of awareness and sadhana. If you naturally jump the line, that is wonderful, but if you try to jump the line, then you will see, you will simply deceive yourself because it cannot be done. It can only happen. It is not a capability that can be made to happen. When you are willing even to drop all your capabilities and your incapabilities, all your likes and dislikes, above all, all the stuff, all the substance that makes you think, "this is me," if you are willing to drop all the substance that is supporting your limited self, then also Grace happens. It is not something that you can do; you can only allow it to happen, but by the process of awareness and sadhana, you can create a situation where it can definitely happen.

The web of bondage is constantly being created only by the way we think and feel. Whatever we are calling as awareness is just to start creating a distance between all that you think and feel and *yourself.* What we are referring to as sadhana is an opportunity to raise your energies so that you can tide over these limitations or these mechanisms through which you have entangled yourself to your thought and emotion.

When I look back, it surprises me that I have spoken so much. It is not like me to talk so much, but I have spoken that much because I did not find enough people who could simply sit with me. So I had to talk and talk and talk; that is the only way they would sit with me. At least those of you who are here should learn, should mature and should sprout into the possibility within yourselves where you can simply sit with me, not gathering, simply sitting. Being a Guru means a burden of thoughts and emotions of a thousand people around him. Please lessen my burden a little bit. Stop your mind's chatter and just be with me.

Unveiling

The morning sun dispels the darkness of the night...

The Master shatters the very foundations of society's limitations in these interactions.

The other day, when you came to invite me for this particular installation function, I was told that this year's motto for Rotary International is, 'Mankind is Our Business'. If mankind is your business, your first business should be yourself, because whatever you do in this world will not be anything other than who you really are. You may have great intentions, you may have great ambitions, you may have many desires, but fundamentally, everything that you do in this world spells out who you really are within yourself.

One thing that I would like to remind you of at this point is, in this world, on this planet, most of the harm, most of the pain, most of the suffering has been caused to people, to humankind, only with good intentions, not with bad intentions. The maximum slaughter and killing has happened on this planet only with good intentions. If you look at the world, the fight is not between the good and the bad. It is always the good people who are fighting. If you are a good Indian, you fight a good Pakistani; if you are a good Hindu, you fight a good Muslim. The better you are, the more you fight. It is not the bad people who are fighting each other. It is always good people with good intentions. The crusaders, who slaughtered millions, also did it with good intentions. Even somebody as brutal as Hitler, who caused so much pain and suffering on this planet, did it with good intentions. He wanted to create a super world – a great intention!

So our intentions are fine, but fundamentally, every human being first needs to work on himself because whatever you do in your ignorance, you are only harming yourself and the world around you. The first and most fundamental responsibility for a human being is to become a joyous human being; because no matter what you are doing, it doesn't matter what you are pursuing in your life, whether it's business, money, power, education, service or whatever else you wish to do, you are doing it because somewhere deep inside you know that this will bring you happiness. Somebody is willing to give his life away to another person, even *that* he does because that is what brings him happiness. Every single action that we perform is springing from an aspiration to be happy. So every single action that man performs on this planet is seeking happiness. Today we are seeking happiness so vigorously that the very life of the planet is being threatened.

In the last hundred years, with the aid of science and technology, much has been done on this planet. There are many conveniences and comforts that could never have been dreamt of a hundred years ago. What royalty did not have a hundred years ago, today ordinary citizens in the world have in terms of comforts and conveniences. In spite of that, it cannot be said humanity is any happier than what it was a hundred years ago. It cannot be said that humanity is any more peaceful or loving than what it was a hundred years ago. So it does not matter with what intentions you do any act, still, fundamentally you are only creating what you are. If man does not take up this project in his life – that he changes himself into a joyous human being by his own nature, not because of something or somebody else – then unknowingly, with good intentions, he will cause much damage to everything around him.

For example, science and technology could have been a great boon for humanity, but today, with science and technology, we have driven this earth to a point where the very life of the planet is under threat. We could be heading for a global suicide. We are on the edge of it in many ways, with good intentions and not with bad intentions. So the first and the foremost activity, the first and the foremost responsibility of a person is to single out his interiority.

Now you have always understood that, to be happy, to be satisfied, to be fulfilled in your lives means you must do what you want to do. You must achieve what you want to achieve in the outside world. Right now, in many ways, people's happiness, people's peace, people's love, is mortgaged to the external situation. Since it is mortgaged to the external situation, they are never going to be happy or truly peaceful.

All those people who depend on external situations to be happy will never know true joy in their lives, because no matter what kind of a person you are, however powerful you are, even if you are a super human, you don't have absolute control over the external situation. Even if there are two people in the family, you don't have total control over the situation. You can manage the external situation only to a certain extent, whereas your interiority can be taken into absolute control. Now whatever you understand as peace, whatever you understand or experience as happiness or love in your life, is a certain experience to which there is a certain inner basis.

There are many ways to understand this. One simple way to know this is: today, if you lose your mental peace totally, you will go to a doctor. He will give you a pill. If you take this pill, your system will become peaceful. Maybe this will last just for a few hours, but you become peaceful. This pill is just a little bit of chemicals. These chemicals enter your system and make you peaceful. Or in other words, what you call peace is a certain kind of chemistry within you. Similarly, what you call joy, what you call love, what you call suffering, what you call misery, what you call fear, every human experience that you go through, has a chemical basis within you. Now the spiritual process is just to create the right kind of chemistry, where you are naturally peaceful, naturally joyous. When you are joyous by your own nature, when you don't have to do anything to be happy, then the very dimension of your life, the very way you perceive and express yourself in the world will change. The very way you experience your life will change.

Now you are not a vested interest anymore because, whether you do something or you don't do anything, whether you get something or you don't get anything, whether something happens or doesn't happen, you are anyway joyous by your own nature. Now your actions will rise to a completely different level. When you are seeking happiness through your actions, you are always enslaved to the external situation. As long as you are enslaved to the external situation, you will always be in some level of suffering because the outside situation is never going to be one hundred percent in your control. Whether it's your own family, your own children, your own business, your own whatever, nothing is ever in your total control at any time. It is in control only to a certain extent. The rest of it is always fluid; anything can happen.

When an 'anything can happen' situation is there outside, man always lives in suffering, many levels of suffering. With this experience, slowly people have started accepting that suffering is a natural part of life. The greatest crime that you can do to humanity is to teach your children that suffering is a part of their life. Once you bring up a child stating that suffering is a part of life, you have taken away the possibility of him being a joyous human being; and if people, if individuals cannot be joyous, there is no question of joy in the world. It doesn't matter what we have, people are still not happy. If you take Western society as an example, anything that you can dream of materially is there, but when I travel there, all I hear are long complaints about life; I hear more misery than anywhere else. So somewhere, all these things that you think will settle your lives, have not settled you.

That reminds me of a story. On a certain day, a sanyasi came and settled down for the night under a tree just outside a village. A man from the village came running to him and asked, "Where is the diamond; where is the diamond?" The swami asked, "What diamond are you talking about?" The man said, "Last night I had a dream.

In my dream, Shiva himself came and said, 'Under this tree, tomorrow, there will be a sanyasi. You go and ask him for a diamond and he will give you the largest diamond in the world, that will make your life.' That diamond, where is it?" The sanyasi said, "Oh! You are talking about that diamond!" and he put his hand into his bag and pulled out a huge diamond, the size of a man's skull, the biggest in the world and handed it to him.

The man received this diamond and all his dreams and desires started projecting as to how he was going to live with this diamond. He hid it in his clothes and went home with great turmoil within him. Now he didn't know whom he should tell and whom he should not tell about the diamond. He didn't know whether he could trust his wife or not. He did not know what to do. He didn't know where to keep it, so he put it under his pillow and tried to sleep. With a stone the size of your skull under your head, definitely you cannot sleep. So all this turmoil plus this stone didn't allow him to sleep the whole night. He suffered and struggled. The next morning he came back to the sanyasi and asked him, "I asked you for the diamond. You pulled it out of your bag and just gave it to me. Such a precious stone, the most precious stone in the world, you just handed it over to me, so easily. For you to do something like this, you must have something within you which is much more valuable than this diamond. What is that? I want to know." Then the sanyasi said, "Sit down here. You just settle down here for a while. I will teach you what that is." Until a man finds this within himself, the most valuable, that which settles his life inwardly and outwardly absolutely, until a person finds this, he will always live as a beggar. It doesn't matter what he has, he is still longing to have something else all the time, and it doesn't matter what he gets to have, always he will remain that way. It is always so.

This will go on even until the moment you reach your deathbed. This process just goes on. People are going on thinking that life is going to settle tomorrow. It doesn't matter what you do. Even for Alexander the Great, conquering half the world, life did not settle. Yes? Alexander, I don't know why they call him 'Great'. Probably they forgot his third name! Alexander the Great Idiot; they forgot that. Why I am saying this is, what did Alexander do in his life? At the age of sixteen he started fighting and went about killing people, unknown people, people who did not know who he was. What was his purpose in life? He went and slaughtered thousands and thousands of people. Sixteen years of non-stop fighting he did. At the age of thirty-two he died a miserable death. He was so miserable because the other half of the world was yet to be conquered.

See, let us say this microphone is your property. Between you and me some dispute has arisen about this property. If we quarrel for five minutes, if you have a little sense, you will feel, "Let this property go. Let me be free from this nonsense first." If you have some sense! For sixteen years if a man has to go on fighting non-stop for something that is not even his, he must be absolutely insane; but it is this kind of people that you have made 'Great'. You are asking your children to read, to believe that this man was great. Tell me, what is his contribution to human life? Unfortunately, all your focus is in this way because this man had the mad ambition of conquering this world and somewhere, everybody is an Alexander the Great, but not potent enough. They don't have the same level of potency. They are impotent Alexanders; but everybody is an Alexander, wanting to conquer something all the time. As long as this is your consciousness, as long as this is the basis of the action that you perform in the world, this world cannot be beautiful. If Alexanders exist here, if your only intention is to conquer everybody in some way, conflict will be the way. This world will always be in conflict. Pain and suffering will be the way of the world.

Even in history books, Gautama the Buddha is only a footnote, he's given just two lines. His whole life was spent for human well-being, but he deserves just two lines in the history books. Even those two lines he earned not because he was a Buddha, not because of his enlightenment, not because of his work, but because he was a king. This has been your attitude; this has been your focus. Unless this focus changes, if mankind really is your business, you yourself must be your first project. The first project is to set yourself right, to get yourself properly focused so that this person is no more a vested interest in this world. If you have to cease to become a vested interest, it is important that you become a joyous human being. When you are happy, you are a very generous human being, isn't it? When you are unhappy, you are a dangerous person, aren't you? I want you to understand this.

Do not go on with the belief that this is a good man and this is a bad man. Is there anybody here who is a good man twenty-four hours a day? This moment you are wonderful, the next moment you turn nasty, another moment you become something else. Isn't that your way? Yes or no? So there is no such thing as somebody being good or bad. It is just that if you bring the necessary awareness and alertness into yourself, if you bring the necessary consciousness into yourself, you will lead a fruitful life. Then you can attend to mankind. When you are happy, you are a very wonderful man for all the people around you, isn't it? Whenever you are happy, you are a beautiful person for people around you. When you are unhappy, you are a nasty and dangerous person to this world. So the first and foremost responsibility is to establish yourself as a joyous human being. If this does not happen, with good intentions you will cause great suffering on this planet, which is happening.

Parents are doing this to their children all the time. With very good intentions, in so many ways they are destroying and distorting a child's life. With very good intentions, not with bad intentions! In so many ways they are ensuring that the child can never enjoy his life, with very good intentions! This is happening simply because they themselves do not know how to be within themselves. If you do not know how to make yourself happy, is there any possibility of you making the world a happy place to live? Is there a chance like that? A man does not know how to manage his body, a man does not know how to manage his mind, a man does not know how to manage his emotions, but he wants to manage the world. It is not going to happen. If you do not know how to take care of yourself, you will definitely not know how to take care of the world. So the first and foremost duty and responsibility of every human being is to settle himself, his inner being.

Every day, I meet many people, and one thing that I see is, they have invented so many ways of torturing themselves. The varieties of sufferings they have created for themselves are unbelievable. The latest news is that God has decided to replace the devil with man in hell because man is such an expert in torturing himself! Wherever you put him, he is miserable. Whatever you give him, he is miserable. He knows how to make misery out of everything. Unless this changes, unless you know how to be within yourself, you will not know how to create the outside because whatever you create will only have the quality of who you are right now.

The whole science of spirituality means to become free from this process where your happiness is mortgaged to outside situations. Generally, people ask me what is the difference between a spiritual person and a materialistic person. One thing I can say is, a materialistic person is one who earns his food, but everything else he begs in his life. His peace, his joy, his love, everything he begs from people around him. A spiritual person is somebody who has everything within himself, he only begs for his food; but if he wants to earn that too, it is no big deal. He can earn that also.

It is very important that the spiritual dimension is brought into 'everybody's lives. Why many people have developed an allergy to spirituality is because somebody always told them, "Spirituality means leaving everything and going to the mountains." Even if you want to go into the forest, there is not enough forest for all of you, and here the forest brigand Veerappan occupies most of it. There is not enough space for you there. Now you had better learn how to be spiritual in your office, in your home, on the streets and wherever you may be. You had better learn that because spirituality is about your interiority, not what you do outside. What you do outside is your choice. How you want to dress, what you want to eat, where you want to be is your personal, individual choice.

Spiritual science is about managing your interiority. For example, now you have modern science to create a conducive external atmosphere for you to live here. Similarly, this is an inner science to create a conducive inner atmosphere because the quality of your life is not dependent on where you are living, or how you are living. How you are within yourself now, that is the quality of your life. Isn't it? This moment, the quality of your life is not decided by what you are wearing, your bank balance, or your educational qualifications. The quality of your life this moment depends on how joyous you are, how peaceful you are. This dimension you have completely neglected.

You came out of your mother's womb, opened your eyes, started looking at the world outside and you got too enamored. You thought everything is out there. It doesn't matter how much you do out there, unless you do something here, to the inner, you will not know what it is to be peaceful, you will not know what it is to be joyous; you will not know how to go beyond the limitations of being just a physical body and a mind. When I say your physical body and your mind, I want you to understand that this body is not yours.

When you were born, this little body that came to you, your parents gave it to you. After that you have just borrowed the big body that you have now from the earth by eating this and that. When you leave, you can't take even an atom of this body. Everything you have to leave. So this body is not really yours. It is a hodgepodge of everything that you have eaten, isn't it? It is on loan to you from the earth. Your mind – this mind is not yours either. Just sincerely look at your mind and see; you will see your mind is society's garbage bin. Everybody who passed your way has thrown some nonsense into your head. That is all you have got. You look into your head and see, your father is sitting here, your mother is sitting there, your teacher is sitting somewhere else, your friend or enemy, the movie that you saw, the book that you read, everything is there, doing lots of things within you. So your mind is just an accumulation of all that you have gathered from the background in which you were brought up.

Now, even if your body and mind are not yours, there is something else which needs to be looked at beyond the dimension of the body and mind. If that dimension is not experienced – once you have come in the human form, if you do not experience yourself beyond the limitations of this body and mind – I would say this human form has been wasted upon you, because, to eat, sleep, reproduce and die, you don't need this kind of a body. You don't need this kind of intelligence. Every worm, every insect, every bird, every animal does these things very efficiently: eating, sleeping, reproducing and dying, isn't it? In fact you are no competition for them. Eating; there are insects and worms which can eat a thousand times their own body weight in twenty-four hours. Now if you weigh fifty kilograms, you should be able to eat fifty tons of food. That would be a real party, isn't it? Right now you have a body, if you eat a little more than what you should eat, you go straight to the toilet or to the doctor. That is the kind of body you have. So in the eating department, you are no competition.

Sleeping also you are no competition because there are birds, insects and animals which can sleep for three months to six months at a stretch. With the most comfortable mattresses, you cannot remain in bed a few more hours than you should, isn't it? Reproduction; to bear one child, how much fuss! They are bearing in thousands, some of them in millions. There also you are no competition. Dying also you make too much fuss about it. That also they are doing gracefully.

So to eat, sleep, reproduce and die, you don't need this kind of a body and this kind of an intelligence. You have come with a different possibility. Now you may be thinking, "No, no. I am not just eating, sleeping and reproducing. I am running an industry, I am a member of the Rotary club." That is fine. The day you have to die – do you know you will die one day? Are you aware of this? Is it okay? Is it all right that you die one day? I bless you with a long life, but you will die one day. Do you know that? So when the moment of death comes, you will see that all that has happened is eating, sleeping and reproducing, nothing else. Generations of people, millions and millions of people who lived on this planet, if you look back and see, that is all that has happened for them also. Very few individuals rose beyond that. Most of the people just lived.

Unless you experience something, unless you know and live with something that is beyond the physical body and mind, human form has gone waste on you. So the most fundamental thing is, if mankind is your business, make yourself your first business. Only then will you see you can do something of lasting value for humanity. If you see in the physical sense, if you look at the lives of Gautama the Buddha or Jesus, and many others like them, they did not do much. In fact they did not do as much work as you are doing – some of you are just overworking yourselves – but their work has remained, simply because they functioned from a different dimension, from within. Either you can work with your body, with your mind, with your attitudes or with a completely different dimension within yourself. If you work with your body and your mind, the life span of your work is just short term. It will be there for some time; it seems to be very relevant today, but tomorrow it might not be of any significance.

See, your father may be a great man. When you were a teenager, you looked at him; he looked like a fool to you. Yes? This is a constant problem that happens between parents and children, isn't it? He might have been a very sensible man, a very great and useful man. Society also thinks he is good, but his children think he is just nonsense, simply because the child has come thirty years later, so he has a different perspective of what is what.

So people who worked with their consciousness, their work has always remained. So working with the consciousness need not necessarily mean you start another movement, another revolution now. With whatever you are doing, whether you are in your industry, your office, or at your home, you can do everything and function from a completely different level of consciousness. Every single act that you perform can come from a completely different dimension within you. When people perform like this, when people perform activity in the world like this, it doesn't matter what they do, this world will be a more blissful place to live. Then really making mankind your business will be truly worthwhile.

It is truly wonderful that you have made mankind your business. Anyway it is your business and everybody's. It is wonderful that you are putting your effort into that. And I once again want to remind you that if mankind is your business, then you, yourself is your first of business.

Questioner: Sadhguru, is there a God? If there is one, where is He?

Sadhguru: Now, if I talk about something which is not in your present level of experience, it cannot be understood. Suppose you have never seen sunlight, and you have no eyes to see sunlight, if I talk about it, it doesn't matter in how many ways I describe it, you will not be able to grasp what sunlight is. Yes? So anything which is not in your present level of experience cannot be understood. So the only next possibility is that you have to believe me. You have to believe what I say. Now if you believe me, it doesn't get you anywhere anyway. If you disbelieve me, still it doesn't get you anywhere. Isn't it so?

See, if you believe me, you will fool yourself. Without knowing you will simply pretend to know. If you disbelieve me, you will destroy the possibility to know something that is not in your experience. If somebody talks about it, this is all there is, either you believe them or disbelieve them. Now, in the world, there are believers and nonbelievers. There are people who believe in God and people who disbelieve in God. There are people who believe in heaven and hell and there are people who disbelieve in heaven and hell. They are not even on different boats; they are on the same boat. All of them are going on arguing about something that they do not know fundamentally, because somewhere they have lost the basic quality of being sincere enough to admit, "I do not know." Yes? And if you do not admit, "I do not know," you have destroyed all possibilities of knowing in your life.

Today, everybody is a believer. Every street has at least three temples; God is everywhere. In your house there are one dozen gods, but still there is fear in your hearts, isn't it? God in your house, fear in your heart; does it really make any sense to you? Now you have become God-fearing also. This is simply because there is no living experience. It is just a belief; because your grandfather said so, and your father said so, and always it has been said so, so you believe. It is convenient; it is a solace, but it has not liberated you in any way, and it will not liberate you in any way.

Why I am setting up this background for you is because I don't wish to talk about anything which is not in your experience. I might be just forcing you or unnecessarily influencing you to believe me or disbelieve me. I don't want you to believe me and I don't want you to disbelieve me. If you want to go somewhere in your life, you can only start from where you are right now. Yes? Is this understood? If you want to get somewhere, you must start from where you are right now. The first thing is to understand, "Where am I right now?" The next thing is to see, "What is the next possible step that I can take?" So right now, your whole experience of life is limited to your body, your mind and your emotions.

You know the physical world around you to some extent: your body, your mind, your emotions, and you know for all this to happen there must be some kind of energy. So these are the only four things which are in your living experience right now. Everything that you have experienced, from your birth until this moment, you have experienced only through the five sense organs. Isn't it so? By seeing, hearing, smelling, tasting and touching. Your senses can perceive only that which is physical, right? Anything that is beyond the physical is not in the perception of the sense organs, but your whole experience of life is limited right now to these sense organs. If your five sense organs do not function now, you will neither experience yourself nor the world around you. This is what is happening to you during sleep. When you sleep, your heart is still beating, your blood is still flowing, you are alive, and your mind is also functioning, but you have no experience of yourself or the world around you simply because the five sense organs have gone to sleep.

So right now everything is limited to your sense perception. Now you are sitting here, looking at me and hearing me. Your eyes and ears are functioning for that to happen. Are your *ears* hearing me or are *you* hearing me? Are your *eyes* seeing me or are *you* seeing me? Which way is it? Your eyes may be the windows through which you see, but still *you* are seeing, isn't it? Even if I erase all your memory, and you forget who your father is, who your mother is, who your God is, who your demon is, everything you will forget, but still *you* will be there. Yes? Still *you* will be there, isn't it? If I erase your memory, your family will disappear, your status will disappear, your business will disappear. Everything that you own in the world will disappear, but still *you* are there, isn't it? So beyond all the things that you identify yourself with, still there is something called *you*. That *you* is not subject to what you learn from outside. It is not subject to who your parents are, to who your gods are, what group you belong to, what background you come from. No. Beyond that *you* are still there; but unfortunately that *you* has been so crowded with other things that you never allowed yourself to look at that. You never thought that was important. You always thought that what you are identified with is much more important than who *you* really are.

Now if your focus shifts from what you are identified with right now to who you really are, then the other dimension can start opening up for you. Or in other words, the whole process of spiritual science, yoga in particular, is to somehow elevate you to an experience that is beyond the five sense organs. If you experience something beyond the five sense organs, you are beginning to experience that which is not physical. The physical existence is like the peel of a fruit.

This moment you are sitting here, this body is very important. You have to clothe it, you have to feed it, you have to decorate it, you have to pamper it; many things you do, it is very important. Tomorrow morning, that something which is inside this body, which you have never experienced, if that something leaves, suddenly nobody wants this body anymore, isn't it? The moment the fruit is gone, this peel has no value, but right now you have focused all your attention on the peel. The physical existence is just the peel of the existence. The fruit is inside, which remains inexperienced, untouched by a large mass of humanity. Unless you taste the fruit of life, you will never know what life is.

You might live here for twenty, thirty, or sixty years. You might just live here without experiencing the fundamentals of who you are, without knowing the joy, the blissfulness of knowing who you really are. Unless a person touches his interiority, unless a person transcends the physical dimension of who he is, and moves into that dimension which is the basis of this physical body, until then, he always remains subjugated to the external situation because the body and the mind which you are identified with are things that you have picked up from outside. They are not yours. They have the qualities of the outside. They don't have the qualities of who you are. You think, "Who am I?" means your personality. Your personality is also something that you picked up from outside, isn't it? The content of your mind, the content of your body and the content of everything that you are identified with doesn't have the quality of who you really are.

So going beyond this is the way. How to go? That is the science of yoga; that is the science of spirituality we talked to you about. Do not think of, "Where is the next dimension? Where is God? Is God there or not?" Thoughts like this will only send you into flights of imagination. This imagination has not liberated the world. We have gods and gods and gods everywhere. I don't know how many hundreds of gods we have in India, but still look at the pathetic state in which people are living. Somehow all these gods are not able to lift you up, isn't it? This is not about gods; this is just your own foolishness, that is all. You have never aspired for the Divine. I want you to understand this. You have never aspired for the Divine. Your aspiration was never for the Ultimate. All your aspirations are just for comfort, for wealth, for power, for pleasure, and you think God is a tool to help you achieve all these things. This has happened because you are not connected to your inner nature.

This will not work. This has happened because you are not coming from your experience; you are coming from a belief system and this can be dangerous. I can make you believe anything. From the day you were born, if I go on telling you this little finger of mine is God, whenever I show you my little finger, you will have divine emotions within you. Isn't it? So what you believe is immaterial; you can believe anything. You can make a man believe anything. He just has to be worked on a little bit, that's all.

Questioner: India was a very ancient and noble country but...

Sadhguru: India is definitely an ancient country. Noble? I don't know. A very ancient country, yes, and much wisdom and many extraordinary things have happened in this country. In this country, people have looked at life with more depth than anywhere else in the world. That is for sure. They have looked at how a man should be inside himself as a science. Nowhere else has any other culture ever approached the interiority with the depth and dimension that has happened in this culture. That is true, but that is not the reality today. Neither inside nor outside are you rich today. Both ways you have become very poor because somewhere you have been stupid enough to always think about the past and not do anything about the present. It is time we do something about the present. I don't want to hear that India *was* a noble country. I would like to hear that India *is* a noble country.

Questioner: Guruji, you have dismissed Alexander the Great as a fool. I have just one doubt...

Sadhguru: No, I can't dismiss him. I am establishing him as a fool (laughter). How can you dismiss a man who killed hundreds of thousands of people? You can't ignore him.

Questioner: Yes Guruji, I just have a doubt. In the battle of Kurukshetra, why did Lord Krishna compel Arjuna, who had laid down his arms? He did not want to fight his own kith and kin, why did he compel him to fight?

41

Sadhguru: Now you have brought Krishna in. First of all, before we bring in Krishna, we need to come to some understanding of who Krishna was. I want you to understand that Krishna does not fit into the logical dimensions of your life. You built temples for Krishna. That's easy. You worship Krishna. That's also easy. You sing songs in praise of Krishna. That's always very easy. Now suppose there was a man like Krishna in your neighborhood, would you accept him? Would you be capable of accepting him? Can you?

Questioner: I don't think I could, Guruji.

Sadhguru: Then how can you worship him? You worship him because your grandfather told you that Krishna is God, but if he walked into your neighborhood now, you would not accept him. So your worship is false. Whatever you think about Krishna is false, because if that kind of a man entered your society today, you would not accept him, you would want to persecute him. You would want to hound him out of the place because your wife may want to dance with him, your mother and children may want to go and dance with him, too and you wouldn't know what was happening! This would be the reality and you are not mature enough to digest the situation, isn't it?

When you cannot even accept a man, where is the question of worshipping him? It's false worship. It's only because he existed five thousand years ago that you are able to worship him now. If he were alive now, you wouldn't worship him. So let us first look at the basics. Krishna comes from that dimension which is not logical. You cannot logically understand him. Now this question will open up too many things, so I will just be brief on this. If Arjuna had eschewed violence, if he had given up violence, Krishna would have touched his feet and said, "Go," but Arjuna was a warrior. He was willing to slaughter anybody. He had slaughtered thousands of people in his life. He was like a sharp double-edged weapon. He didn't know anything else except fighting. Even on the battlefield, he was willing to slaughter almost everyone.

It was only five or six people – his grandfather, his Guru, his brother, his friend – except for them, he was willing to slaughter everyone else. So Krishna was saying, "If you want to kill, kill those who are dearest to you. You will realize life. If you want to kill, kill your own child, then you will realize what life is. But if you kill somebody who doesn't mean anything to you, you will remain a fool forever." So Arjuna was asking these questions, "How can I kill my Guru? How can I kill my brother? How can I kill my friend? How can I kill my grandfather?" Krishna says, "Only if you slaughter your grandfather will you go to heaven. Only if you kill your Guru will you attain enlightenment." In truth Arjuna had not given up violence. He only wanted to save those few people; he was willing to kill the rest. So that's why His teaching is like that. I want you to understand what importance Krishna gives to one man's realization. If you realize, and in the process, ten thousand people die, it is okay; it is of so much value to the world. It is that value that he is establishing. He is not propagating violence; he functions from a completely different dimension, which is not logical. Logically he will not fit into your mind at all. It is only because this happened five thousand years ago that you are able to worship him. If he was here today, you could not.

Questioner: I would like you to throw some light on dreams. Are they the projections of the soul?

Sadhguru: On dreams? All dreams come from your mind. Dreams cannot go into your soul, if there is one. They don't even touch the two soles of your feet. Much importance has been given to dreams today. In the West, especially in the process of psychoanalysis, Freud and Jung have given too much importance to dreams. In the East, the enlightened have always ignored dreams because they are just another outcome of the madness that you call 'mind'. Your mind, as I already said, is just a garbage bin that gathers things from the people around you. This mind is of appropriate significance as a good survival tool. That is all. To survive in the world you need this stuff, but in terms of life itself, it is of no real significance. Generally most people live their lives like a dream and they even have an investment in their dreams. It is like this.

Have you heard of Jack Stevenson? Once Jack Stevenson was sharing his dreams. He was regretting, "Today I made a big mistake in my dream." People asked, "What nonsense. How can you make a mistake in a dream? A dream is a dream and how can anyone make a mistake in a dream?" He said, "No, you don't know. Do you know what happened? I went to the Vatican and the Pope himself offered me a drink. We sat there and he offered me a drink and he asked me, "Do you want it warm or cold?" I said, "Warm." So he went inside to heat the water, and that was the mistake." Someone asked, "What is the mistake about that? In the dream you asked for a warm drink, what about it?" Jack said, "By the time he could heat the water, I woke up. If I had just told him, I would have it cold, you know, I could have enjoyed the drink." Life is going on like this for most people. People think that before the water heats up they can have another drink. They think, before the water really heats up, they can have a drink on the side – a cold one; and they miss both.

All your dreams are straight from your mind. So it doesn't matter what kind of dreams you have. Whether you see a god or you see a demon in your dreams, it doesn't matter. Whatever is utmost in your consciousness reflects itself. Generally, ninety percent of dreams are just an expression of unfulfilled desire. There are certain other dreams which happen on a different level which could be intuitive. There could be some amount of intuitiveness in your dreams.

In dream states, accidentally, sometimes you can touch your subconscious mind. When you touch your subconscious mind, you transcend the limitations of time and space. Time and space are a creation of your conscious mind. You may have a dream like this: early morning you saw yourself sitting in a garden, your friend came and said something to you, something, an ordinary situation. Tomorrow morning you are sitting in the garden and the same friend comes and says the same things to you. Things like this happen. You dreamt something and then it happened. This may happen simply because you transcend the limitations of time and space when you touch the subconscious. It has got nothing to do with the deeper dimensions of who you are. Dreams always come from the mind. Do not attach too much importance to dreams. Stop dreaming and start living, it's time.

Questioner: Is there life after death? There are a few people I know who communicate with the dead by using a medium. These people who act as mediums also meditate. Is it the right thing to do?

Sadhguru: Now, life after death. Most people don't know how to handle their life here. Do you see this in the world? Most people, ninety-nine percent of people, don't know how to handle their life. These people, why are they pursuing life after death? What is the point? Fundamentally, all these things have come because somewhere people are seeking immortality. Millions of people in the world are seeking immortality, though most of them won't even know what to do on a Sunday morning (laughs). Isn't it? Most of them, if they're given a break, if they're taken away from their routine and are left alone, they wouldn't know what the hell to do with themselves. These people are seeking immortality. The sixty or seventy years that they live here, they don't know how to handle. If they live forever, what a mess they will be! Do not worry about life after death. If such a situation arises within you that it opens up certain memories, if certain things happen for you, just leave it. It is okay.

All these people who are claiming to be mediums need to understand: the mind has many dimensions. It can play many tricks with you; that, you know. Any number of ghosts, devils, spirits or any number of gods can be created. You can actually make them a reality with your mind. The mind is very much capable of creating these illusions. So it's just a mind game. It's a psychic game that you play with yourself and you can play it with other people also. It will not lead to any kind of evolution for human kind. It is only another way of getting caught up with life, another kind of entertainment for you, that's all. It is like a movie, just watching another movie. It will not lead to any kind of growth. Let us say you contacted five dead people, okay? When there are so many people living here and you have no contact with them, why are you interested in contacting the dead? Leave them alone. At least they are free from you. Just leave them alone. With people who are here, you have no contact, but somewhere else you have contact, or you want to have contact. Those people who are mediums, ask them to become mediums here, to the life around them so that life here is connected to you.

Questioner: I have a wife and two children. Half my earnings I give to charity, but there is no sleep for me. The reason why I enrolled myself for the yoga program is because of this. I have consulted many doctors and undergone many treatments, but to no avail. I spend much of my time, money and energy on charity, but still there is no sleep for me. What should I do for my sleep? I do not want any wealth or comfort; I just want sleep. Please Swamiji, tell me what to do!

Sadhguru: Now, when you say I do not want any wealth but I just want sleep, it means sleep has become wealth in your life.

Some time ago in a high school, the schoolteacher asked a question to his students, "If you get a chance to ask for something that will come true for you, what will you ask for?" Some of the students said that they would ask for a car; some said they would ask for one million rupees. Like this they answered depending on what they wanted. For that the teacher replied, "Oh! Fools, why are you all asking for these things? You should ask for brains, intelligence." Then one student stood up and said, "But sir, everyone will only ask for whatever they don't have!" Now what you don't have in your life is your wealth. Only that appears as big wealth. Isn't it? Now for you, sleep is a big wealth and comfort. For people on the path of meditation this is not a problem. Meditate everyday, sleep will automatically come.

Questioner: What is this Dhyanalinga at Isha, do you really need it? Aren't your teachings enough?

Sadhguru: Now, the Dhyanalinga is an attempt to touch all beings without having a teaching. Above all it was my Guru's dream to establish this. It did not happen during his lifetime. So we wanted to do it. For life times we have worked on it. In the process of creating this, we've lost many precious things in our lives because this will not come easy, it will demand a price. It is almost like trapping Shiva and keeping him in one place, an exalted being who you have to create and establish in the form of stone or in the form of energy webs. So, when we do this, he will not come easy. He'll demand a price and we are willing to pay any price because we know it is worthwhile. Another reason why this has been established is, Isha Yoga is a powerful way of imparting a teaching, but after a few generations, we don't know what people are going to do with it. Obviously, they'll distort it. When they could distort Jesus, when they could distort Gautama, when they could distort Krishna; do you think they won't distort me? They'll twist it out of proportion and do some other nonsense

47

with Isha Yoga. We are taking a lot of care to keep this Guru-Shishya paramparya alive and to train people in the proper way, so that there is no distortion as far as possible. Still, we won't have control a few centuries from now. People will distort it. Isha Yoga may get lost after sometime; but now the Dhyanalinga is here and its energies are forever.

Questioner: Isn't the Linga shape a Hindu symbol? How are you able to call it a multi-religious temple and expect a Muslim or a Christian to accept this form? If Isha is all about dhyana, or meditation, why couldn't we have a symbol of Buddha?

Sadhguru: Yes, one aspect of the Linga is that it is symbolic as you mentioned, but there is a science behind the symbolism. The importance of this symbol…for example if you want I can charge this handkerchief with energy and give it to you. The problem is that it cannot retain this energy for very long. After sometime it will become just a handkerchief again. There are certain shapes and certain materials which can retain energy extremely well. Of all shapes, the Linga retains energy the best. You ask me, why not a symbol of a Buddha or his scriptures at Isha? What you need to understand is, Buddha spent all his life demolishing all gods. He demolished all gods. The moment he left, his people made him into a god. They started building temples just like Hindu temples, and it was about the same kind of worship, too. Only the mantras are different and making the mantras different is not a sensible thing to do. This is because the mantras in the Sanskrit language have more science behind them than in any other tongue. Generally, most mantras have an emotional significance to people who utter them rather than any scientific basis. Definitely, this is not what Gautama intended. He wanted you to experience everything as it is, so he demolished all forms of worship. He wouldn't like it if he came back and saw the Buddhist temples, he just wouldn't like it. Whether it is his picture or form or anybody's, he wouldn't appreciate it.

Have you noticed the shape of nuclear reactors? They have simply arrived at the conclusion that this shape retains energy best, but they do not know the whole of it. There is a whole science behind it, experientially that they do not know; but some calculations have been made and they have come to the conclusion that this shape is the best for storing energy. Why have we used the Linga shape? It is not something that we have concocted in our head. If you go deep into science, the energy around your body, your aura, naturally takes the shape of a Linga. Out of this understanding, a religion has created a symbolism; otherwise, people would not experience the science as it is.

Not everyone can understand the fundamental truth about your energy. So stories have been created around this that they say this form is God. The ultimate meditative energy in a person always takes this form. This you don't have to believe. Just sit and meditate and if you are aware enough, gradually you will come to know that, your energies will take that shape. Once it becomes like that your energies get crystallized. Everybody has energy, but only with the right kind of support will this vibrancy be able to be sustained; otherwise, this energy dissipates. However, once a person's energy becomes crystallized in this form, he is always vibrant. Even if he leaves the body this energy will not go.

Now the nature of the Dhyanalinga is such that all seven chakras are manifested and at their peak. It is just like an ultimate being sitting there. Once the energies of the Linga were locked, even if the stone form is destroyed the energy will always remain. The form is only an initial support. Afterwards we can remove the form if we like, but we will not because so much work has been done on it. Another reason is, not all people can relate to just some empty space. They need something to see. Very few people can enter a place and feel the energy. They need to relate to something, some kind of form, only then they can feel it. So we will retain the form.

The question of whether Muslims, Christians or others will accept it, I would say, nobody, not even the Hindus should accept it. I want everyone to experience it. Every human being can experience it. If you are prejudiced it cannot be helped. This is not about any Hindu god sitting here. You must understand that the Linga form was created during the Vedic times when no gods, existed in India. When there were no gods there were also no images of gods. It's during that time the Linga was formed. It is a basic experiential science. This Linga is just an outcome or an outside manifestation of looking inward.

Perhaps this symbol has been branded as Hindu and in the process we might be branded too. Maybe to some extent it cannot be helped, but the Linga form is not Hindu. This is the very nature of your energy, this must be understood. Whether you are a Hindu or not, if you are human this is the peak of energy one should strive toward. I think its time we reinstate the science behind the Linga, about a deeper understanding of the self, a deeper understanding on how this body is controlled, how this mind is constructed, how all these things are put together and made into a human being.

It's time people went deeper into this science. We are spending too much time creating external comforts with science, but miseries have come along with that. If science was used for human well being or for the well-being of the planet then it would be valuable; however, today science seems to be losing its value because man has in no way grown internally, it has happened only with the external. Along with this growth of the external, man needs to develop the inner science. If inner sciences do not develop along with the external sciences, then there will be calamity in the world. It's bound to be so, isn't it?

Questioner: People are taking Vaasthu Shastra to the extremes these days. What do you say about it? To what extent have you gone by the Vaasthu for the Dhyanalinga temple? (Audience applauds the question).

Sadhguru: What is this? You are clapping for the question itself? I understand the perversion of the question. Many of you would be extremely happy if I say we followed Vaasthu for the Dhyanalinga temple. Maybe I have to disappoint you. There is one type of Vaasthu in Tamil Nadu and if you see in Karnataka, there is a different type of Vaasthu there. Even in Karnataka, if you go into the mountainside, there is a different type of Vaasthu. In the plains it is different. What is Vaasthu? See, in the olden days there were no architects in the villages. Now, for example, there is a man who wants to build a house for himself. So he built one which was five feet in width and fifty feet in length. The door is at one end and he forgot to put in a window! If you go and live in this kind of a house, what will happen to your mind and body? It will rot, isn't it? If you remain within two walls like this all the time, wouldn't your body and mind decay? So they developed a Shastra or the basic guidelines.

Shastra means a guideline. If you want to build a house, it should be in a particular way depending on the climatic conditions of the place where it is being built. If the western sun is very strong, then the walls on the western side should be thicker. The other side can be a little thinner. They created Shastras pertaining to the situation there. People followed it to some extent and it was good. It is just an architectural guidance to ensure that the house is well ventilated. As there were not any architects in every village, they created some architectural guidelines, rules to say that if it is built along those guidelines it will be good.

There are various types of Vaasthu in India. Depending on the area, they created the guidelines, the Vaasthu for that place. Only in the

51

last ten years, people have started taking it to the extremes. This Vaasthu was not followed to such an absurd extent ten years ago. Only in the last eight to ten years they have made this into a big business. Vaasthu has come into your life only because you exist in fear, isn't it? Only because you are in fear all the time, you have gone and built a toilet where a kitchen should be and a kitchen where a toilet should be. They have done it like this, isn't it? Now I hear that people are even changing the direction of the water closet in the toilet, because the Vaasthu says it brings well being, sitting in that direction and defecating. Ridiculous!

When I first came into Coimbatore, I was invited to a home for lunch. It was a big house. There was a small garden inside the house – a courtyard. A beautiful house, but right in the middle of the garden there was a huge flagpole. Without serving any purpose, it was just standing there. I asked the lady of the house why they have kept this flagpole there like that. The lady hesitated to tell me. She was very embarrassed to tell me the truth. She said, "Had I done the Isha Yoga class earlier, I would not have done this." I asked her, "What is it?" She told me that it was about twelve years since the house was built and they have lived well all those years, but just about six months ago, a Vaasthu scientist visited them. People who find things that do not exist are supposed to be big scientists, isn't it? What is the big deal about discovering what is already there? Yes, people who discover things that exist are scientists, but those who discover things that do not even exist are very big scientists!

Now this Vaasthu scientist came and said, "Everything is good about the house except that the southwestern side of the house should be at a slightly higher level than the rest of the house, whereas the northwestern side of your house is higher. If it is like this, your son will die." This lady had two sons. The scientist said this and went away. Now the lady became highly disturbed, but her husband who is a doctor refused to budge. He did not want to demolish and rebuild the house.

The scientist allowed this to boil within the family for a week. Within that week this lady became a bundle of emotions; she almost went mad. She had dreams where her sons were taking turns falling down dead. Imagination ran riot in her mind. She became terribly afraid. She became terrified that her sons would fall dead at any moment. So after one week she wanted to call the scientist back. That scientist knew how long it would take for the reaction to whatever he had said earlier to set in. After a week, the man called them on the phone and these people told him to go ahead and do something to counter the ill-effects of the construction.

This man said there is a *pariharam*, a remedy, and charged them about twenty thousand rupees, took great care to ensure that the son does not die, and brought a huge flagpole, about twenty-five feet long. Then, with the help of the family members, with great difficulty, they brought it into the house. Only if you pretend great difficulty the drama will reach its finale, isn't it? They brought the flagpole and put it in the courtyard. Now because of this flagpole the southwestern side became higher and they saved the life of the boy!

There is a science behind building a house, definitely. There is definitely a science to ensure the well-being of our physical and mental health, our general well-being. It is not that it is not there, but because of fear, you have taken it to ridiculous proportions. It is also a science. I am not denying that. Now anyway they have given up the local Vaasthu. They have imported something from China. Now you no longer have to convert your toilet into a kitchen! They just put a mirror in front of the toilet. You can now see the kitchen inside the toilet! If they do this, everything will become all right. They are even more intelligent. There is no more breaking of walls. Just mirrors and stone would make everything all right. You are not doing what is required to be done. You are doing lots of unnecessary things. You are wasting all your energies and intelligence on activities like this.

Questioner: Dear Swamiji, in our religion it is said that you yourself are nothing but Shiva. Now where is the need to establish an idol relating to Shiva here at Isha? Can a shape or a symbol be given to God? I understand within myself that there is no shape for God. I have come to a conclusion that I myself am God. Then why this Linga rupa, why this form here at Isha?

Sadhguru: Is the question over? (Laughter) And if it is over, stop with it. With your limited understanding, there is no need for you to frame the answer too. Now, when you go to a river, if you take a pot to fill with water, the water will take the shape of the pot. If you take water in a jug, water will form the shape of the jug. If you take some other vessel, it will take that shape. There is no permanent shape for water. Whatever contains it, it just takes its shape. Similarly, what you call God, though it has no shape, for you to relate to it, idols are created.

In the Indian culture there is no particular belief that God is sitting somewhere and doing something. At least it wasn't so a few centuries ago. Saying only this or that is God has happened only in the last six or seven centuries. Shiva always meant 'that which is not'. That's how the name was given. How can the common man relate to that which is not? Only if you give some identification to it can he relate to it. Even when idols were created, they were scientifically created so that the energy could be retained and experienced.

There are many stories pertaining to Shiva. The stories are said in such a manner that you can neither call him good nor bad. Generally, in all cultures God is depicted as good, very good, but if you see this world you don't see it as good. At times Shiva is a true yogi, the next time he appears as a drunkard and the very next time you see him as something else. You cannot come to a conclusion about him. You cannot say he will do this or he will not do this. Sometimes he is an utter rogue, sometimes he's Divine, at other times he is something else. Shiva has been attributed with every kind of nature and character.

Why it is so is because he does not belong or fit into anything; he has no shape. Now for that which doesn't have any characteristics, some form has been given to it so that you can relate to that energy. Why we have depicted Shiva like this is, if you can accept Shiva, then there is no problem in accepting any other being. Do you understand that when you say, "God," for you he means, good, good, and nothing but good. Now, where is the problem in accepting that which is good? When it comes to Shiva, here he falls down drunk, there he kills in anger. He does many things which are not in your understanding, which are beyond you; but if you see, he is operating from another dimension, a higher dimension which is beyond your logical perception. Why we have created God with these characteristics is, if you can accept him totally, in all totality, then you can totally accept any kind of human being also.

We have given a shape to the Divine, which in reality is only a tool. There is nothing wrong with using a tool. Only when you differentiate and say that only *this* is divinity and *that* is not, out of your foolishness, you will miss out on life and, in the process, miss out on experiencing the Divine.

Question: What is the difference between space and emptiness?

Sadhguru: Do you know what space is? Right now there is neither any direct experience of space nor of emptiness. If you know at least one of them – see if you ask me the difference between a mango and an orange, if you neither know a mango nor an orange, I can start talking around it. I can tell you a mango is like this and an orange is like that, but if you have not known a mango or an orange, talking about them is a waste of time; it will become senseless talk. Space is still a physical quantity. What you call *Shoonya* is not a physical quantity. That much I can say.

Questioner: Sadhguru, what is samadhi? When people just slip into it, can they come out by themselves?

Sadhguru: Samadhis are of eight different types. If a person goes into samadhi out of his own sadhana, definitely he will have sufficient awareness to get back. Now if you look back at spiritual history, you will notice that there were people who went into samadhi and were not able to come back by themselves. This is because samadhi dropped them somewhere, in some blissful state and after two or three days they were out of it, but by themselves they don't have the maturity to come out of it nor do they wish to. The path of samadhi itself is a path of unawareness, generally.

There are people who go into samadhis in full awareness. They decide the time at which they are going to come out. One can just sit down and go into samadhi deciding beforehand the date and time to come out, and it will be so. You can come out of samadhi at the time and date you have chosen. This is done in full awareness. There are many beings who go into samadhi states who somehow learned how to go into samadhi, but are unable to use that energy in any particular direction. They stay there for a few hours, a few days and then they are out of it. Just being there is sufficient for them. They do not care to use it either.

For example, Ramakrishna Paramahamsa. Whenever he goes into a samadhi state he doesn't want to come out of it. He doesn't care to do any work here. He just wants to enjoy that samadhi, but somewhere the samadhi drops him and then he'll cry and yell and beg to get back into samadhi. He's in samadhi for three days, and once out of it he'll really beg. He's a Kali bhaktha and he goes begging to Kali, "Ma give me samadhi! Give me a taste of samadhi once again." So somehow, in another week or ten days' time he'll get back into it. This is how life passed for him most of the time, but towards the end he grasped enough control over himself that he could get in and out of samadhi when he wished. Not only that, he gave samadhi to other people also.

The word samadhi has been largely misunderstood. People think samadhi means a death-like situation. The word samadhi literally means *sama* and *dhi*. *Sama* means equanimity and *dhi* means the buddhi. If you reach that kind of equanamous state of intellect, it is known as samadhi. What we mean by an equanamous state of intellect is this: only when the intellect is functioning, are you able to discriminate between one thing and another. The discrimination that this is this and that is that is there only because the intellect is functioning. The moment you drop the intellect or transcend it, this discrimination does not exist anymore. Now everything becomes one whole, which is reality. Everything just becomes one whole. In this state there is no time and space. So you may think the man was in samadhi for three days. For him it is just a few moments, it just passes like that. Lifetimes can pass like this. There are legends where it is said that there have been yogis who lived up to four or five hundred years and that some of them are still alive today. Is such a thing possible? Theoretically it is possible. Whether there is such a person or not, is not the point, but it is definitely possible. These four or five hundred years is according to your calculation. For him it might seem to have been just a few minutes.

If you want to understand these things, you have to pull yourself out of the world. Staying in this world, whichever way you look at it, you cannot understand, because you are bound by time and space. When there is no time and space, there are no physical quantities. This world as you understand it today, as you see it and experience it today is a complete falsehood. It seems to be there, but it is not really there. It just *seems* to be there, including yourself; it just seems to be there. Now the whole struggle is to see that it is just nonsense. The whole thing is just an illusion. This is what is meant by 'maya'. It just seems to be there. Today physics proves it beyond any doubt that there is no such thing as matter in the existence. Everything is relative. It just seems to be there, but it is not there. But it is so real, isn't it? It seems very real. Who is going to believe this story that it is not really there?

It is there, very much there. The whole existence, the many forms of creation, can you say they are not there? They are very much there, but only as long as the intellect is there. The moment you dissolve your intellect, everything dissolves into one.

Questioner: What is Zen and how is it different from Isha Yoga?

Sadhguru: The word *Zen* comes from the Sanskrit word *Dhyan*, and Gautama the Buddha taught *Dhyan*. Bodhidharma transported *Dhyan* to China. There it became *Chan*. This *Chan* went further down into Far East Asian countries, where it became *Zen*. You can say Isha Yoga is pure Zen in its own way. Zen is one form of spiritual path which has no scriptures, no books, no rules, no particular practices, nothing. It is an uncharted path. It is nothing very different from what yoga is. It is just yoga.

Questioner: But Jaggi there is a path in yoga, isn't there? You say if you do this and this, an enlightened being can be manufactured. We are doing sadhana only for this purpose, aren't we?

Sadhguru: In yoga, we are presenting the same thing as a science. In Zen it is handled as an art form. Now to appreciate art you need to be evolved in a certain way, but everyone can enjoy the fruits of science. What we call yoga, they call Zen, but Zen became popular because at a certain time a few very wonderful Masters came, a lineage of Masters. It was a miracle that for a few centuries, for about four to five centuries, continuously, a series of Masters came, which was a rare happening. Because of these very extraordinary Masters, Zen has taken on a different kind of aura, a different kind of quality.

Otherwise, fundamentally it is simply Isha Yoga, where there's nothing to be done. That's what Zen is all about, but it has taken on a different dimension by itself simply because of the series of Masters who came. Each one evolved Zen in their own way, taught or transmitted Zen in their own way. Every Master had his own unique way of giving it to another person. Probably, once in an eternity such a lineage happens. Continuously, for about four to five centuries, many of them, dozens of fully enlightened Masters came and they created wonderful methods of transmitting this knowledge, which cannot be repeated again. If you repeat it, then Zen is meaningless. Zen is something that happens spontaneously.

Like this, in the path of Zen, there was a person whose name was Huitti. He never taught Zen to anybody, but he was known as a Master. Everybody respected him as a Zen Master, but he never had any teachings to give. He carried a huge bag on his shoulders, a huge sack. There were a lot of things in it and some were sweets. So in every town, in every village where he went, children would gather around him and he would distribute sweets and then he would leave. That's all. People would come and ask for teachings; he would just laugh and walk away. That's all he was. One day, another Zen Master, Nbanin, who was of great repute, came and met Huitti. He wanted to know whether Huitti was really in Zen or not. So he asked him, "What is Zen?" Immediately, Huitti dropped the sack and stood straight. And then he asked, "What is the goal of Zen?" Huitti took the sack on his shoulders and walked away. This is what yoga is also about; that is what every spiritual sadhana is about.

Now when you want to attain to yoga or to Zen or whatever you call it, you have to drop your load, discard everything that is on the way, remain free, and stand up straight. This is important. With your load you may never be able to do it. One can also do it with their load on their back, but that is very, very rare. I do not know in how many millions there is such a person. You drop the load! What is the goal of yoga? Then, take up the whole load once again! But now it is no more a load; it doesn't feel like a load because you know the whole thing is there, but is not really there. Anyway it does not matter. Whether you live or die, it does not matter. Tomorrow morning if all of us are going to disappear from this planet, it really does not make any difference. "Oh! If I am going to disappear, what will happen to my children? What will happen to this, what will happen to that?" So many things are there, isn't it? But really, it doesn't matter. Nothing will happen. A few more fools will cry, a few more fools will yell and once again they too will die. Once again they will be born, "*Punahrapi Jananam, Punahrapi Maranam.*" Maybe if you die, at least they will start thinking, "What the hell is this life about?" If you go on living, probably they will never even think along those lines. Lots of people have settled down into their comforts so well, they even think they are immortal. The arrangements you are making in your life, it is as if you are immortal, isn't it? As if you are going to live here forever, this is the kind of arrangement many people are making, isn't it? This is absolute stupidity.

Okay, you have not realized the nature of this existence, but at least you must know that you are going to die. If you have not even realized that much, you are not fit to live. Maybe you didn't have any great realization, not an ounce has melted for you; it is still solid. The world is still solid for you, the transient world, the solidity of which modern science has proven beyond any doubt as false. Reality is relative. At least you must know that you will die one day. Even that, people have forgotten. You're going about in this world – every action of yours is like you are going to be here forever. Even at the age of seventy, or ninety or even one hundred, when death comes, still you are not willing to die and you never did anything worthwhile.

Life has only been about misery and complaints. For most people in this world, let us say, sixty is the average life span. In their sixty years of life, I don't know how many moments they have really enjoyed themselves without any hassles. Hassle-free enjoyment – how much have they had in sixty years? In your thirty to forty years, how many totally hassle-free moments of enjoyment have you had? Forget about love; even your laughter is measured, your tears are measured, whatever you do is measured. All actions are calculated. So whether you are going to live for sixty years or six years is not really going to make any difference. If you become realized and go, then again it doesn't make a difference; but if you live, at least you will be useful to somebody else. For yourself you are never useful. You cannot be useful to yourself. What use can you be to yourself? The only way is to evaporate and disappear. Really, the Ultimate is to dissolve into nothingness.

Questioner: Many holy men here in India do yagas and yagnas for relief from drought, to bless barren women with children, to prevent earthquakes and so on. What is your contribution towards this or how do you ascribe to these practices?

Sadhguru: I think I should go one by one: drought, barren women and earthquakes. These holy men, these so-called holy men have always been in excess in this country. In spite of these holy men, this country has seen too many droughts. In spite of all these yagas and yagnas and all kinds of very complicated expensive poojas that they are doing, we had very severe famines until 1964. After that, we have never had a famine, but we have had droughts, leading to bad agricultural years. Since 1964 we have not had famines, not because somebody did a yaga or a yagna or a pooja, but because our agriculture became a little more organized. We are approaching it with a little more sense. Instead of calling for the gods to take care of our crops, to some extent we started taking care of the crops ourselves. That is the reason why, in these forty years or so, we have not had a famine. Otherwise, this sub-continent was ravaged by famine every other year, which took hundreds of thousands of people's lives every time. When it came, it took many of them away.

As far as barren women are concerned, I think yagnas seem to have worked! We are definitely over-populated! That one thing seems to have worked! I hope they can do some yagnas to make them barren once again. I think that is the yagna we need in this country: some poojas to make everybody barren for a few years, so that they don't bear children. They did yagnas to make barren women conceive, but they did not do yagnas to feed those children who happen to fall on the streets. For that you need aid from some other country. Even if they send cattle-feed you are happy. Yes! Many times Western nations have sent cattle-feed and you were happy! Our children ate and lived. Somewhere, even the so-called holy men went on supporting the foolishness of the people. Science played a role in controlling famine, floods and other things. Once epidemics were taken away, it was your business to control your population, but you didn't come to your senses and the holy men egged you on to produce more children. One reason for this probably was, these so-called holy men are thriving on the number of people who come to them. There is a big fight always about who is going to convert how many into their fold. Ultimately, the whole thing is about having more people around you, and the more stupid they are, the better it is for you.

Now, earthquakes. After the recent Gujarat quake, wherever I go, this is one question they have been asking me, "Such a great calamity; what can we do? Are the gods angry with us? Is there some spiritual process that we can do to avoid earthquakes in this country?" I want you to understand, an earthquake is not a calamity. An earthquake is just a natural process; Mother Earth is just stretching herself a little bit. It happens everywhere. Since almost two-thirds of the planet is covered by water, and as most of the earthquakes happen in the ocean beds, you do not notice it. Tidal waves arise, disturbances happen. Many times it is because of the tectonic movement that an earthquake happens in the ocean. You don't notice it because it is far away. Two-thirds of the earth is under water anyway. Only one-third you have to manage, and see what a mess it is! Now, especially in India, just see how deficient we are in managing these things. Earthquakes are happening in many places all over the world, in some places almost on a daily basis. For example, in California, earth tremors are happening almost every day. Nobody dies. It is because people have organized themselves sufficiently to handle those situations.

One quake happens here in India and hundreds and thousands of people die, simply because we have over-populated this place, and we have absolutely no preparation for a situation like that. In no way are we prepared. When something like this happens, people die just like insects. I would like to tell you an example. About two to three years ago I was in Tennessee in the US for a program. That evening the Bhava Spandana program was going to start and we were on our way. That afternoon, a tornado struck the city of Nashville. The tornado is total fury, absolute fury. It just comes twisting and you have everything flying, trees, cars, everything. It was like that! It seemed to be taking just about everything into the sky. It hit the very center of the town; the downtown area was hit. Within the city, over eight hundred large trees were uprooted in a matter of ten to fifteen minutes. Almost every building in the downtown area had its windows and doors blown out. Hundreds of cars were piled up because of the wind. We were driving and about half a mile away the tornado was moving; we could see it. It was just blasting through homes. They were just being blown like matchsticks. Seeing this, I thought hundreds of people must have been killed. All the traffic sections were choked. Everything was scattered on the roads – trees, vehicles, broken glass. It was total havoc. The next day in the news it was announced that seven people were missing, and in two days' time all those seven people were found. Not a single person was killed.

If such a tornado strikes the city of Coimbatore, I can imagine, at least fifty thousand people will be dead for sure. This is not because they are doing good yagnas and you are not doing yagnas properly. This is simply because they are handling things sensibly; that is all. What needs to be done is being done. You are not doing what needs to be done, but you are doing everything else. You don't need an earthquake. The nation itself has become a calamity today because you are not running your country the way it should be run. You are still thinking the gods will run the country. You are still waiting for the gods to handle everything for you. All the mess that you have created, you are expecting that some gods will come and clean it up. It is not going to happen. The Creator has done a wonderful job with creation. You cannot complain. So perfect and so exuberant it is! You could not have imagined a better creation. Something so tremendous has been created. Now it is time that you take your life, your home, your social and your national situation into your hands and do what needs to be done. Unless we take this country into our hands and away from God's hands, these things will go on happening.

Somebody performs a yagna in Andhra Pradesh so that earthquakes won't happen. I am telling you, in the next five years there will most probably be no earthquakes in Andhra Pradesh. Anyway this man gets the credit now, "No earthquake because I did a yagna." Some other holy man in Tamil Nadu predicts that after a hundred years there is going to be a big flood in Tamil Nadu. In a hundred years there is going to be a flood and this man announces it now. Everybody is around him because he has made a big prediction about what is going to happen after one hundred years. Anybody can predict what is going to happen after a hundred years. Predict what is going to happen after ten minutes, then let us see. It is easy to predict what is going to happen after one hundred years because neither you nor he will be there to see it anyway, and anyway there may be a flood somewhere in a hundred year's time.

These yagas, yagnas and poojas, there was some scientific basis to them. These rituals had some basis as a way of creating a conducive atmosphere for people. When people did not have their own ways to create an inner situation, those who knew how to create a conducive atmosphere outside did so during the Vedic times with certain yagas and yagnas. Slowly, the Bhrahmanic culture took this beyond all sense and it became a big business because the Bhrahmin was the only one who could utter all those words. Nobody else could. Even during the time of Rama, you heard about how a Shudra who came and saw the yagna and was killed just for witnessing it. For hearing what was being said, that man was killed. This was because somebody wanted to maintain the monopoly of that business and they made it so complicated and elaborate that people would really think there was actually something to it.

Somebody told me this a few years ago: it seems there was one doctor somewhere in Kolhapur. As you enter his clinic – he has got a huge hospital-like place – there are all kinds of complicated tubes and flasks like in a laboratory. Many things are happening there. Red, blue, green liquids going here and there. So if you go to him as a patient, the first thing is, before you see him, you have to go through many passages where you view all these things. Many experiments are going on. By the time you reach the consultation room you are too impressed; something very big is happening here. When you get there, he will make you lie down and all kinds of multi-colored lights will come on, noises will happen, so many things will happen. You are going through all kinds of scans with just light bulbs. When all this is done, he gives you a thin bottle about three millimeters in diameter with about three or four milliliters of liquid inside –red colored liquid or some bright colored liquid. You have to take just two drops of this liquid a day and every three days you must get a refill.

Many people found this man to be a miracle healer. They got rid of all their diseases. One day something happened and he was caught.

They found that all this was just colored water and it was working very well! Hundreds of people were saying it worked for them. Anyway, most of the people are pretending to be diseased; they like to be diseased. Really, you won't believe this, but that is the truth. Lots of people like to be diseased because that is the only way they can get attention. They don't have any other means to get attention from people. This is a deep psychological process. This is something that you have been trained to do, something that you have always been encouraged to do. In many homes, when you are a child, when children are there, when they are joyous, nobody pays any attention to them. The moment they are sick, the whole family is around them, saying all the nicest things, doing all the nicest things possible and pampering them. Somewhere inside, unconsciously, the child learns that sickness is a great investment. If you become sick, everybody will show the best side of themselves to you.

Unfortunately, most of the time, if somebody is joyous, if the child is joyous, nobody pays attention. They think he is trouble. In fact, he is put down if he is too exuberant and happy, but sick people are always getting extra attention. This is a very unhealthy trend, which is in many ways a big source of illness on the planet. Right from their childhood, people have been trained to become ill. If you are ill, you get the best. You must always ignore sick people. Yes, don't celebrate sickness. If they need medicine, if they need care, yes, that should be offered; but don't unnecessarily attend to the sick. If somebody needs medicine, needs care, and needs good food, that much care you take, all right, but there is no need to give unnecessary attention. It is not necessary. If you are sick, just lie down in a place. What else is there to do? You are not good for anything else. Pampering the sick is a wrong thing to do, especially for children, because it just gets built into their psyche and they go on seeking attention unknowingly. Whenever they badly need attention, they will really fall ill. They are not pretending; they really fall ill. I am not saying they are pretending to get attention. They have actually become ill. Medically they are sick, but it is caused because of psychological reasons.

So, performing poojas, this or that, has not helped our country to be free from these things, isn't it? It is time you do what is needed to be done. Now, what is my role towards stopping the earthquakes? I don't want to stop earthquakes. Instead, I want people to become sensible enough that even if earthquakes happen they know how to handle their lives sensibly to begin with. And I definitely do not want barren women to become fertile. This earth is better off that way. Many senseless people who don't even know how they should live are going on producing more children. They have not even learned how they should live. Forget about enlightenment; they don't even know how to keep their physical body! They don't know what the human form is. They don't know how to keep their emotions; they don't know how to keep their mind in balance. Why are these people going on producing children?

Producing another being is a tremendous responsibility; it is not to be done wantonly. If you want to produce a child, first you better handle yourself well. If you know how to keep yourself, at least if that much is there – forget spiritually; at least physically and, mentally – if you know how to keep yourself, only then you have a right to bring another being onto this planet. When you do not even know how to keep yourself physically, mentally and emotionally, why are you going about producing children and creating more and more havoc and problems in this world?

One reason why people are producing children is because they think they are going to be fulfilled by it. If you produce one dozen, you will still not be fulfilled. You have seen those people who produced a dozen? They are not fulfilled. You don't see any fulfillment on their faces. You don't even see peace on their faces, isn't it? They are just harassed by their children. That is what I see. Most of them are simply harassed. They are not able to handle it. It is time we take our lives and our situations into our own hands, instead of always calling upon gods to do this for us.

What is my contribution for human well-being? My contribution is to make you understand that no power on earth or beyond can do anything for you unless you are in a certain way. Unless you become receptive, grow, and create sense within yourself, no holy men, no gods, no enlightened beings are going to do anything for you. You may adore them, you may worship them, you may sing praises of them, but you will continue to exist in the same misery. There will be no release for you.

When Krishna, Rama, Gautama, Jesus and many other sages and saints have come into this world – truly wonderful and powerful beings – still most people around them lived ordinary, suffering lives. Just a few rose above their limitations; all others continued to exist in their suffering. So it really makes no difference to you if your yagas and yagnas bring even God down, you will continue to be stupid. Unless you do something about yourself, the situation is not going to change.

I want to tell people, I want to put it into them, I want to provoke their mind, body and energies in such a way that they become a little more alive, because without aliveness, people will not stand up for their lives. They will lie down and wait for God to do it for them. I am here to make them a little more alive, to make them a little more sensible, to make them open to the possibility of going beyond. The first thing is to stand up and be sensible. To handle this body, to handle this mind, to handle these emotions, things that are within you right now, to handle them sensibly.

If you don't know how to handle these things sensibly, forget about going beyond. Such a thing will not happen. It is just an illusion. It doesn't matter which God appears in front of you, if you don't know how to be, if you don't know how to receive this, you will continue to be the same. No gods need to come, because whatever you refer to as God is always here, within you, but dead. To make him alive, first you have to become fully alive. If you want the Divine to become alive within you, first of all you, as a human being, have to become absolutely alive.

So my work is just to make you alive. If you become alive, truly alive, then the Divine in you will also become alive. Then earthquakes will not matter for you; you will know how to handle them. It is not that these things will not happen. They will happen; they should happen. It is just that you should learn to handle your personal lives, and your social lives, and the national situation, and the world situation more sensibly. This is possible only if you know how to manage your mind and body sensibly. Otherwise, you will not know how to manage this world sensibly, isn't it? So that is my yagna. I think the next question should be how to avoid sleep when we are in a sathsang (laughs).

Questioner: To seek the Divine within is it necessary to withdraw from worldly affairs? Does it not imply running away from one's responsibilities?

Sadhguru: To seek the Divine, should you withdraw from worldly affairs? How can you withdraw from worldly affairs anyway? It all depends on what it is that you are calling worldly affairs. Now, I am tending to this coconut tree, is it a worldly affair or not? Very much. It is a worldly affair, isn't it? I am cooking my own food, is it a worldly affair? Yes or no? I wash my own clothes, is it a worldly affair? So you have to do these worldly affairs. Otherwise how will you live here?

What kind of worldly affairs you want to do is your choice; it is your individual choice. Everybody need not join politics, isn't it? Even in the social situation, somebody is in politics, somebody is just a clerk in an office, somebody is running a whole industry and somebody is just sweeping floors. All of them are doing worldly affairs. So you cannot really withdraw from worldly affairs. It is just a choice of what kind of worldly affairs you want to do in your life and how much you want to do. Why shouldn't a person have that choice? Every person has a right to choose what type of worldly affair he does and how much of it, isn't it? Every person definitely has the choice. It is only those people who do not know what they are doing with themselves and are just doing what everybody else is doing, who complain in this manner. They are just doing what everybody else is doing. They don't know what to do by themselves. They neither have the intelligence nor the awareness to do their own thing.

Such people are always complaining about spiritual people. "Oh! These people are not being responsible. They are not doing worldly affairs, they are doing their own affairs." The man who is in his own house or in his office is also there just to do his own affairs. He is not interested in the well-being of the world. He is also there just to take care of his own affairs. He doesn't know what his real affair is and has gotten himself into such a mess that he doesn't even know how to get out of it. Because he is unable to get out of it, he thinks that somebody who is able to manage his own affairs the way he wants it in his life, to the extent he wants it, is on the wrong bus.

It happened like this. One day, a drunk somehow pulled himself onto the bus, stumbled around over the passengers, dislodged suitcases and briefcases, came and landed on a seat next to a prim and proper old lady and fell on her. The old lady pushed him off and said, "I hate to say this young man, but you are going straight to hell!" The drunk suddenly sprang up and blurted out, "Oh no! I'm on the wrong bus!" So drunken people do not know who is on the wrong bus. If somebody manages their lives the way they want, to the extent they want, these people who have made their lives unmanageable, enslaved and entangled to the situations around them, become very jealous.

They will always complain. They will say these people are running away from the world. Right now, the way the world is going, if a lot of people continue doing too many things on this planet, this planet will not even last another ten years. Ten more years it will not last if all six billion people become over-industrious. Fortunately, fifty percent of the people are lazy. The other fifty percent, who are too industrious, are busy destroying the world. Probably only one in one thousand is spiritual. We want to make at least fifty percent of them spiritual in order to save the world.

People who are withdrawing from excessive activity are not causing any damage either to themselves, to the society, to the world, to the environment or to the planet. It is only people that are doing activity in absolute unawareness who are truly destroying this world, isn't it? In total unawareness, not knowing what they are doing, simply imitating somebody, they are doing more activity, more briskly than anybody else. They are the people who are causing tremendous damage to this planet. They are the people who are really threatening life on this planet. They are the people who are taking the whole of humanity toward global suicide. So right now, the most responsible thing you can do in the world is to withdraw from activity. Withdrawing from activity is not so simple. It takes tremendous maturity to simply sit quietly. It doesn't happen because you are lazy or irresponsible, it happens because you are aware and conscious.

Questioner: Dear Sadhguru, how can the science of yoga and meditation make the world a better place?

Sadhguru: The world was always a great place. The world has always been a great place. From whatever little knowledge we have about this existence or the other planets, we know this world is a great place compared to anything that we know of. It is just these over-ambitious fools, who, in absolute unawareness, went about slaughtering every other life form that existed on this planet, thinking that they are going to create human well-being. That human well-being is still a dream. After thousands of years of civilization, after thousands of years of slaughtering so many other animal forms, and sometimes our own race, still human well-being is far away. We are no closer to it than we were ten thousand years ago. With all the science and technology, we have altered the external situation very much, but still, we are no closer to human well-being.

It is definitely time that we look inward and see how to create it. From your own experience of life you can clearly see that true well-being will come to you only if your interiority changes. Right now the quality of your life is not being decided by the clothes that you wear, or the educational qualifications that you carry, or what family background you come from or what bank balance you hold. This moment, the quality of your life is simply decided by how peaceful and joyous you are right now within yourself. That is all that decides the quality of your life.

So meditation is that dimension of science which handles your interiority, where the focus is on creating the right kind of interior, so that you can live a joyous and peaceful life. Or in other words, you can just live well. If you become a peaceful and joyous human being, will you consider that well-being? Now yoga and meditation – it is improper to say yoga and meditation: when we say yoga, it includes meditation. This yogic science is of utmost importance now, like never before. I am not saying it was not important earlier. Why I am saying this is, today we have tremendous tools in our hands to do things in the world. With modern science and technology, we can flatten this mountain (points to the mountains behind him) tomorrow if you want. When we have this kind of power in our hands, it is very, very important that we have an inner sense, an awareness of life, and that we experience life, and every other being as a part of ourselves. Otherwise, you can create a calamity for yourselves, which you are, in many ways right now. You are creating such a calamity that just to breathe is becoming a problem in the world. Just to exist here is becoming a problem in this world. This has happened because you have attended only to the external science. You never looked at the inner science of creating the right kind of inner situation. So definitely yogic science is more relevant than ever before, because today you are powerful. When you are powerful, it is very important that you are sensible.

That reminds me of very powerful people on this planet. Dictators are always held as very powerful in their times and in their countries. One day, Mussolini got all the trains in Italy to run on time. He achieved this by having a few railway engine drivers shot. Then the trains started running on time in Italy. It had never occurred in their history and suddenly it started happening. Mussolini was so thrilled with his achievement, he decided that they must release a postage stamp with his face on it. With his picture he wanted a postal stamp in commemoration of all the trains in Italy running on time for the first time! They released the stamp, but they started noticing a certain problem that wherever the mail went, the stamp always fell off, and in the postman's bag there was always a huge collection of stamps. When this came to Mussolini's notice, he called the Postmaster General and asked him, "Why aren't you using the best quality adhesive, the best glue? Why?" The Postmaster General, with great fear and hesitation told Mussolini, "We are using the highest quality of glue, but most of the people are choosing to spit on the other side of the stamp, so the stamps are not sticking." So it is time that you apply yourself to the right side. The science of yoga will make that dimension become active within you so that all the conveniences and comforts that science has brought can truly lead to human well-being.

Questioner: Dear Sadhguru, what is true bliss?

Sadhguru: How can I tell you! Maybe this question springs from so many influences, that you ask, "What is true bliss?" This is probably because even psychedelic drugs today are being named 'bliss' or 'ecstasy'. If you say 'ecstasy', in the West they will think that you are talking about a particular tablet, a particular drug. So now you are asking what true bliss is.

There is no such thing as true bliss and false bliss. When you are in Truth you will be in bliss. When you are really in touch with Truth, you will naturally be in bliss. So being in bliss and not being blissful is like a litmus test for you, whether you are in Truth or not. Probably this question is coming from a certain mindset, "If by just watching the sunset I become blissful, is that true bliss? When I am saying my prayers if I become blissful, is that true bliss? When I am meditating and have become blissful, is that true bliss?" How you become blissful, it doesn't matter. Somehow you become blissful. That is all that matters.

Now the question is to sustain it, to be able to sustain it. Most people misunderstand pleasure as bliss. You can never sustain pleasure, it always falls short of you; but blissfulness means it is not dependent upon anything. Pleasure is always dependent on something or somebody. Blissfulness is not dependent on anything, it is of your own nature. Blissfulness does not really need any external stimulus as such. Once you are in touch with it, you will know that all your needs were actually a childish attempt to become blissful. When you are blissful, it is absolute. Blissfulness is not something that you earn from outside. It is something that you dig for deep into yourself and find. It is like digging a well. When it is raining, if you open your mouth and wait for raindrops to fall into your mouth, a few of them may get inside, but still, it is quite frustrating to quench your thirst by opening your mouth in the rain. And the rain is not going to last forever. It lasts an hour or two or three and then it is over. That is the reason why you dig your own well, so that you have water throughout the year. So whatever you are referring to as true bliss is just this: you draw water from your own inner well. It sustains you all the time. It is not something like opening your mouth in the rain, no. All the time you have water with you. That is bliss.

Inner Freedom

Women on the path of Freedom… the Master breaks centuries old shackles and speaks on children.

Just because women are physically weaker than men, man has done everything to make them psychologically weaker than himself, spiritually lost and financially nowhere. This attitude of people has continued for thousands of years. All this, just because women are physically weaker than men. There is nothing else. There is no other way a man can claim superiority over a woman except that he is physically stronger, he has more muscle on him. This has gone on for thousands of years. I think it is too long. It is time people stood up and did something about it. Until we learn to respect our women, until every man learns to respect a woman, he will never know himself; there is no way, because half of him is just that.

Indian spirituality has always been a rich mixture of men and women reaching the heights of their consciousness. It is proved beyond doubt that a woman is as much capable as a man when it comes to the inner nature. It is only the peel that you can call a man or a woman. The self is the same. Either you wear a masculine peel or a feminine peel. That is all it is. The peel is not going to decide what your spiritual capabilities are going to be. Maybe there are certain biological disadvantages, but as we see now, psychologically, women are better equipped. Right from the Vedic times there have been many women who have been great saints, who reached the very heights of consciousness. The earliest form of worship always started as worshipping the Divine as a mother, holding the ultimate divinity as the mother. Right from then on, it has continued that way. Even today worship of the feminine aspect as mother is more dominant than worshipping masculine gods. Even today, the ignorant man, when all gods fail him, he goes to the Amman temple (enshrined femininity) to get quick results. How to deal with enshrined femininity?

During the Vedic times, a woman also wore the sacred thread as a Brahmin wears today. She was also eligible to wear the thread, because without the thread you are not supposed to read the Vedas and the Upanishads. Spirituality was not available only to the man; even a woman wore the sacred thread. There have been many great saints; Maitreyi is one among them.

It is said that one day there was a spiritual debate going on in the court of King Janaka. All the saints and sages of that kingdom had assembled there to participate in the spiritual debate. You can even call it a contest to find out what the Truth is and what it is not. King Janaka was a realized being, a king who had realized Truth within himself. So he created a situation where every human being in the country who was on the spiritual path could participate. As the debate progressed, it became very subtle. In the beginning every person in the assembly participated in the debate, but as time went by, people were just sitting and watching the events and eventually no one could understand what was actually going on because it had become so subtle. No one could understand what was happening. In the end only two people remained. One was Yagnavalkya and the other was Maitreyi.

The debate between these two people went on for days. Without sleep or food the debate went on and on. Everybody sat and watched the proceedings, but nobody could understand what was being discussed, it had become so subtle. In the end Yagnavalkya could not answer the questions put forth by Maitreyi. A man who was renowned in the kingdom for his spiritual prowess, most important and well known for his sharp mind, he could not answer the questions. He became angry and agitated. He told her that if she asked one more question she would be blown into bits and pieces. Then King Janaka interfered. He told Yagnavalkya that though he seemed to know everything, it was not a living experience within him and that was the only reason why he could not answer her questions. Then he honored Maitreyi in the presence of the full court.

Yagnavalkya realized his limitations, fell at her feet and asked her to take him as her disciple. Maitreyi chose him as her husband. She said, "You can be my husband, not my disciple," because she saw there could be no other man this close. He had still not found what she had found, but there was no other man she could see at the time, who was this close, so she decided to take him as her husband. They lived together for many years; they raised a family. In the Vedic times, all the practices that were available for men were also available for women. After a certain age, Yagnavalkya one day came and told Maitreyi, "I have decided that I have had enough of this world. Everything that we have, I will give to you and I am going into the forest to find myself." Then Maitreyi asked, "What makes you think that I will settle for mundane things? When you go for the real treasure, what makes you think that I will go for petty things? Will I settle for trinkets?" Then both of them went into the forest and lived as realized beings.

Like this, there are many stories, which make it very clear that during the Vedic times a woman was on par with a man in every way as far as spirituality was concerned. These were well-settled societies. Wherever things are well settled in a society, naturally a woman will dominate. Not necessarily dominate, but she will be on par in every way. Only when strife is created and societies are disturbed and migration comes, then survival becomes the top priority and then man takes over. Whenever such situations occur, a woman becomes highly dependent upon a man. When life becomes very gross, then man will naturally be dominant; but when life becomes very subtle, many times you have to look up to a woman to know what is what. It is so. Maybe it is one of the reasons why man always creates strife, more and more strife everywhere, because that is the only way he can keep up his dominance.

Right from the year 3000 B.C.E. that we know of history, a woman was on par with a man in India. Then barbarian hordes invaded the country from parts of Asia like Mongolia, Central China and Indo-China. They were outsiders who were totally gross, whose ways were to grab things and live. Then somewhere along the way, in this atmosphere, a woman slowly lost her freedom. The invaders would take or grab anything and go. So man started becoming protective. Slowly the process became so biased that they started changing the rules and rewrote the Shastras, the Smruthis. Vedas are the Shruthis; they talk about the Ultimate Reality, and not fixing lives in any way. But then they wrote the Smruthis and we can say a large segment of the Smruthis are only about fixing a woman in many ways. Maybe for a certain period it was a compulsion because the physical situation was such that some restriction had to be put on a woman, but, unfortunately, it was made the law. In the Shruthis, the first let down for a woman was when they declared that a woman cannot wear a sacred thread. It should have been written over a period of time, not all at once. Slowly they went further, saying that the only way a woman could attain to mukthi or her Ultimate Nature was by serving her husband. There was no other way, they decided.

During the Vedic times, a woman could dissolve her family whenever she wanted. As a man had the freedom, a woman also had this same freedom. There are many instances where women have done this without any social reprisals. It was accepted in the society. A woman took her mate when she wanted to. Once she felt she had grown out of the need, she left it, the same way a man was doing. A man got married, he lived within the marriage for ten to twenty years, and when he had the urge to become spiritual he renounced the family. Similarly, a woman also had the same right. When she got the urge to grow, she also would renounce the family. This was perfectly accepted during the Vedic times.

Somewhere along the way, somebody fixed it that only a man could renounce. Nobody ever asked, nobody ever answered if you asked questions, "Okay, a man can renounce a woman when he wants to become spiritual. It is everybody's right to renounce whatever they have. If a man can renounce a woman, who is going to take care of the family?" These questions are never answered. It was left just like that. If both have the same freedom, it is different. If only one person has the freedom and the other person doesn't, then it is simply exploitation. I think since this kind of law was passed, unfortunately, very few men and women have been really happy together. Yes, because two people can be happy and joyous, only when they meet in freedom. When they meet in bondage, you marry a slave who has been a slave from the day she was born. You have trained her only to be your slave, nothing else. There is no way you can enjoy your life. Maybe at the most she is convenient, she caters to your needs, but you cannot enjoy your life.

Unfortunately, even today, in the twentieth century, the same continues. It has been made clear that the moment you are born as a woman, you are born either to serve your father or your husband. Beyond that, you have nothing else. This has been taught by people who are talking about *advaitha*, the non-duality of existence, that everything is one, but a woman is less. I don't know what sense it made to them. Nobody can be an advaithist; nobody can be a non-dual person if he cannot even accept a sexual difference out of which he has come. He knows his existence depends upon the woman and if he cannot accept her, his accepting all the dualities in the existence is simply out of the question.

The very existence depends upon her. In fact she has a bigger role to play in perpetuating human existence than a man does. A man's role is very limited. When he cannot accept her, I think he is either crooked or terribly ignorant. Mostly it is out of crookedness because there is some advantage. When there is an advantage, why give it up?

Whether it is fair or unfair is not the point. "When I have the advantage, why give it up?" If this attitude does not go, there is no spirituality. It cannot be, it simply cannot be.

It is still true that the same man who goes and prostrates in front of the Amman temple returns and beats his wife at home. He may be ignorant, but he is also crooked. Without the crookedness this will not happen. Now it is not about a woman going out and doing what a man is doing. That will become obscene. This is happening in the West and to some extent here also. Women are trying to become like men. If that happens, the damage will be even greater. If a woman loses her femininity, her feminine nature, she will become ugly. The idea that a woman wants to become like a man is itself a sick idea. Why does she want to become like a man? Because somewhere she still thinks that she is inferior and man is superior, so she wants to become like him.

Questioner: But Sadhguru, man has proven to be superior in all fields. So now women think they can imitate him and then maybe become his equal.

Sadhguru: That is not the point. The question of inferiority or superiority only comes in a prejudiced mind. It is just a question of two qualities. It is not a question of who is inferior and who is superior. From the day a woman is born, you are making sure that she will have nothing to fight with, isn't it? It is not just with marriage alone. You do this from the day she is born. In every aspect, you make sure that the slave mentality is imposed upon her. When it happens in front of me, it just burns me up. Now, if you think that a woman, out of whom you are born, is inferior, how can you be superior? That possibility just does not arise.

The problem is not just between one man and one woman. The problem is universal. It is not just about one gross man thinking like this. You have made this your way of life. You have made this the fundamentals of your homes, your society and everything. You have made this a part of your very culture, your very religion! It looks like your very souls are affected, to that extent you have taken this. It has been ingrained into everyone for ages. It is time people stand up and do something.

As Vivekananda said once when he was speaking, a certain social reformer came and said, "It is great that you also support women, what shall I do? I want to reform, and I want to support." So Vivekananda said, "Hands off, you don't have to do anything about them; you just leave them alone. They will do what they have to do." Yes, that's all that is needed. It is not that a man has to reform a woman. If he just gives her room, she will do what is necessary. Right now, I see she is more refined.

Questioner: Aren't women also contributing to this unfortunate situation that they are in right now?

Sadhguru: Yes, at times, though unfortunately, a woman is again her own greatest enemy. This is also true. Women are their own greatest enemies. In moments of tenderness, in moments of love, man breaks his monopoly and lets her free; but if there is another woman around, she will make sure it does not happen. The whole culture has done this to her one way or the other and she has been conditioned for centuries to settle for petty things. Maitreyi asked Yagnavalkya that question, but most women are just settling for petty things in life. So man definitely thinks she is inferior. He goes for big things in life and she goes for petty trinkets, because we have made it that way that a woman desires only these petty things. Her whole life is about that. Women have made themselves like that and men have supported it.

Questioner: Sadhguru, why is walking on the spiritual path looked upon as revolutionary? Why is it seen as such a big step to walk out of the standard way of life? Is it because nothing is certain here and we don't even know whether we will reach or not?

Sadhguru: Probably in your life it was a revolution. For me, when I walked out of it, it was one more step, a natural step for me to take. That is all. Maybe for you, the way you have been brought up, the way you have lived, it is a big step. I acknowledge that. It is a big step. In this kind of a society, a girl stepping out and saying, "I am going to do something other than what others are doing," must be a great step, but don't think your problem is over the moment you step out. The problems have just started, okay? Do not think just because you have stepped out of one structure, your problems are over. It is just the beginning of the problems. So many things will come when you have to make a new path. If you just tread the old path, everybody's path, which the majority of people also walk, everything is wide open. It is a highway. Maybe it doesn't get you anywhere, but you can walk easily. When you have to make a new path and walk, you know it involves risk. Do you know there are risks here? Don't think Isha is safe. There is risk. Yes? Suppose I die tomorrow, I don't know what these people will do to you when I am gone. I am not talking about my death, but I am talking about your security. I am talking about you looking at it.

Questioner: I don't foresee such a thing happening.

Sadhguru: I am not saying that you must plan for it right now. I am asking you, do you know life is uncertain? Things may not go as you plan. I am not trying to threaten you. I am just telling you to look at every aspect of life. Whenever you take a step you must know, if you have so much trust that anything is going to be okay, "Whatever happens is okay with me," then it is different; but if there is fear, you have to look at everything, every aspect of it you have to look at before it happens. If there is no fear, "I don't care what happens, whether I live or die, this is what I will do," then it is okay for such a person. Once a person doesn't care whether he lives or dies, that person has no limitation. He can do anything he wants. People who want to live well, they have to think. Yes, they have to think hundreds of times; just once is not enough.

Someone who walks the spiritual path is one who does not care what happens. His only wish and desire is to take one step now. He doesn't care whether he is going to attain mukthi now or he is going to come back for a thousand lifetimes; he is not bothered. He does not care, but now he wants to take this one step. That is the only goal in his life. He is not bothered about the end result. That person has no problem. Somehow life takes care of him. Are you like that? If there is fear, you must look. If there is no fear at all, you don't care what happens, then it is okay. For such people there is something else that takes care of them.

People used to ask Ramakrishna, "See, my job, family and work, what will I do?" He would say, "So you must go and work." If they asked, "But then, my spiritual path?" He told them, "Yes, then you must go on the spiritual path." If they say, "But then my office," he says, "Yes, yes, then you must go to the office." "Then what shall I do?" He used to go on doing this; he never used to give them any answer. When the day came, when just the name of God, just if you say, 'Ramakrishna', tears will flow in your eyes, that day you don't have to work. Do you understand? You have reached such a point that if you just utter the name Ramakrishna; tears will flow from your eyes. Now you don't have to work. You come, God will take care of you; but if you are thinking what will happen, how, when... then you must work. If you come unripe, you will suffer here. It is better if you suffer there. So unripe fruits don't pluck yourselves. Let it ripen and fall by itself.

Are you a ripe one or a raw one? If you have enough maturity to tell your family what you are going to do with life, that this is not just something that you have jumped into because somebody told you, then go ahead. If you have made a decision about it and you know the ins and outs of it and still you arrived at the decision – you know the risk, but still you are making the decision, then yes. If you are really there, if there is no question of making a decision for you, you have reached a point where you cannot make a decision, then yes. There is only one decision you can make in your life. If you have reached that point, then also there is no problem. Okay, there is something else here which takes care of you, but if you are still thinking, calculating which is better, choose the other one. This is not the better path.

The spiritual path is not a better path. It is a different path. It can't be compared with anything else. If you are a thinking kind – if I become an engineer, a doctor – if you are thinking on those terms, you had better choose that. That is safe; but if you have reached a point that you have no choice, "This is the only thing I can do and there is nothing else for me in my life," then this is the best thing in life. Do you understand? Make sure it is clear within you. If you think doing yoga is better than going to the office, no, it is not so. If you cannot do anything but this, if you have reached that point, then this is a great path.

Questioner: But I don't know how to convince my people. They don't seem to understand anything.

Sadhguru: If that is so, tell them in the way they can understand. All these days it has been food, office, work, and suddenly now you go and tell them that you want mukthi. What sense does it make? How you tell them is up to you.

Questioner: They seem to be very skeptical about this path; and also every time you put me on a new process, I fail. The others progress, I feel ditched.

Sadhguru: Their skepticism is different, but within yourself, you should be one hundred percent clear about what you are doing. If you are not clear, then every time we do a new process, you feel ditched. Yes. Every time there is a new turn, you feel you have been ditched. It is not about ditching anybody, no question about ditching anybody because first of all, there is no promise, so how can we break it? If there is a promise it can be broken. Love cannot be broken; promises can be broken. Somebody who is loving, how can you break it? Whatever you do, it does not break. Whether you are here or there, you can love from anywhere. So it should be like that. Ramakrishna puts it correctly. Ramakrishna says, "When it is everything for you, now you don't worry about food, security... for such a person things will be taken care of," but if your mind is thinking, "Which is better? Which is better?" then this is definitely not the better path. This is a great path, but not better than something else. Those worldly things are safe, but there you will die and here also you will die. Okay?

When you are young, you might not know that you will die, isn't it? Maybe you know that on certain days, but experientially, moment-to-moment you don't know, isn't it? But you must know. Everybody should know; never forget that whichever way, you are going to die. So what little time you have, how you are going to spend it, is what you need to decide. Just see, if you just look at it, there is no guarantee for you. My life is guaranteed. For a certain period, my life is guaranteed. For you, you don't even have that guarantee. Yes? So it can happen any time. So whenever it is going to happen – I wish you a long life– but whenever it is going to happen, it is still a very short period of time! It could be just three days, it could be thirty years, we don't know. Actually the time that you have is only this moment, because death could be in the next moment. Yes? Actually, the living time you have is only this moment. So how do you want to spend this moment? That is all the question is about life. This is the fundamental question about life. How do you want to spend this moment?

People are always planning how to spend the next thirty years. I am asking how do you want to spend this moment? Free, bound, joyous, stuck, miserable, attached, loving – how do you want to spend this moment? See only this moment is guaranteed. The next moment is not guaranteed for anybody, isn't it? How you want to spend this moment? That is all you can plan and it doesn't need planning. When I say this moment, this moment you can't do anything. That is there. The way it is, that's the way it is, but how do you want to live? Many times you may not have the choice of doing what you want to do. At times, external circumstances will decide what you may have to do in life, isn't it? All those are outside things, but how you are going to be internally? This you need not allow the external to decide. This you can decide now.

Questioner: I see a lot of women wearing *rudhraksha* here. Can a woman wear them?

Sadhguru: Why I am particularly encouraging women to wear rudhraksha is to let them also wear what a man wears with pride. Not chains. When what a man wears, you also wear with freedom, they don't like it. When you wear a rudhraksha mala it means that you have gone beyond all the petty things in life. Now if you wear ten gold chains and on top of that you wear a rudhraksha mala also, it is just stupid. That person who wears the mala, she cannot be chained. Yes, a person who wears rudhraksha cannot be chained any more. They are walking on the path of freedom, but it has to be made clear that rudhraksha is not one more fancy thing that you wear when you want to, and take off when you don't. They must understand the seriousness of wearing it.

Questioner: You have said that in spirituality there will usually be more women than men. But there have been many Masters such as Ramana and Ramakrishna, and nobody has spoken about any women being Masters. Why is this so?

Sadhguru: A woman can generally never make an effective Master. Her femininity will not allow her to be an effective Master, but at pursuing the path, she is very good. To grow on the path you need a way of receiving. That receptivity comes naturally to a woman. Whatever you call masculine or feminine is just the body. Nature has created it like this to fulfill its purpose of procreation and so on. So when you say a *woman*, basically you are talking about physiology, a body, nothing else.

When we say body, in the body we also include the mind, because without creating a feminine mind, a feminine body cannot be nurtured. It is not possible. The receptivity has to be on all levels. Otherwise, she cannot carry the womb. The womb itself is receptivity. It is because of the womb that she has become a woman. The word *woman* comes from the word *womb*. It is only because of the womb that she carries, that she can bear a child. That is why she is a woman. The womb means receptivity. A *wo-man* is a man with a womb.

Man cannot receive anything. He can do things here and there, but receptivity is less for him. It is not that he cannot prepare himself; he can, but a woman comes with that natural quality. So naturally when there is a Master, more women will gather because they are more suited for receiving; but rarely do you find a woman Master. Even if you find her, she will be very entangled in social situations, which will not allow her to function as a Master. She will not be very good in terms of truly opening up a path. At the most, she will teach devotion, bhakthi. See, being a Master and being a butcher are not very different. He must be of that kind who brings things up lovingly and then slaughters them when it is necessary. This, a woman cannot do.

It is not in her nature to do so. I am not saying she cannot do this at all. When I say a woman, her quality cannot do that kind of an act. And though every Master is always talking about surrender, devotion, going beyond the logical, he is very logical himself. He may be rooted in an experience beyond logic, but he is extremely logical in everything because construction and demolition involve logic. Now a woman will talk about dissolution right from the beginning. So she will never make a good Master. She cannot construct and then demolish. Whatever she constructs, she becomes extremely possessive of it.

That is a problem with a woman always. Anything she constructs, she becomes extremely possessive of it. There is no way she is going to demolish it. This story illustrates the possessiveness of feminine nature. There was a Buddhist nun. She was always traveling, always moving. She had her own Buddha statue with her. Once, she went and stayed in a temple where there were thousands of Buddha statues. In the morning she lights incense. She sees that it is spreading to all the other Buddha statues. She doesn't like it. She makes a funnel so that the incense goes only to her Buddha. After some time, Buddha's nose turned black. A little later his face became black because she funneled incense into his face. In the process of funneling incense into her Buddha, slowly she turned her Buddha's face black. Because that was her nature, she became very possessive. It was not that she could not transcend it, she could.

I am just talking about why there aren't too many women Masters and even if there are, usually they are on the path of devotion. There have been some very wonderful Masters among women, but they are of a different kind. We have always found that they operate in a completely different way. They cannot operate the way a man operates. They have to find that kind of a situation, that kind of a support system in the society.

Another aspect is that society has never supported a woman as a Master. They killed them before they became anything. Especially in the West, whenever a woman started expressing her wisdom, wherever a woman started having access to something beyond what normal people had, they were labeled as witches and burned at the stake. Thousands of women have been burnt at the stake in Europe especially. Even today, in modern countries like the United States, if somebody is looked upon as a witch, that is it. They won't burn them today, but the whole community sort of excommunicates them. Once she just starts exhibiting some other qualities, she gets labeled like that. Once she evolves into a certain state, she may become so open, she may become physically free in many ways, that people think she has lost her morals. That is the only way they can understand her.

So once they see that, they will do many things to suppress her. Usually, they were killed. Now you can't kill them, there is a law against it. So in many other ways they get fixed. She has that disadvantage. At the same time, there are a few women who have more masculine fire in them than most men. There are women like that. These kind of women can become very wonderful Masters, if the social support is there. There are such people, but in all these centuries of human history that we know of, that support was never there for them. Probably in the future it should be possible. We may see many women as spiritual Masters.

Questioner: If we have to bring up our children without making them distorted or rotten like us, what kind of situation should we create for them?

Sadhguru: If this much realization has come to you that your life is distorted, then the first thing to do is, do not touch your children, do not influence their minds with your distorted minds. That is the first step you need to take.

Questioner: But Sadhguru, if I don't influence my child, there are many other rotten minds around; they may be more rotten than mine.

Sadhguru: Yes, the possibility is very much there. The child can get exposed to all the other rotten minds. You can't isolate him totally from the rotten minds, because they are everywhere in the world, yes? Yes, they are everywhere in the world. You definitely cannot isolate your child. Now the questions: "What should I do? What should my child's education be? How should I bring him up? How should I guide him?" You just encourage him to be intelligent, to be aware. Every being has been given the necessary intelligence to fulfill his life. An ant is born, you study it and see. It has all the intelligence to live an ant's life fully. It may not be able to do what you are doing, but as an ant, the necessary intelligence for being an ant is there for it. The same goes for every creature. Similarly, it goes for you, too. You too have the necessary intelligence to live your life to the fullest.

Now the problem is that you want your child to be intelligent your way, not his. You want the child to be intelligent the way you understand intelligence. Now, your idea of intelligence is, your child should become a doctor. Maybe he would have made a wonderful carpenter, but you want him to become a doctor, not because doctors are needed in the world, not because you care so much for the suffering that you want your child to dedicate himself as a doctor, but simply because you have a stupid idea in your head that in the social structure, a doctor or an engineer means some kind of prestige or some nonsense for you. This is because you yourself have found no substance within yourself. You want to live your life through your children. "My child is a doctor!" This is a sure way to destroy children. This is a definite way to destroy children.

Now, every child does have the necessary intelligence. You create an atmosphere for him to grow into his intelligence rather than superimposing your rottenness on him. When it comes to influencing him, the teachers will have a role, his friends will have some, and the other sections of society will have some influence on him. You can't help it totally. You can't build a sanatorium for your child, but still, as a parent, you can play a very important role in allowing the child's intelligence to grow. First of all, if you have come to the idea that when a child is born it is time to teach, then you will ruin the child. When a child comes into your life, it is a time to learn, because you have missed much in your life. So much of you has become distorted.

Now a child is just there looking at life fresh. You sit with him and look at life fresh. Your rottenness will also go to some extent, too. His intelligence will grow. The only thing that you can do to your child is to give him love and support. That is all. Create a loving atmosphere for him where intelligence will naturally flower. That's the only thing that you can do. Your child need not do what you did in life. Your child should do something that you did not even dare to think of in your life. Yes? Your child should do what you did not even have the courage to think about. You did not have the courage to even nurture a thought like that. Your child should do that. Only then this world will progress and something will happen, isn't it? Especially in India, where we have a vast humanity of children.

Actually, today it is a crime to produce a child in this country. One billion people! You have not done this out of love. You have done this probably because you have nothing else to do. You have found nothing else worthwhile to do, so you are going on producing children. Not out of love for life, only out of insecurity or because you had nothing else to do, mostly because of insecurity.

People understand that to bring up a child lovingly means to get him everything that he asks for. This is very stupid and disgusting. First of all, you are not even looking at your child with intelligence. If you look at your child with intelligence, do you see that to get him everything that he asks for is sheer stupidity? To this, you have given the name 'love'. How should you bring up a child? In whichever situation he is put, he should be able to live joyously, isn't it? That is the way he should be brought up.

If you want to bring up your child well, the first thing is that you should be happy; but you, by yourself, do not know how to be happy. In your house everyday there is a demonstration of tension, anger, fear, anxiety and jealousy. Only these things are being demonstrated to your child. What will happen to him? He will learn only these. If you really have the intention of bringing up your child well, you must first change your way of being. You should change yourself to be a loving, joyous and peaceful being. If you don't know how to keep yourself as a joyous, peaceful and loving human being, what can you do for your child? Your child will only imbibe your tensions, anger, anxiety and every other nonsense. If you are really concerned about your child, first you must be willing to transform yourself. If you are incapable of transforming yourself, where is the question of you bringing up your child? So is it not better that you think it over before giving birth to a child, whether you are capable or not, whether in this life you need it or not? Isn't it?

Questioner: I did not think on those lines.

Sadhguru: Only when you think we can say that you are intelligent. Otherwise, we will say you are only a goat. If you are an animal, you will think only after giving birth. If you are a human being you have to think beforehand. If you are a human being, before doing anything you have to think whether you want to get into it or not. Only then it will be the human way of being. After doing everything you think, it is animal nature, isn't it? First of all, in this nation today, to give birth to a child itself is a crime. In this department alone you have succeeded. You have created one billion people; there's no place to sit or stand!

Questioner: Yes, Sadhguru, even in this hall they said there is space for only two hundred people, but actually there is more than five hundred of us sitting here.

Sadhguru: (Laughs) That is what I too am asking for this country. We should have stopped at half a billion. It is a shame that you have created such a situation in this country. It pains me to see this. Such a rich culture, but today the way it is, is disgusting. The man on the street in any country, if you compare the state of an ordinary man, he is much better off than the man on the streets in this country. Such a rich culture with so many religions. We claim that all the religions were born here. We know everything about God, but our situation is like this. This is basically because we have no control over our population. We have become like cows and goats.

Questioner: But Swamiji, cows and goats are also life!

Sadhguru: Yes, everything is life, but what is disgusting is that such an evolved being – this being can realize Divinity – such a being is now kept like an animal. This is only because of our over population.

Questioner: Dear Sadhguru, these days on any given television channel, whether they show God or not, they show ghosts. Are there ghosts? My little son who watches this is scared to enter dark rooms. The other day when I was traveling with my son, he pointed to a pig and asked, "Appa, what is this?" Only then I realized that he did not know what a pig is, but this ghost, which neither I have seen nor has my father seen, has become a reality for my son because of television shows. What to do about this?

Sadhguru: Now, because of this television, the characters and people that you normally do not allow into your house otherwise are making a forceful entry. All of them enter your house. A drunk, a murderer, a devil, a ghost, everyone comes into your house and dances. Normally, you won't allow such characters inside your house. Everyone has now come into your house. It is you who has to decide to what extent you should allow them, what their role is going to be. Otherwise, they will take over your house. They will occupy your children's mind. It will be so because they are seeing only devils and ghosts every day.

The childishness and immaturity of modern science is such that anything that is discovered, they want to spread it to the world. One thing is that the scientist has patented it and there is much money involved in it. Another thing is that someone else can manufacture it and make more money. It is projected as, "Whatever I know, everybody should know." Unfortunately, this is freedom of knowledge.

This is not the way the Indian culture had handled situations. For example, in yoga there are many levels of being. It is a vast science. When you come for a thirteen-day or a seven-day program, you are taught only the fundamentals of it. After that, based on your capacity we lead you to higher and higher levels. Now modern education is not like that. Everything is made available to everybody, but the human mind lacks the maturity to handle the vast knowledge that is available. Today, even children can search the Internet and collect data. Now they make bombs at home, shoot at each other because we said all knowledge should be made available to everybody. You think all this is openness. It is not so.

See in the Vedic science there is a very detailed description of how to create an airplane. A similar kind of airplane was created by someone in Bombay in 1896. They even flew it. This news appeared in the newspapers in England. After the airplane was made to fly it was just discarded. They made sure that it would not be available to anyone. What they said in the Vedic science was that an airplane could be built and flown, but if these airplanes are allowed to fly, they will create unnecessary disturbance in the ether, which will further lead to unnecessary disturbances in the minds of humans. Because of this, it was said that these airplanes should not be used unless it was an absolute necessity. They had written this in the description itself.

Now is this possible today? When something is discovered, you dance in celebration, but when it is said, after ten years, that only because of this all these other problems have come, you cry, and to rectify the situation, you do something else. This has been happening all the time in history, because your understanding is fragmented. You are just going on like this because your understanding is not in totality. There is a specialist for everything, a specialist for the right ear, another for the left, another for the eyes, the nose...there is a specialist for each. These days you don't have the capability to see what is needed for the whole human being. In the future, we will probably have thirty-two specialists for all the thirty-two teeth. For every tooth, one specialist. Science is getting fragmented, and fragmented, and fragmented.

The same thing is happening with the television. Somebody invented it. Somebody made a big industry out of it, an industry that runs twenty-four hours a day. What can they telecast for twenty-four hours? How many programs can they invent and telecast? So they have created their own versions of ghosts and devils which are not there. Now these two hundred-odd channels that are available today have to do something to run the show. So all that transpires on the television screen is nothing but distorted versions of the human mind. You have to decide whether you want to see it or not, whether you want to expose your child to it or not. Naturally, when your child is exposed to this, he develops fear. Mental sickness can also arise out of this. You need to judge to what extent you allow this into your house.

Questioner: What is a full and complete life? What is used to measure this and how does one recognize that person?

Sadhguru: Your lives will not attain fulfillment by some action. In every stage of your life you thought, "If this happens, my life will become complete." This thought may have come up within you. When you were a child you thought, "If I get this toy, my life will be complete." You got that. After three days you took it and threw it into the dustbin. Life did not attain fulfillment. When you were in school, you thought that if you passed your examination, life would be complete. That happened, and nothing happened. Then you thought if you complete your education, your life would be complete. That too happened. Then you thought, what is the use of all this education if you are not able to stand on your own two feet? That happened. After three months you began to think, what is the use of working like a donkey? If you get married to that man or woman who is in your heart, your life would become complete. That happened and then you know what happened!

It has been going on like this. For slightly older people, they believe that their lives would become complete if they get their daughters married. Only when you get your daughter married all your problems will start, isn't it? It has been going on like this. Whatever action you may perform, life has not attained any fulfillment. Fulfillment will not come because of some action that you perform. Only if your inner nature is complete, your lives will attain fulfillment.

If your inner nature is unbounded, your life is also unbounded. You can either sit with your eyes closed and your life is complete or you perform different actions and your life can be complete. When man has reached a state where within himself he does not have the need to perform any action and his actions are only to the extent required for the external situation, then that man has become complete. Once a man has reached the state where he does not have the need within himself to perform

98

any action, then that man is a complete person. Why have you been performing one action after another? It is towards fulfillment, isn't it?

There are many people who perform actions to excess. When you ask why they are doing all that they are doing, they answer, "What to do? Food, wife, kids, who will take care of them?" Then we tell them, "Come to the ashram. Your food and your family will be taken care of. You just come and sit quietly." This person cannot sit for a day. He cannot even sit for three hours! He has to do something. If we ask him, "Why are you doing all this? All your needs have been taken care of, why don't you simply sit?" He cannot sit, he has to do something. Why this is so is because his inner nature has not attained fulfillment and he is trying to do so through actions. Your actions are not happening for food or comfort, they are all happening in search of fulfillment. Whether this has happened with awareness or without awareness, the actions indicate the search for unboundedness.

If within you, your inner nature has attained fulfillment, there will be no need for action. If the external situation demands some action, you can do it joyously. If it is not needed, you can simply sit with your eyes closed. When a person has reached a state where there is no need to perform any action, we can say that the person has become unbounded. That does not mean that this person does not do any work at all. If the external situation demands it, he can work twenty-four hours a day, but action is not needed for his inner nature. He is not bound to action. He is not something because of his actions. He is the same, even without any action.

Questioner: What is the need for a person to be born in this world and then to die?

Sadhguru: They are born, so they have to die. It is easy to say why a person dies. It is because he is born, he has to die. Why is a person born?

Now the question has come up, "Why is there life?" Always when questions like, "Why is life there? Why should a person be alive? Why is there a universe?" are asked, then I will have to tell you only stories like: one day, God was sitting without any work to do. He was playing with marbles. One marble fell here and became our earth. Another fell there and became the Sun and he did something else and there were human beings. Like this, I can go on telling you stories. Whatever stories I tell you, some may believe them, some may disbelieve them. Whether you believe these stories or not, your lives are not going to be enriched in any way.

Many of you have always believed in many things all along. Now how many of you here believe in God? (Many hands go up) Okay. How many of you don't believe in God? (Very few hands go up) You are very few! Some people believe in God and some people disbelieve in God. In this group how many of you believe that you have two hands? All those people raise one hand. Do you believe you have two hands, or do you know you have two hands? Even if we don't have eyes to see the hands, experientially we know we have two hands, isn't it? Can someone start a discussion with you and prove to you that you don't have two hands? Is it possible? If the discussion gets very heated, all you have to do is give one slap to the man and he will know that you have hands. You know you have hands but you believe in God, why? All that we do not know, we believe. Some people believe there is God and some believe there is no God. Whether you believe or disbelieve, it is of no use. If you see that you don't know, then a search will begin within you. Once the need to search has come, then an answer is not far off. Once you begin to believe in something, then the search within yourself has been destroyed. Isn't it so? If you say, "This is so," you have come to a conclusion. Once you have concluded something, then even the basic quest to know the truth has been destroyed within you.

Once, Gautama the Buddha was sitting in a congregation of his disciples early one morning before sunrise. It was still dark. One man came there. He was a great Ram bhaktha. All his life he had said, "Ram, Ram, Ram." He had said nothing else all of his life. Even his clothes have "Ram, Ram," written all over. He had not only been to temples, he had also built many temples. He was growing old and a little doubt had come. "All my life I have said 'Ram, Ram,' but those people who disbelieve in God, even for them the sun rises. Breath happens for them too. They are also joyous and have had lots of happy occasions in their lives. I have just been sitting saying, 'Ram, Ram.' Suppose that, like they say, there is no God, my whole life would have been wasted!" He knew there is God, but a little doubt had come, that was all. "An enlightened being is here, so let me clear my doubt." But how to ask the question in front of everyone? So he came in at dawn when it was still dark and standing in one corner, asked this question, "Is there God or not?" Gautama looked at him and said, "No." There was an, "Ooof," amidst the disciples, a big sigh of relief. This struggle, whether there is God or not, had been happening daily with them. Many times they have asked this question to Gautama and every time this question was asked, Gautama would remain silent. This is the first time he clearly said, "No."

How joyous it is to be without God! You can do anything in your lives. There is no one to keep tabs on you as to what you are doing and what you are not doing. There is no one to put you in hell and torture you. You are absolutely free. If there is no God, you are absolutely free, isn't that so? You can do anything in your life. Absolute joy amidst the disciples. That day was a happy day for everyone. In the evening, again Buddha was sitting amidst his disciples when another man came. He was a *charwaka*. Do you know who a charwaka is? In those days there was a group called the charwakas. They are out and out materialistic people. They don't believe in anything. They believe in only what they can see.

Nothing else exists. They will come to your town and throw a challenge at you: "If you can prove there is God, I will give you ten gold coins; but if I prove to you that there is no God, then all of you together should give me one hundred gold coins." His whole life, he had earned only this way. He kept going from one town to another town and proves that there is no God, no God. This was his job. He was a big man in his field and he had proven to thousands of people that there is no God.

Now he was growing old and a little doubt had come. "I have been telling people there is no God all my life. Suppose there is God? Will he leave me when I go there? People were saying there is something called Hell." Little doubt. He knows there is no God; he had been proving it all his life, but a little doubt had come. "Suppose there is God? Why take a risk? There is an enlightened being in town. Let me ask him." So, late in the evening, when it was dark, he came and stood there and asked Gautama, "Is there God?" Gautama looked at him and said, "Yes." Again a big struggle began amidst the disciples. All morning they were very happy because he had said there is no God, but in the evening he is saying there is God. Why is this so?

If the need to grow is deep within you, if that is your aim, first of all you should be clear about what is there in your experience and what is not. Clearly mark what is there in your experience and what is not. What is there in your experience, you know. What is not there in your experience you need not say it does not exist. Just say, "I don't know." If you have reached this state, growth will happen by itself. What you don't know, if you accept that you do not know, then there will be growth. Instead, if you start believing in whatever you do not know, you will think you know everything. You know God, you know where He is, you know His name, you know who His wife is, you know how many children He has, you know His birthday, you know what sweets He likes for His birthday. You know everything, but you don't know what is happening within you; and that is the whole trouble right now.

You even know the address of heaven, but there is no awareness of what is happening within you at this moment.

Now, if growth has to happen within you, you should see what is there in your experience right now. Right now, what is there in your experience? You have experienced your body to some extent. You have experienced your mind to some extent. You have experienced the world to some extent. In some moments, you might have also experienced to a certain extent the energy which makes this body and mind function. Beyond this you have not experienced anything. Everything else is just imagination. Whichever way the society has taught you, your imagination is that way. Look into what is there in your experience and what is not. All that is not there in your experience you accept as, "I do not know." This is very, very essential. Otherwise, this whole life will pass in pretensions.

Though you believe in God so much, why has your life still not become complete? In your own house there must be at least one dozen gods. Isn't that so? Not one or two. There must be a minimum of one dozen gods, isn't it? One dozen gods in the house and fear in the heart, does it make any sense to you? If gods are sitting in your house, is there a possibility for fear? Is there such a possibility? You have one dozen gods in the house and still you are in fear. What is the meaning of this? You are always pretending something or the other and the real search has not begun within you. You just go on believing what is comfortable for you.

You don't have to come to any conclusion. What you do not know, if you accept as, "I do not know," then the search will happen within. Whether it is God or whether it is Truth, if you have to search, where should you search? You should search within, isn't it? If you have to search within, if you have to realize within, you need an appropriate tool. Let us say you have an urge to know the depth of the ocean. Is it possible to do that with a foot scale? Is it possible? Is it possible to measure the depth of the ocean with a foot scale? You will come back with the conclusion that the ocean is bottomless. Yes? You will only come to the conclusion that it is bottomless, but that is not the truth. To go inward, you need to have the necessary tool. What is there with you right now to go inward? Just your five sense organs. You have nothing else to search with. Whatever you have to experience, what tool do you have right now? Just your five sense organs. These five sense organs can realize only materialistic things. Isn't it so? There is no chance of experiencing what is beyond the materialistic world with these limited tools.

Now this body is sitting here; this is very important right now. You have to feed it, you have to clothe it, you have to decorate it and you have to do so many things to it. There is something invaluable within you, and until now you have not experienced that. This something which is within you, if it goes away tomorrow morning, nobody wants this body after that. Even your city municipality does not want it after that. Isn't that so?

Only because the fruit called life is inside this peel, this skin has so much value. What happens if the fruit within is gone? There is nothing after that, but you are not bothered about the fruit. You are very much preoccupied with the peel. If you keep on eating the peel all your life how will it be? Bitter isn't it? The problem with the peel is that there is some sweetness here and there. Because of its association with the fruit, there is sweetness here and there. Now your whole life is about searching for that sweetness. If you struggle a lot, you will find some sweetness here and there. Instead of this, if you are able to realize the fruit beyond the peel, you can always be joyous. There is every possibility that you can always be in this sweetness. Had this peel been completely bitter, you would have all been enlightened by now. The trouble is, there is some sweetness here and there and you have gone after that sweetness and forgotten the very source.

Questioner: Will a horoscope be a reason for a man's success or failure? Will there be any positive result from altering a name according to numerology?

Sadhguru: In this crowd, if there is one intelligent human being, can you predict what he is going to do the next second? Can you predict it? No, because he may do something which nobody has ever done before. There is every possibility for that, isn't it? If there is an intelligent being here, there is every possibility that he can create an event which has never happened in the world before. Is there such a possibility? Yes. Now there is an idiot here. The moment you see him you can predict right now how he is going to live his life. Isn't that so? Now they have written it for you on a piece of paper as to how you are going to live. What does that mean? It does not necessarily mean to say that you have no intelligence, but it seems to me that you have decided not to use it. It seems as if you have decided not to exercise your intelligence.

For example, if there is a form, there is a vibration associated with that form; and because of that vibration it acquires a certain quality. Now if I hold this handkerchief this way, it acquires one kind of vibration. If I hold it another way, it acquires another kind of vibration. If you are a little subtle you can experientially feel it. The very vibration itself will change according to the way it is held. Each form has a unique vibration to it. Similarly planets have certain vibrations. Because of this, when planets are in different positions, they have a certain effect on your mental status when certain happenings occur on this planet.

How this is so is, during *pournami* and *amavasya*, on a full moon day and a new moon day, people who are slightly imbalanced tend to become slightly more unbalanced. Do you know this? Are you aware of this? Those who are slightly unbalanced will get a little out of control on those particular days. Do you also become like that on those days? Do we have to hold you on amavasya and pournami?

105

Is it necessary? No? When you compare yourself with them, you are a little stronger mentally, because of this, wherever the moon may be, there is no big change within you. Similarly, if you are a little more balanced, let any planet go anywhere, you will be the way your quality is and not be dictated by any lesser force. All these planets and stars, what are they? They are all inanimate things, isn't it? Just inanimate objects like stone and sand. Is an inanimate object stronger or is human nature stronger? You will have to open your mouths and tell me now.

Questioner: Definitely human nature, Sir.

Sadhguru: Then what is the problem? Should human nature have control over an inanimate object or should an inanimate object have control over human nature? Which should have power over what? Which should rule which? Should human nature rule inanimate things or should inanimate things rule human nature? Human nature should rule inanimate things, isn't it? Then let the stars go anywhere, let the planets go anyhow, why should you bother? If your inner nature is firm and balanced, there is a very definite possibility that you can create your life the way you want it to be.

The science of yoga is a possibility where you can take your whole life, the nature of your body, the nature of your mind, the nature of your life, everything, totally into your control and create it the way you want it to be. To what extent you can take it into your hands is, you can even determine the womb you are going to be born in. You have the power to determine to that extent. There is a science behind this, too. You can even determine when you are going to be born and when you are going to die. There is a science for that, too. This is an inner science and we call this yoga. There is such a possibility for a man.

Now coming to numerology, will it be good for us if we change our names according to numerology? When you asked me this question, I remembered an incident. Four to five years ago. we were doing a program in Tirupur. There was a participant in our Isha Yoga Program. When I saw his nametag, his name was spelt "B a c c h a." I kept calling him, "Baccha, Baccha." The class finished and it was the last day of the program. He came and met me and said, "You kept calling me Baccha, Baccha in the program. My name is not Baccha, it is Badshah." I could not help laughing. Where is Baccha and where is Badshah! Do you know Hindi? *Badshah* means king of kings. *Baccha* means a kid, amateurish or incompetent. Where is the comparison? I asked him why he had spelt it "B a c c h a." He said, "A numerologist asked me to change the spelling of my name this way saying it would be good for me, so I'm spelling Badshah as Baccha." In your life, when you could be a Badshah, when there is a possibility to be a Badshah, you are just choosing to become a Baccha.

Who created these numbers? Was it there in nature? For our convenience, at least to count with our fingers, we created numbers. This one to ten numbering came mainly because of the ten fingers. If we had fourteen fingers, we would have counted eight, nine, daam, doom, too. Because we have only ten fingers we have created the numbers in this way, for our convenience. The tool which we have created for our convenience, can it rule us? I would like to tell an example for this. About six to seven years ago I was driving a Maruti car and I decided to sell it. A person that I knew decided to buy the car from me. I told him that the car had been used very extensively and that he should take a proper look at it and then buy it if he still likes it. He said, "No, no, there is no need to look at anything. I had decided the day you bought the vehicle that I should buy it when you decide to sell it." I asked him why and he told me, "Your car has got a tremendous number." I didn't know that I had been driving a car with such a tremendous number. I told him, "Let the number be. You should drive it and see if you like it before you buy it." "No, no. The number is sufficient." I was wondering how a person could be this way. He told me that the number is three hundred thirty-three and his birthday falls on the third, and it is the third day of the third month, so on that day at eleven forty-five a.m., he would come and collect the car. I told him to ask the rate in the market and give me the money. Seeing the way this man was, I felt he shouldn't be left at that, so I told him that the registration number is only outside, but the real number of the car will be on the engine and the chassis. I said the registration number could be changed anytime, so he should look at the engine number and the chassis number. Now he became very confused. He went to his numerology Guru and told him that I said it is not sufficient to just look at the registration number alone and that he should look at the engine number and the chassis number. His Guru told him that all those numbers were not needed and that the registration number alone would suffice. That man did not even know that the engine and chassis had a number. Only what is seen is needed! So he came and told me, "My Guru said this is sufficient," and bought the vehicle. He told me he would buy it for one hundred thousand rupees. When he brought the money he had brought one rupee less because he wanted to give the amount of ninety-nine thousand, nine hundred and ninety-nine rupees. I said, "Okay," but he was very embarrassed for giving me one rupee less and had brought a huge gift along with the money. I said, "Okay, I am happy as long as you take the car happily." As he was driving along one day, the reclining seat suddenly went backwards. When the seat went back suddenly, he got terribly frightened. He thought some evil spirit had caught hold of him from behind. I happened to visit his home a month later and casually asked him if the car was running well. With great reluctance he told me that he had sold the car as such an evil thing had happened. He could not understand that this had happened only because the reclining mechanism had failed.

Why astrology and numerology are ruling your life is because you are always living in fear. You are not living in love, in peace, in joy, but mostly in fear. When fear is the basis in you, I can make you believe anything.

I can make you believe just about anything. "Every day when you go out of your house you should put this little finger thrice inside your mouth, otherwise you don't know what can happen." If I tell you this, I should actually tell you this as a story with a lot more suspense. I just said it in ridicule. If I say the same thing with a certain graveness and give a mystical explanation to the act, most of you will definitely begin to do this. Many little fingers will get very busy! You don't have any respect for your inner nature. The inanimate objects and numbers that you have created have become very important for you. They are ruling you. That one thing which is above all is within you and you don't have any respect for that. One, two, three, and four have become very important for you now.

Questioner: People who have a negative influence generally turn out to be very close relatives, like my own parents, my wife. If they have a negative influence on me, how do I get relief? How can I not be influenced by them?

Sadhguru: Why do you say they are close to you (laughs)? When you believe or if it is true for you that these people are creating negativity for you, they are not close to you. It is a lie to say that they are close to you. Maybe you are living in the same house, but they are not close to you, obviously. Isn't it? I am not here to tell you how to avoid this person or that person, how to avoid this quality or that quality. What I have been talking right from the beginning is, you cannot become free by giving up something. Even if you leave your home and go, liberation will not happen. Whatever you may leave and go, freedom will not come. If people in your house have become very negative towards you, you should see why they have become this way in the first place. You may be the main cause!

see what you have to do about that. If you have become negative towards each other, then why should you stay together?

Questioner: Then should I leave them and go?

Sadhguru: I am not asking you to leave anything. First of all, however the other person may be, your quality, your inner nature has not become strong enough yet. Your quality is such that whatever a few people tell you, you will become that. If four people tell you that you are a stupid man, you become that. Yesterday in a meeting somebody was telling me that someone called him an idiot. He said, "Someone came all the way from America and called me an idiot. For the last week, the peaceful man that I used to be, has been shattered. Now I plan to file a lawsuit against him. What do you think, Sadhguru?" Somebody said one word and your peace has been shattered for more than a week! What can it mean? It means whatever that man said is true, isn't it? Aren't you being stupid? Your quality, your inner nature is not firm; you become whatever somebody tells you to become. Nobody can do anything negative to you. They are saying whatever they know. They are expressing themselves the way they have understood life. If you are intelligent, you should be able to decide what to do irrespective of whatever they are saying, isn't it? Why do you become negative just because they are telling you something? For you, this quality of *self* is not firm within, and you go in whichever direction the wind blows. That is why this whole struggle.

If you leave your house and go somewhere else, there somebody else can also influence you in a negative manner. Nobody leaves you alone in this world. Wherever you go, they catch up with you, isn't it? After all, what is it that they are doing? They are doing whatever they are doing based on the extent to which they have understood life. That is all they are doing. They cannot do anything else. Isn't it you who is making it negative and positive and creating problems?

Questioner: Dear Sadhguru, you have spoken very harshly about religious conversions which are happening in India at the UN peace summit in New York. But in India you have not spoken about this nor have you identified yourself as a religious leader. Why?

Sadhguru: In the first place, I am not any kind of leader. I want you to know this. I am not a religious leader or a leader of any kind. Nor have I spoken harshly about it. I just said that everybody should choose their religion out of their intelligence, out of the particular needs they have within themselves. They should not choose or be influenced to choose their religion because they have no money, no education or no food to eat. They should not choose their religion based on these factors. Now I don't belong to any particular religion, for that matter. I don't identify myself with any particular religion. Any person who is truly on the spiritual path can never identify himself with any particular group or religion.

Now why is it that I spoke about conversions? Just make all religions available to people. Let them choose whatever they want to. First of all, I feel there is no need to convert anybody into this religion or that religion, and there is no need for anyone to belong to any party. What you are seeing as religion is not a religion. Fundamentally the word religion means an inward step. Religion is not something that you do on the street. It is something that you do within yourself. So if it is an inner process, there is no need to convert somebody, there is no need to form groups, there is no need to be desperate to add numbers to your group, whichever group is doing it. I am not talking about any particular group.

This was spoken in the United Nations in the context of uprooting cultures. In the name of religion, in the name of spreading religion, people are going about rampantly uprooting cultures. Once a culture is uprooted, most of the people will lose their bearing in life. Some of the countries, some of the societies which have been deeply affected by this kind of forceful conversions are the Aborigines in Australia and the Native Americans in North America. The way they have been treated and what has happened to their cultures is truly sad. India: such a rich, gentle culture! It can include any number of cultures. It can include any number of religions into itself. There is no problem, but in the name of spreading religion one does not have to uproot this entire culture. This culture is one of the most colorful; it has taken thousands of years to create this variety. It is so chaotic and yet so beautiful. You cannot make this happen overnight. It has taken thousands of years to evolve into this.

We have a culture, we have a tradition, we have a lineage of people whose maturity is such, it cannot be matched by anybody because it comes from inner realization, not from thinking. Understanding life from within and understanding life from outside are two different things. They can never be compared. It doesn't matter how much you think and how much you propound theories about it. In India, philosophy was not *tathwam*, it was known as *darshana*. Darshana means a vision. You simply look at something, that is all. That is the only way to know the tathwam. You can only know it by vision. That is known as *darshana*. So all Indian philosophies were known as darshanas, not as tathwas. Tathwas were created by scholars. Scholars took over only later; the earlier part of the civilization was pure consciousness. It was only somewhere on the way that the scholars took over and made philosophies out of everything.

When you refer to somebody as a Hindu – I want you to understand this – it is not a religious identity; it is a cultural identity, it is a geographic identity. The word *Hindu* comes from the word *Sindhu* which is a derivative of *Indu*. Whoever is born in the land of Indus is a Hindu. You don't have to ascribe yourself to any particular belief system to be a Hindu. You can believe in God and be a Hindu and disbelieve in God and still be a good Hindu. This is because it is not a religious identity. It doesn't ascribe to any narrow belief system.

belief system. You can be anything and still be a Hindu because it is a cultural identity.

Right now, this Hindu is slowly trying to become an *ism*, trying to become aggressive. This is only because of aggressive religions that have come from outside which started converting people aggressively. With this insecurity, the Hindu community is trying to organize itself into another aggressive group, which is a very sad thing. It is a sad thing to happen to this culture, because they have always welcomed everything that came into this country with open arms. They had no problems, but now, a certain fear has come into these people that if they remain passive, their culture will be wiped out. Now they are trying to organize themselves into groups, violent groups, and do what others did sometime ago in history.

This is very sad and unnecessary for this culture because it has not been afraid of welcoming anything. They have been open to every kind of god, every kind of belief and every kind of philosophy. Any kind of philosophy in the world is accepted, since in this culture, spiritual sciences have been looked at in such depth. Nowhere else has such a thing happened. This culture knows how to manufacture an Enlightened Being. We know that if we do this and this with a person, he has to attain to the Ultimate. No other culture has looked at the inner science with as much depth and understanding as this culture has.

So this culture is definitely very precious – I am not saying this because I belong to it. Any culture, for that matter, is precious, because that is what gives people some roots in life. Everybody is not enlightened and able to live without any identification. They need some identification. It is better to have a cultural identity than a religious identity because the so-called religions have become just a narrow set of beliefs.

Once religions start conversions forcefully and go to the extent of saying, "If you believe this, you are in religion; if you don't believe this,.you will be killed," it ceases to be a religion. It is just a political party. There are so many kinds of parties; similarly religious parties have come up. So when I spoke at the UN, I was only talking about not unnecessarily distorting the culture. Anybody talking about alleviating poverty, if they are concerned about poverty, if it is compassion which is making them give food to people, providing education to people, they should do it without disturbing the local structure. They should use the local structure, the indigenous structure, whatever the indigenous culture is, use that and make education happen, make food happen, make prosperity happen, not by erasing cultures.

Why does one have to use education, money and other kinds of resources as an inducement to convert somebody into some belief system whether he likes it or not? When somebody is poor, when somebody is hungry, to go tell him, "I will give you food, but you must worship my God," is obscene. It is not necessary. If he wishes to worship some other God, let him do it. I know numerous Hindu people who have Jesus in their homes, who have Mohammad in their homes, who have so many other religious icons in their homes since the Hindu culture doesn't resist anything. It includes everything. It is good that everybody who is in this country is like this, rather than belonging to this group or that group. And it is not that I have not spoken about this here in India.

Normally, my work is not to talk about political issues or even social issues for that matter. Generally, my work is to support people on the spiritual path, to support individuals spiritually. So in India, I don't have much opportunity to talk about it. When I went to the conference I voiced my opinion on the injustice of forceful conversions. It is not that I am avoiding the subject here. I want you to understand that I am not speaking this from being identified with this religion or any other religion. Just as a person who was born in this country, I know the wisdom, the depth of wisdom that exists in this culture, the uniqueness of this culture.

Unfortunately, today people are living a stupid life; but if you just scratch the Hindu culture and look a little deeper, you will see every bit of life has been so deeply looked at. Every bit of life has been scientifically understood and created. If you see this, you will see in India, every action that you perform, every single act that you perform in your life is actually a spiritual process leading towards your liberation. How to sit, how to stand, how to eat, how to study, for everything there is an asana, there is a mudra and a certain attitude which will lead you to a higher level of consciousness. Every aspect of life has been thoroughly looked at. For example, music, dance and many fine arts are not just for entertainment. They are all a spiritual process in this country. If you look at Indian classical music and dance, if you perform them properly, if you involve yourself in them, you will become sage-like. It can lead to liberation. It is not just entertainment. It is not just body-shaking music or body-shaking dance. If you go deeply into this, you will become sage-like. You can see that musicians who are deeply involved in their music will become naturally meditative, because that is the way the culture has been created.

It is very precious, not just for us, but for the whole world that this culture is preserved, nurtured and allowed for everybody to experience and know what was the depth of life that existed here a few hundred years ago or a few thousand years ago. Unfortunately, today you are trying to imitate somebody else. This imitation has come simply because somewhere along the way you have become economically poor

This country was one of the most prosperous countries. Four hundred years ago, before the British invaded India, India was one of the richest societies in the world. Do you know this? In four hundred years time, it has become one of the poorest nations in the world because this nation has been plundered, so badly plundered that economically it has become poor. Once you have become economically poor, you start looking up to the economically rich, irrespective of him being a good man, a bad man, a crude man or a cultured man. Whoever is rich, their culture becomes dominant. Unfortunately that is happening in the world today. I am concerned that such a thing doesn't happen because you will regret it after some time. You will regret adopting the gross attitudes of the rich cultures after some time if the subtle aspects of this culture disappear.

Questioner: Sir, can you tell me how many stages are there in realization and which one are you at?

Sadhguru: (Laughs loudly) I am in the one hundred forty-forth stage! Realization does not have any stages. Either it has happened for you or it has not. That is all. If there are lots of truths then there can be different kinds of realizations, but there is only one Truth. There can be only one fundamental Truth, isn't it? If that is so, how many types of realizations can there be? Now who has this level problem? Only fools have problems with levels. The problem of levels is for people who do not have respect for their inner nature. The problem of levels is for a person who has not understood the value of what is within. Where is the question of any level for a person who has realized?

Questioner: What is the difference between doing sadhana while being a *grihastha* and doing sadhana while being a *bhramhachari*?

Sadhguru: If you are a grihastha and you want to do sadhana, you have to get permission from many people. They may give permission or they may not. There are many difficulties in that, but if you are a bhramhachari, you can determine for yourself. Certain types of sadhana will be a little difficult to do while you are a grihastha. It will not be possible to create the necessary environment. So should everyone become a bhramhachari to realize the Truth? No. That is not needed. What does it matter how the outside situation is to realize the Truth within yourselves? For your convenience what is needed, and what is necessary for your needs, you can look at and have it that way.

Someone gets married and someone else takes up bhramhacharya. Which is right and which is wrong? Or which is better? There is no such thing. Everyone is the way their individual needs are. Some have the need to marry and so they get married. For some that is not needed and they take up bhramhacharya. The same rules do not apply to everybody. If a person who needs marriage is given bhramhacharya, life will become hell for him. A person who does not want marriage, if forced into it, will go through another type of hell. It will be hell for both him and for the other person involved, too.

Many people have become this way, just like sheep. They never give it a thought, whether they need the marriage or not. They just get married because everybody else gets married. Many people do not look into this deeply. They do not look into whether there is a definite need for marriage or not. Everybody gets married, so they also get married. After three days, the person can no longer bear it; he cannot seem to manage all the things that come along with marriage. Marriage means many changes in lifestyle. Shouldn't one get into this only after they are fully prepared to face these changes and take up the responsibilities? It is not a single day's matter. Many things come with it.

It so happened that it is the twenty-fifth wedding anniversary of a couple. And on a day like that, however the relationship has been, on that anniversary you are supposed to, or rather forced to celebrate. However it has been all these years, it does not matter, on that day you

117

encounter the ENLIGHTENED

day!'" He said, "That is not why I have tears in my eyes." Her father was a judge. "Twenty-five years ago, your father threatened me by saying that I had been fooling around with you and that if I didn't marry you, he would slap some case on me and put me behind bars for twenty-five years. If I had taken that proposition, today I would have become been a free man."

If something goes wrong, it becomes a misery. It is not that the marriage is wrong. It is an opportunity for two people to share and live together. It is a good way to live and can be made into a wonderful way of living. Because people are not mature enough, they get overly possessive – what to say – above all, they try to make a life out of each other. If you have a life of your own, then you can share your lives and live together, but people try to make a life out of each other and the marriage is bound to fail, maybe not in court, but in life. Either you must be a very stupid person that you don't know anything, you simply live on, or you must be a total surrendering kind of person. If you have surrendered to the other person, then it goes on well or if you really love each other so much that everything is fantastic between the two of you, whichever way it is, it is okay. Otherwise, it is simply not possible. Two people sticking around for years simply because of a social commitment is madness. People are just destroying each other this way.

I have seen both men and women, for both men and women this is true. When they are young they are such vibrant and alive people. Then they get married – I have seen these lovers in college. They thought they were just made for each other. They went ahead and got married amid much opposition. They went against the parents, against society and got married. These vibrant and lively people, after marriage, within four to five years of marriage, both of them become such miserable people. You can see the misery on their faces, all liveliness is gone. It is unfortunate to see people like this. Because once you make a structure out of it, once you make this relationship

118

all liveliness is gone. It is unfortunate to see people like this. Because once you make a structure out of it, once you make this relationship into an investment in life, nothing worthwhile in life remains with you.

If you love somebody, immediately you want to make an investment out of it, isn't it? Why? You want to get all the securities that you can get out of it, but then it is finished. That is the whole thing. If you try to extract something out of love, love will be gone; only extraction will be there. Unfortunately, everybody tries to do it. They pay a big price, but people don't learn. People really pay a big price. Your misery is the greatest price you can pay, isn't it? What else is left? You have lost your love and lost the joy in the process. Above all you have lost your love. What other price do you have to pay? You don't have to go to hell. This is enough, isn't it? At least, if you just remembered that love affair in college that would have been a source of joy for your life. Yes, but when your dreams came true you made commerce out of it. That beautiful person, who meant everything to you once, turns into an ugly person for you. It is so unfortunate that such a thing should happen, but people – generations and generations – go on like this, doing the same thing. It is time to change. It is really time to change and decide what is meant for you and what is not.

See whatever actions you perform, there is a whole stream of consequences. If you are an intelligent person, you should see whether you are ready for the whole stream of consequences which will follow this action and then decide whether it is necessary for you or not. Think and decide whether you are ready to face the consequences and happily accept them. You should look into this and then decide. Something common cannot be fixed for everybody.

Questioner: What is the basis of prayer and why does one tend to pray more during times of difficulty?

Sadhguru: You should look at this a little more deeply. You don't have the urge to know God at all. The basis for your prayer to God is because from your childhood they have taught you that if you pray to God you will pass your examination. If you pray to God, money will come easily to you, you will be healthy or your child will be healthy. They have told you there is a lot to gain. That is why you pray to God. It is true, isn't it? If they had told you that if you pray to God you will lose whatever you have, or that if you pray to God you will get all unwanted problems, would you be praying to God? No. So all your search is simply to live comfortably and happily and somehow carry on.

If someone told you that you would become joyous if you pray to a donkey, you would pray, wouldn't you? Your urge is not to know God. You're praying or going to temples is either out of fear or greed. There is no connection between this and God. Your fear and greed are the only underlying reasons for this action of yours. Don't think it is thirst for Divinity. You have looked for a way and found one for your greed and fear. That is all. This is not Divinity. You will realize this Divinity within you, in your life, only when you experience this life as a joyous one. When you realize this creation joyously, only then the urge will come to know the power which created this. Let us say you saw a painting, a work of art. It was beautiful. As soon as you saw this you want to know who created it, isn't it? You look at a flower. You feel it is very beautiful and you immediately want to know who created this. Once this question has come up within you, once the question arises within you, the search for God can begin. Now you can search for God. Only when a man is joyous can he search for God.

If people are searching for peace and happiness, they need not search for God. Let them first create peace and happiness in their lives.

You must create it out of your intelligence and out of your awareness. After creating it, if you experience life as a joyous state, and the question arises within you, "A life which can be so joyous, who could have created it?" Then that is the path to Divinity. Don't think that by praying to God out of fear and greed is Divinity. You are not praying to God. There is no prayer in it. You will do anything to get whatever you want. Somebody has taught you this prayer and you are doing that now. You praying everyday or you praying more when in distress is at your convenience.

Questioner: This is a personal question. We had a son who underwent heart surgery at the age of ten, but died at the age of fourteen. In memory of the boy, on the date of his death we distribute many things to orphanages. We are doing whatever we can to help such organizations. How do we know if the boy's atma is peaceful, whether it is satisfied with whatever is being done here?

Sadhguru: These religious rites, karmas, have a certain science behind them. If somebody dies here, in India, either the children or some family member will perform the religious rites. This act of performing karmas for the dead is ninety-five percent or even more, purely psychological. It has psychological benefits. Now somebody whom you loved is here today and tomorrow he is gone. Many people, though they have seen death many times, still when it happens to their loved ones cannot accept it. Their attachments are such, they just cannot accept that suddenly somebody who was close to them is gone. Now, suppose your mother, father or somebody dear to you dies and when you sit for your meal, you feel, "Oh! He is not here to eat this." These emotions are there within people. Most of you have them, don't you?

So at least one day a month, in the first year of his death, you offer food to him. Whether a kaka (crow) eats or a cow eats, it does not matter, but in your heart you offer food to him so you don't feel guilty about eating without him. Do you understand? People feel guilty. Once a month, for the first year you offer food. After twelve months slowly you start getting used to the idea of your loved one not being there and, with time, you settle down. After that, just once a year you offer food and you are at peace with yourself. Now after three years you don't really think about him. So it helps you to at least remind yourself of your elder, or child, and once a year in his name you offer food. In his name, you will feed some other creatures. You never thought of feeding a crow. You always threw stones at him. At least that one day, that poor crow, you feed it, you give it a good meal. You do this not just for the crow, maybe for others, too. This is good both for those fed and for you.

Somebody told you, your ancestors have all become crows. Then at least you would feed these crows, otherwise you would never think of feeding them. A person who is conscious, a person who has become a little aware, may take a little of his breakfast everyday and feed it to the birds and animals. This is there in many houses. In my house, everyday my mother used to make about one extra breakfast and leave it out for the ants and sparrows. She would feed all these creatures before she feeds us. It is just ingrained into these people, because these creatures have been there before you came and built your structures. You suddenly built your buildings and you don't know how many of them are deprived of their homes. So you just leave a little food here and there and it makes a tremendous difference for you. It brings a tremendous amount of caring into you, which is a great karma. It changes your attitude towards life. They too, maybe when they find so much food in one place offered everyday, I am sure they will have some gratitude.

Whatever you want to do for anyone, do it when they are alive. It is not just this boy's case. Many of you, when people are alive, you don't even look at their face. You don't talk to them nor do you spend one joyous moment with them, but after their death, you have this big urge to do so many things for them. When a person has left his body, there is no contact between you and him. You must understand this, because even when he was alive, you did not realize anything else. You have realized him as a human being only at the level of his body and mind. You have not realized the Divinity within him, isn't it so? It may be your mother, father, wife or child. You have only known them at the level of their body, mind and feelings, isn't it? What have you known beyond that? They have left all that behind them here and gone. Once they have left their body and gone, there is no contact between you and them. So whatever you want to do, do it when they are still alive. Do it now, do it right now. Who knows about tomorrow? But you won't do it now; you won't talk, you won't see their face, but after they are dead and gone, you will send food for them to heaven, in a carrier.

For some reason somebody died. They either died when they were young or they might have died when they were old. At whatever age they died, you might have been fond of them and they could have been important to you in your life. You want to remember them and there is a need within you to do something for them. For that, you may feed a few poor people or educate a few children in that person's name. Whatever you can do, it is good, but the beneficiary is never going to be the person who died. It is going to be the people who are here now.

It would be good if you understand this. You cannot do anything for the dead; there is no need to do anything for them. They don't need your service. They have gone beyond all of that. They don't need your action; but then, it is someone who has been close to you, someone you know very well, and you want to remember them at least once a year. You want to express your gratitude to them. So if you want you can do something on their behalf. All these are your sentiments. You can express it whichever way you want to, there is nothing wrong in that; but doing it for people who are alive is better. There is no need to do anything for people who are dead and gone. See what can be done for yourself, for your growth.

Questioner: In this competitive world, compassion and honesty are things which are very difficult to practice in life. What should we do about that?

Sadhguru: If you leave out compassion, what is left? You can only be an animal. Society is in that state right now. If you survey the challenges of today's world, one can easily come to a dismaying conclusion. There is competition. Those who want to compete can compete. If you don't need the race, why don't you come out of it? Or at least why can't you slow down the pace? No, you want to race with everybody because you want to be one up on everybody, especially your neighbor, but you do not want to face the difficulties that arise due to this competition. You should understand this very clearly: whatever action you perform in your life, there is a consequence to it. There is no such thing as you must perform only this type of action and you must not perform another type of action. You can do anything, but you must be in a state to accept the consequences joyously.

After performing the action, cribbing or crying when you have to face the consequences will not do. Do whatever you want in your life, but tomorrow, when you have to face the consequences, you should not cry and complain. If you can accept this joyously, you can do anything. If you don't have the energy to accept the consequence, you don't have to perform that action. It is not needed. Just because somebody else is doing something, you don't have to attempt it or do it. You do not know the kind of energy they have. Isn't it? So the society has not become competitive; you have gotten caught up in the rat race. You can compete to the extent you want to, but if you don't have the need for competition, we will teach you meditation. We will set you on the path of meditation, not because you are useless for anything else, only because the need to compete, the need to be in the rat race has dropped away.

Questioner: A lot of political leaders rule using the advice of Swamis like you. So who is ruling the world? Can we say that in the name of leaders it is the holy man who rules?

Sadhguru: (Laughs) I wish sages were ruling the world. Politicians in the garb of sages are ruling the world, unfortunately. I truly wish that sages were ruling the world, then the world would be very different. Unfortunately, this is not so.

Questioner: How can a person go beyond *maya* or illusion? Even when a person is truly good, a good bhaktha, however much he tries, he is unable to elevate his status in life. Is this because of *maya*?

Sadhguru: It is not enough if you are a good person. If you have to live in this world you should be capable also, isn't it? You have always been thinking that you are a good man. In the first place what makes you think you are a good man? Not just a good man, a truly good man at that! It is time you come out of this *maya* or illusion. First of all, on what basis have you concluded that you are a good man? Sitting here, how could you conclude that you are the only good man in this crowd? Only when you see that the ten people sitting around you are not okay for some reason or another, or in comparison with them, you can conclude that you are a better person. Isn't it so?

When you have concluded that you are the most wonderful person in this world, it means in your mind there is no other good person on this earth; you are the only one. When you are in such stupidity, anything can happen to you. You need not be a good person. In your life, if your inner nature is peaceful, loving and joyous, it is enough. You need not attempt to be a good man. The problem on this earth is because of the good people, isn't it? The people whom you think are bad commit some crime, murder or whatever, and leave it there.

You don't have to come to the conclusion that you are a good person. You just have to see if you have lived a peaceful, loving and joyous life, truly. The good people cannot even laugh. That is how they have become. Do you know why? Because they are very good people! What to do with this kind of goodness? You don't have to be a good person. If you are a peaceful, loving and joyous person, it is enough.

Being a good bhaktha has got nothing to do with you succeeding in elevating your status in society. Now you want God himself to come and run your business to boost it! In return you give your devotion. Stop the bartering. When any being calls, really calls, existence answers. If you really reach out, God always answers. It is so. It is just that nobody really reaches out. They are all accountants. People are all accountants. They are always thinking in terms of balance sheets. Profit and loss, how much to keep, how much to give. Their calls do not go anywhere. With a logical mind when you shout, even if you yell God's name or do whatever you want, God is deaf to logic. He has no ears for logic. When love calls, immediately it is answered. There are some people for whom every prayer they make is answered. Do you know this? There are lots of people like this. They may be very simple people. Their genuineness is such that anything they pray for is answered.

There is a man in Namakkal, a Hanuman bhaktha. I never meddle with him because he is a very simple being. Hanuman is the path for him. Hanuman is everything for him and anything that he asks for gets answered for him. For him it is like this. Even this yoga program – he does not know what yoga is. He is too simple a being. For him

Hanuman is everything. So he went to Hanuman and asked him if he should go to the yoga program and apparently Hanuman told him that it is good and he could go. It gets answered for him somehow, it does not matter whether a flower falls, or something else. That is not the point. That man is so simple and so sincere that it will definitely work. Somebody just has to say, "Hanuman" and tears will flow out of his eyes. It is fantastic for a man to be like that. If I just hug him, he will go into ecstasies because he is just on the verge. I make fun of temples, I say, "Hanuman is a monkey, he is not God." I say many things in front of him, it does not matter to him because he sees Jaggi also only as Hanuman. That's how he sees. For him, Jaggi is also another form of Hanuman. He feels the same vibrations here. You say whatever nonsense you want about Hanuman, he will happily sit and listen. It is okay with him! Immediately after the program he will go straight to the temple. It is fantastic for a man to be like that. It is very easy, just like that everything will fall in place for such simple folk.

It is not Hanuman; it is your own consciousness. How you hold yourself is everything. What you hold as you is God. If you are sincere enough, if the logical mind is eliminated and you ask this question with love, God is right here. Because you cannot see it directly, if you see it in the form of Hanuman, it is okay. It is a beautiful device if it works. If Hanuman is just about going and putting *vada mala* or *jilebi mala* and then you start the barter, then you are a fool. For you, temples should be destroyed; but if there are people like this Hanuman bhaktha, we must build temples. It is needed. If people are like this, a temple is a great instrument.

Religion and Harmony

Moving into the realms of religion in its true form, the Master with a group of missionaries visiting him at Isha Yoga Centre.

The very basic purpose of Isha Foundation has been in many ways to remind people that whatever has been followed as religion is towards human emancipation. It is to reach to his highest peak and not to identify with certain beliefs. The moment man became religious, it should have been the end of all conflict, but unfortunately, religion has become the main source of conflict everywhere. It has taken the maximum number of lives, caused the maximum amount of pain on the planet for thousands of years. This is so because people believe in something that is not a reality to them. If somebody believes in something and somebody else believes in something else, naturally conflict cannot be avoided. Today or tomorrow they are going to fight. They may avoid conflict for some time, but some day they will fight. As long as you believe that only your way is right and somebody else believes something else is right, you are bound to fight.

So, though all religions started as an inward path, over a period of time they got twisted up in many ways and simply became a set of beliefs. Though all religions taught the value of a human being, for the sake of the same religion, today you are willing to take each other's lives. Unfortunately, much pain and conflict has risen on this planet because of this. Somewhere, I feel that the basic problem has not been addressed properly. People are always trying to do patch-up jobs between one group and another, but these patch-up jobs do not last for long and somewhere conflict will arise. The basis of this fight is that people just believe in something. Something that is not a reality for them, but they believe in it. If you come down to reality, it is the same reality for everybody: the Christian, the Hindu and the Muslim. When you come to belief, each religion has its own belief of what is right and what is wrong, what is true and what is not true.

Things that you have not seen and experienced, you believe. That has become the basis of all conflict in many ways.

So, the basic purpose of Isha Foundation has always been to pursue religion as an experience, as an inner experience, not as a belief. Don't start with any belief; start looking inward. Whatever is true, you experience and go further, approaching it as a science, not as a belief. It is unfortunate, but most ancient religions have always given much importance to faith. Almost every religion gives much importance to *bhakthi* or devotion, but this devotion, this bhakthi, will only work when people are very innocent and childlike. Every religion has made it clear that innocence is needed. I think, for you Jesus made it very clear that this path is only for children, "Only children will reach the kingdom of God." This means only those who are childlike can walk the path of devotion. Once the intellect develops, then you start thinking. That kind of mind can never pursue faith. It will just deceive itself in many ways.

In yoga we just see that fundamentally a human being can approach and grow or reach his Ultimate Nature, God or the Divine, or whatever you like to call it, by any of these four ways: either through the body, the mind, his emotion or his inner energies. These are the only four realities that you know. Everything else is imagined. Everything else has been taught to you. The only four realities that you know are, your body, your mind, your emotions and the energy which makes these things happen. These are the four dimensions available for people to grow in. These are the four basic ways of yoga. If the body is used for growth, it is called *karma* yoga. If the mind and intelligence are used, it is called *gnana* yoga. If emotion, or devotion and love are used, then it is called *bhakthi* yoga. If you transform your energies and grow, it is called *kriya* yoga. So these are the four fundamental ways in which a human being can grow to his ultimate nature; either through intelligence, devotion, selfless service or by transforming his inner energies. This is just like referring to head, heart, hands and energy. That's what you are; that's what every human being is. There is nobody who is all head, or all heart, or all hands or all energy. You are a combination of these four dimensions.

So if a person has to grow, he needs a combination of these four paths of bhakthi, gnana, kriya and karma. All the four need to be there in your life. Only then there is growth. Only then there is a possibility of reaching the Ultimate nature. Otherwise we have groups, and groups, and groups; quarrelling groups everywhere. Spiritually, there is nothing happening. Unless something of true value happens within you, you can't do anything of tremendous value to the external world. Whatever you do, it is only your quality that you are going to spread. Whether you like it or not, that is the reality. Who you are is what you are going to spread everywhere. If you are concerned about the world, the first thing is that you must be willing to transform yourself.

It is based on this that the whole process of yoga starts. Whatever we are calling *the silent revolution* is just this. There have been various types of revolutions in the world; the famous ones: the French, the Russian, the Chinese, and others. All that happened in these revolutions is, one tyrant has been replaced by another set of tyrants, but the basic human condition has never changed. This inner revolution is not about changing somebody else. Everybody everywhere wants to change somebody else. It is like the mother-in-law wanting to change the daughter-in-law and the daughter-in-law in turn wanting to change the mother-in-law. This is an age-old problem. In the same way, the so-called revolutionary reformers and religious people are always trying to change somebody else.

This is about, "I am willing to change myself." This is not about wanting to change the world; you are willing to change. Only when you are willing to change, a change can really happen in this world, but when you say, "I want everybody else to change," then, only conflict will arise. Only when you are willing to change there is transformation.

There is a real solution. So it is from this basis that Isha Foundation functions. Everybody here is a volunteer and everything that is happening here is only out of their volunteering. You know how the programs are happening here; you have experienced it.

Questioner: Sadhguru, what school of thought do you belong to? How are your teachings imparted?

Sadhguru: I don't belong to any school. This whole teaching springs from inner experience. We don't come from any particular tradition or any particular school. This has come from an inner experience. So, as it is needed for an individual, accordingly it is given or imparted. The practices that I give to one person, if given to another, it is not going to work, isn't it? So scholars and philosophers are teaching something because they belong to a certain school of thought or whatever. This doesn't belong to any particular school of thought. This is something that comes from an inner experience. So as people need it, accordingly they receive.

Questioner: Isn't the energy you are referring to, nothing but God?

Sadhguru: See, you have never experienced any power beyond yourself, except nature. Now, if you see, outside this room the wind is blowing. You are not blowing it, isn't it? That is very clear. Yes, the wind is blowing right now with tremendous power; you did not start this wind, that much you know. And you did not create yourselves; you happen to be here. Without energy or that something which is beyond you, nothing can happen. Yes? Something must have created you.

Now that you do not know what created you, the next immediate thing you will say is, "God must have done it." Where has God come from? Since you are a human being, you think that God is a big human being. If you were a buffalo, you would think God is a big buffalo. Isn't it? So whatever your idea of God is, is simply coming from the limited experience of who you are right now. It is not coming from any true experience. It is only coming from your limited imagination. You are in human form, so you think God is a big human being. Your imagination is now saying God has four hands because you have only two. Two hands seem too few for God, so you think maybe he has four hands. He looks better to you with four hands. So whatever you call as God, or power, you are only either thinking or imagining. It is only in the mind. The only thing that you can experience is that which is within you; and that which is within you, you have never really looked at in real depth.

Whatever you have known right now, your experience is only limited to your five sense organs. Yes? Whatever you have known either of the world or of yourself has come to you only through seeing, hearing, smelling, touching and tasting. If these five senses go to sleep, you will neither know the world nor yourself. The sense organs are limited perceptions, that much you agree with. They feel everything only in comparison to something else. Now if I feel this steel rod (pointing to the microphone stand) it is cool, simply because my body temperature is in a certain way. Suppose I lower my temperature and touch it, it will feel warm to me. So this is not genuine experience. This is an experience which is just sufficient to survive in the physical reality. Whatever experience you receive through the five sense perceptions is a sufficient experience for your survival in this existence.

If you are seeking something beyond survival, then sense perceptions are not enough. So all yogic practices are fundamentally aimed at giving you an experience beyond the perception of the five senses. Whatever you experience beyond the five sense perceptions is not in terms of physical reality; it is in a different dimension. That dimension, if you want to call it God, call it God or if you want to just call it power. Or if you want to call it 'myself', call it 'myself'. You call it whatever you like. Everybody gives a different name to it; but whatever name you give to it, it always gets misunderstood by people. The moment you give a name to it, people misunderstand it

133

in some way, always. It does not matter what you call it. If you call it *Shiva* or *Allah*, *God* or *Divine*, the moment you say it, within ten minutes, misunderstanding will happen within people's minds.

So right now, the whole experience of transcending your limitations, does it come from within you, or does it happen from outside of you? That is the basic question. If you want to transcend, only if you are truly willing can it happen, isn't it? Otherwise, no power on earth or in heaven can move you. Neither a Krishna, a Buddha, nor a Jesus could move you; when they were here they were just ignored. Many stories are told today, "When he was there, this happened, that happened." Somewhere you have to come down to reality. When they were here, most people just ignored them. Only a handful of people went behind them. Even today it is the same. Even if they come today, the reality is going to be the same. Only a few people will choose to go behind them and experience what they are. The rest of the people will just ignore them. Later, after thousands of years, people will take up the cause. Now everywhere around the country you see temples for Krishna, temples for Rama. It does not mean much because after thousands of years it is convenient. When they are here, to be with them, to follow them and to know them is a different experience altogether. It is challenging; it is life threatening in many ways because you have to drop everything that you know and move into a totally different dimension.

Questioner: Are you implying there is some other power that moves us? If so, how can we trust it? All our lives it has been Jesus for us.

Sadhguru: Is there another power that moves you? Obviously, there is so much more than you in this existence, isn't it? Yes! Obviously, there is so much more than you, than what you call 'myself'. What you call 'myself' is still a limited experience of what you are. If you transcend this identity of who you are, then there is no distinction between you and what you are referring to as the power beyond. There is no distinction.

I think Jesus made it clear. All the time, he went about talking about himself and his Father up in heaven. At one point, he said, "Me and the Father are one." That which is you, beyond these limitations and that which you are referring to as the Almighty are the same. It is not different once you transcend your limitations. It is not about your desire to reach somewhere that gets you somewhere. If you transcend your limitations you are there naturally. For you to transcend these limitations, it definitely has to be you, isn't it? You must become willing. This we call surrender. In many ways this surrender has been talked about. It is a simple method for very simple human beings. When Jesus said, "Come, follow me," not many followed him. Only very simple fishermen and farmers followed him. All the scholars, the intellectuals and the thinking people never did, because they could not. Only very simple, childlike people followed him.

All others either ignored him or persecuted him because that is the only thing they could do. Even today the truth is the same. This kind of path, the path of devotion is only for very simple human beings, it's only for childlike people. Others need to see, to look at other possibilities. Just devotion will not get them anywhere. In every culture, we have celebrated devotion in a big way because it is very beautiful. The path of devotion is always very beautiful, but it is also very entangling in so many ways. In the name of devotion much deception can happen within you because the thinking mind can never be devout. It is not possible. Look at yourself and see sincerely. No thinking mind is ever truly devout. It is just that you have reduced devotion to just asking for money, asking for a job, asking for solace, asking for peace, asking for comfort, that's all. That is not devotion. That everybody does. When they need something, they will ask, isn't it?

Devotion means – the word devotion comes from the root word dissolve or dissolution. The only object of the devotee is to dissolve into his object of devotion. He has no other objectives in his life. He just wants to dissolve. So, only if there is such a simple human being, the path of devotion will work. "Come, follow me," will work only for children, childlike people. A thinking mind cannot follow anybody. A thinking mind cannot dissolve into anything.

Questioner: Dear Sir, with the mind that I carry, is liberation possible for me too?

Sadhguru: Definitely it is possible. Why would it not be possible? It is possible for every human being in this life. It is just that you have to make it possible. If you have to make it possible, the first thing is, it must become the only priority in your life. People have so many other priorities; they've got spirituality going on the side. If it is so, it will never happen. Only if it is the one and only purpose in your life, it is not far away. In a moment it can happen. If all your energies are focused in one direction, it is not far away. After all, what you are seeking is already within you. If this mukthi or liberation is sitting on a mountain, you can ask this question, whether it is possible or not. When it is within you, is somebody stopping you? The only barrier is you, isn't it? If you are willing, who can stop you? So all the sadhana is just to make you willing. That's all. Sadhana is not for enlightenment.

Enlightenment is not far away, but to make a person one hundred percent willing, it takes time because you have layers and layers of resistance. It takes time to work through the resistance, to make them absolutely willing. If you were a very simple human being, "Come, follow me," would have worked wonderfully; but now calculations have come into your minds.

Questioner: Sir, this yoga that you are talking about, is it an exercise or an experience?

Sadhguru: Yoga is neither an exercise nor an experience. It is a certain state. The word yoga means 'union'. When you are one with everything, then you are in yoga. Now when you are here, whatever you may say about your body not being of any importance to you, you still have to attend to it, isn't it? Can you deny it? You can talk God, you can talk religion, you can talk philosophy, but for example, when your body gets hungry, you forget about God, you forget about philosophy. The first thing you want is food. Even if you pray, you will say, "Dear God, food." Isn't it? So, your body is an undeniable reality for you. You can't deny it. By denying it, you can't get anywhere. You can't get rid of it. Can you leave it here and walk away? It is there with you all the time.

Similarly, you have a mind. You can't deny that either. Wherever you go, whether you go to a temple, or a church, or somewhere else, your mind comes along with you. Even if you go to mountain caves and sit and think it is peaceful, your mind will go on with its own nonsense. So your mind also is an undeniable reality. And you have emotions which are always there with you, too. You may think you are controlling your emotions, but they are there. You can hide them for some time. They are there, isn't it? At the right moment, they come out. To make all these happen, your energy is there. If you want to transform yourself, you should not deny any of these. That is why there is a physical yoga, a mental yoga, an energy yoga and an outward, action yoga. You have to accept all these four types of yoga and work on all four levels.

If there is a live Guru, he knows and understands what is required. He looks at the combination that works for a person. It is constantly looked at. He mixes the right combination for each person. He tells this person, "For you, this much activity, this much meditation." All the people here at the ashram do not work to the same extent, do not meditate to the same extent. They have been given different types of meditation, different levels of work depending upon their nature.

One should not deny somebody's nature and go against it. A common prescription will not work; people will only get suppressed. There will be no enlightenment. It is not going to happen. Suppression has happened in the name of spirituality everywhere in the world. Much suppression has happened. Mostly, ninety percent of it is suppression. This is simply because without any understanding you want to go head-on against your own nature. It is not going to work. You don't have to become slaves of nature. You have to transcend nature. You can't go head-on with it. You have to approach it with understanding and awareness.

Questioner: Where organized religion has failed to succeed on the experiential level, Isha Yoga has succeeded. It has brought about real transformation in each individual. Why don't you take it out on a larger scale to the society?

Sadhguru: It is not that we are not doing that. We want to spread this experientially, not as information, but as a genuine experience. For that to happen, much training and dedication is needed. This cannot be done as a profession. This yoga should not be just a part of your life. This should become more than your life. Only then it works. One can't take this yoga as a part of their life and do it on the side. One must hold it more valuable than one's own life; only then it works. Otherwise, it will not work.

You know the nature of the program you have gone through. Unless a dedicated person stands there, it will not happen. This training takes, normally for well-educated intelligent people, four to five years to make them into full-fledged teachers. We are working towards it, and today dedication is scarce material in the world. You have to search for people, for the right kind of people. So it is taking its time, but definitely we want to spread it. At the same time we do not want to hurry it to a point where it would become just information.

We want to take it as a live knowledge. The moment you make it information – if you print books about it and publish them, it may reach millions of people, but then it will reach nobody. So, keeping it as a live knowledge and keeping it as information are very different. Unfortunately, the whole of modern education has just become information. There is no experiential dimension to anything. People know everything but they don't know anything. Slowly they are reaching that condition. They know everything about the world and beyond but they don't even know how to live their lives. They don't know how to get up, come out and enjoy the morning. Even that they don't know.

Questioner: We have gone through this seven-day program. We are doing asanas and pranayama. Our habits have changed for the better. We are very conscious, aware at least to a certain extent. Where do we go from here? What is the next step?

Sadhguru: Yes, this is just preparatory work. If you want to move into a higher level of consciousness, a higher level of awareness, you must prepare the body, the mind and your energy. That is what you are doing now. With asanas you are preparing the body; with pranayama you are preparing your energy. The yoga program you went through prepares and matures your mind in a certain way. If this maturity reaches a certain level, then you will naturally move into the next level of experience. Practice is a tool which can take you a very long way. The pranayama that you are doing right now could be just for health and well-being. You feel a little more healthy, active and alert, but that is not the end of pranayama. Pranayama can take you beyond this body. Pranayama is a complete path by itself.

Among the eight limbs of yoga – do you know there are eight limbs of yoga? Are you aware of this? These eight limbs of yoga are termed as: yama, niyama, asana, pranayama, pratyahara, dharana, dhyana and samadhi. So, yama, niyama are for a beginner. They are the do's and don'ts.

What to do and what not to do, more like a moral teaching, "You must be like this, you should not do this, you should not do that, how you should be with the people around you," that kind of thing. This is for a beginner, for a person who has no awareness of himself. For such a person we fix a simple moral code as to how he should be.

Asanas are about the body. The body is a big factor to you. Whether people accept it or not, the body is a big aspect of you. The physical dimension is a big aspect of you; it rules you in many ways. Isn't it? So if you don't keep your body in a certain level, it will not allow you to think beyond the small realities of it. Suppose your leg is paining; it doesn't matter what enlightenment I talk about, or even if I bring God here, the only boon you will ask for is, "God relieve me of my leg pain." Isn't it? The body has this kind of power over you. So we better handle the body and elevate it. The idea of doing asanas is not just for fitness. It makes the body subtle, from a grosser level to a subtler level.

Similarly, the energies can be gross or subtle. Right now, if you look at the creation – today modern science proves to you beyond any doubt that the whole existence is one energy. The same energy is lying here as mud, the same energy is crawling like an ant, the same energy is standing up as a tree and the same energy is sitting here as me. The energy you refer to as God in heaven is also the same. It is the same energy manifesting itself in different ways. So, from the grossest level to the highest level, the energy has moved. The lowest you call physical substance, or inanimate things. The highest you refer to as God. The whole process of yoga is to cultivate your energy, to make it subtler, subtler, and even subtler so that from being just earth, you become God. You become Divine. If transforming your energy to the subtler planes within yourself has to happen, your body has to cooperate, your mind has to cooperate, otherwise it won't happen. What is being done with Isha Yoga is to make your body, mind, and energy cooperate, so that it moves into a subtler plane. You will see, if you do six months of pranayama, definitely you will be a subtler human being than what you were, in every way. You will feel life much more sensitively. With much more sensitivity you can experience life.

Now it doesn't matter how much preaching people give you, like, "Don't get angry, don't do this, don't do that." When the situation comes, you will get angry. If you continue with your sadhana, one day even if you are put into the most extreme situation, you will see your energies are able to remain very calm. Because whatever you call love, whatever you call hate, whatever you call anger, whatever you call lust, whatever you call compassion – from the lowest to the highest, all types of emotions are a certain expression of the same energy which is you right now. It is a certain type of expression of the same energy. This energy can become anger, this energy can become love, this energy can become hatred, this energy can become compassion. Now if you transform the energies in a certain way, it naturally becomes compassion. If it naturally becomes love, nobody needs to teach you morality. Then slowly, as this process goes further, you will not experience yourself within this limited physical form anymore.

Suppose you start experiencing yourself with the people who are sitting around you. After that I don't need to teach you morality, "Be good to this person, don't harm this person, don't kill this person." This will not be needed for you. Once you experientially are a part of everything, then nobody needs to teach you morality as to how to be with them, isn't it? So the whole process of yoga is based on this. To cultivate your energies in such a way that gradually it will break the physical limitations and you will start experiencing life beyond the physical. The pranayama and asanas that you are doing are to cultivate your body and energy. Already the mind has been prepared in Isha Yoga. The mind is prepared to look beyond your physical reality, to accept everybody as a part of yourself, to see everybody as your own. This is just a preparation so that when the energy begins to move, the mind doesn't resist.

So the practices will slowly elevate you that way, but there are other boosting experiences we can create like Bhava Spandana. It is in the same direction and a very powerful experience. We can allow people to experience that in a powerful way, which sets the basis for what they are seeking further. All these talks just look like a far away thing, so we are creating Bhava Spandana. It is like making the person jump and look beyond the wall. He sees beyond his limitations experientially. Once he sees that, he knows that he must go over the wall one day to see what is on the other side. Otherwise, when he is on this side of the wall, however much we talk, after some time he loses the initiative to go over the wall, "Why should I do it? This is okay with me." He will settle with this. But once we show him what is beyond the wall, then he will not settle for this; he wants to go there.

Questioner: Swamiji, many of us are involved in social work where we strive to create awareness which is only limited to the outward. Don't you think it is more important to make them aware of the inward so that it can lead to deeper social change?

Sadhguru: Definitely. If you are aware of what is happening within you, you will transform yourself. Now you are only aware of what is happening with your neighbor. You want your neighbor to change, and he wants you to change. That's where the whole problem is. All conflict has come from only that. You are aware of what is happening with somebody but you don't know what is happening with yourself. The awareness that we are referring to here is not talking about what is happening with somebody, or what is happening with you. This awareness is to become aware of who you are, really. From what basis have you come, what is your beginning and what is your Ultimate Nature?

To become aware of *nithya* and *anithya*. Do you know what nithya and anithya mean? What is the permanent nature of who you are? Right now you are engaged in a temporary situation and you are so involved in this temporary situation that you have never paid any attention to where it has begun and where it is going to end. You are just settling for some kind of belief or whatever somebody told you. I am not questioning what they have told you. Whatever Krishna said, whatever Buddha said, whatever Jesus said, whatever Mohammed said, might have been true for them, but unless it becomes experientially true for you, until then, you do not know whether it is true or not. Isn't it? Yes, you may just believe, but it is not the truth for you.

This is the reason why it has not worked, but if whatever Jesus said was actually true for you, experientially true for you, this world would have been different. Isn't it? We are talking about somebody else's truth. That is why it has not worked. If it becomes your truth in your life, if it is true, then that's what is needed. We don't need more Hindus, more Christians, more Muslims. We need Buddhas, Jesuses, Krishnas – real ones. We need live ones! That is when true change will happen, and that potential every human being carries within himself. Who those beings were is also your innermost nature. Realizing this latent potential that you are – realizing this and realizing it in this life, is what I'm talking about.

Questioner: Something personal, Sadhguru. What is the cause for your constant eternal happiness?

Sadhguru: (Laughs loudly) Tell me, give me one reason why I should be unhappy.

Questioner: There are so many things that we are unhappy about, don't they affect you?

Sadhguru: Like what? Give me one reason why I should be unhappy.

Questioner: Like the administrative problems.

Sadhguru: Oh! They are plenty, probably more than you have. People around me are not perfect people; they have their problems, their nonsense, and the world around us is not a perfect world.

People have their problems; they give us their troubles, they do many things to us. We are persecuted, we are – you know everything happens. You know what we have been put through (laughs), they don't use a cross and nails anymore, but why should I become unhappy?

Questioner: If something goes wrong?

Sadhguru: Like what? Even if something goes wrong why should I become unhappy?

Questioner: Not that I want you to become unhappy, but it happens. Doesn't it?

Sadhguru: So if it happens, it happens. It affects you because you are deeply identified with the situation. This is so because you have found nothing that you can call 'yourself'. What you call 'yourself' right now is the situation that you have landed in. So situations are everything for you, as you have become them. You have not found anything in you apart from what you identify yourself with.

So what if somebody around you becomes miserable? People are miserable wherever you put them. If you put them in hell, they will be miserable; if you put them in heaven, they will be miserable. They always find an excuse to be miserable, isn't it? Anywhere you put them, even in the best of places in the world, they will still be miserable. Everybody in India wants to go to America. In America you will see, everybody is full of complaints. They are in a different state of misery, but people in India think that if they go there, they will be happy forever. Now if people around you are miserable, tell me, what should be done? Do you become more miserable than them? What is happening is one thing; what should happen is another. If you become miserable is it of value, or is it if you are able to make them happy irrespective of the situation? Which is important? Which is more valuable to this world?

Questioner: Making the others happy, Swamiji.

Sadhguru: Yes. So the best thing that you can do to this world is not service, not spiritual teaching; the greatest thing that you can do to this world is for you to become a joyous person. The best thing that you can do to the people around you is that you are a joyous person. Isn't it so? What kind of people do you want to work with? What kind of people do you want to live with, miserable people or joyous people?

Questioner: Joyous people, for sure.

Sadhguru: So the best thing that you can do to anybody in this world, the greatest thing that you can offer this world is to be a joyous person. Isn't it? So why are you becoming miserable? Everybody wants to be joyous. By choice they want to be joyous, but they have become miserable because they are unconsciously choosing misery. Their whole life happens in unconsciousness. In twenty-four hours time, how many moments are you truly conscious of who you are? How many moments? Very few, isn't it? Very, very few. So your whole life is happening unconsciously, and the majority of the people around you are miserable anyway. So this is a democracy and in a democracy the majority rules (laughs). When it happens unconsciously, your whole life is accidental. When it is accidental, whatever the situation around you, you become that. When you are an accident, at any moment you may become a calamity.

Now you came here with nothing. Whatever all these things, your identity, your name, your clothes, your gods, your beliefs, your heaven, your hell, you picked up everything along the way. Everything that you know has been taught to you, including your gods and demons, everything. You only picked it up on the way. When you go, anyway you have to go empty-handed. When you came with nothing, whatever is happening here, you are in profit. Isn't it? So you must be happy always. You are going about your life as if you came here with a big investment. You did not come with any investment.

Did you? You came with nothing, so whatever is happening, you are always in profit. It doesn't matter what is happening with your life.

Questioner: But, Swamiji, I am not alone; I am living with people in the society.

Sadhguru: I am also in the society.

Questioner: So, okay, one has to be aware of oneself. What about the other people and the society that I am working with and mingling and dealing with?

Sadhguru: You deal with them. You tell me, if you want to deal with them effectively, do you do it when you are happy or unhappy? So even if you want to, if you are concerned about the society around you, if you want to deal with them intelligently and effectively, the fundamental thing is that you are happy. Isn't it? Otherwise, in your unhappiness, it does not matter what good intentions you have, you will only spread misery in the world. Once you are miserable, knowingly or unknowingly you will only spread misery. You can't help it. So being happy and unhappy is actually by choice.

People have chosen to be unhappy because they think that by being unhappy they will get something. So it is being taught that if you suffer you will go to heaven. If you are a suffering human being, what will you do in heaven anyway? Hell will be better home for you. Isn't it? Once you are unhappy, whatever you may get, what does it matter? If you are happy, if you don't get anything, what does it matter? This is not a philosophy. This is your nature. By your nature you want to be happy. This is not a teaching that I am trying to give you, "Be happy, be happy." By nature, every creature wants to be happy. Isn't it? Everything that you are doing, every single act that you are performing is seeking happiness in some way,

Now you want to serve people, why? Serving people gives you happiness, that is why, right? Somebody wants to wear good clothes;

somebody wants to amass money, because that gives them happiness. Whatever every human being is doing on this planet, it doesn't matter what, even if he is giving away his life to somebody, he is doing it because it gives him happiness. So happiness is the fundamental goal of your life. You want to go to heaven, why? Because somebody has told you that if you go to heaven, you will be happy.

The fundamental goal of every single action that you are performing is for happiness. After doing all that you are doing, if you are still not happy, somewhere you missed the ABC's of life, somewhere the fundamentals of life have been missed. When you were a child, you were simply happy. Without doing anything, you were happy. Then somewhere along the way, you lost it. Why you lost it, you must look at it. You got deeply identified with many things around you. You got identified with your body and mind. What you call your mind is just garbage you picked up along the way as I have repeatedly said. I don't know what kind of garbage you picked up – social garbage, sexual garbage, spiritual garbage, religious garbage – it doesn't matter what kind of garbage you picked up, you picked it up from the social situations around you. Depending upon what kind of society you have been exposed to, that is the kind of mind you have.

Everything in your mind right now, whatever you have, is something that you picked up from outside. That did not come with you. You picked up this nonsense and got identified with it. You got so identified with it that now it is causing misery. You can collect any kind of garbage you want. It is okay, but as long as you are not identified with it there is no problem. This body is not yours; you have picked it up from the earth. Isn't it? You were born with a tiny body which your parents gave you. After that you ate all these plants and animals and grew so big. You borrowed it from the earth; it is not yours. For a while you have to use it, enjoy it and go; but you are so deeply identified with it, you think it is you. So it is no wonder you suffer. The basis of all your misery is you have established yourself in untruth. If you are in touch with truth, how can you suffer? You are deeply identified with that which you are not. That's why the suffering.

So the whole process, the whole spiritual process is to dis-identify with what you are not, but when you don't know what you are, you can't search for it. If you search, your imagination will run wild. If you start thinking, "Who am I?" somebody will tell you that you are one of God's children. Somebody else will tell you that you are a demon's child. Somebody will tell you something else, endless beliefs. Only imagination will run wild. So the only thing that you can do is, whatever you are not, start discounting that. When everything is discounted there is something which cannot be discounted. When you arrive at that, then you will see there is no reason for misery in this world.

Questioner: Yes Swamiji, but you see, I am working in a school, and if a child comes late, I become miserable thinking that I am not able to discipline these children or control them. If a child in my class gives me trouble, in the evening I go home very tired saying, "All these children, they make my life so very miserable."

Sadhguru: See somebody can tire me as well, but they can't make me miserable. People can tire you, but they cannot make you miserable. You can be tired and still be happy. If you climb up this mountain – we should have taken you on a trek – by the time you reach the top, you will be tired, but very happy.

Questioner: Is that because we have achieved something?

Sadhguru: It is not because of achievement, it is not necessarily so. It is just that you can be happy. Happiness need not be only because of achievement. It is your nature. When you were a child, you were simply happy. Isn't it? So that is your nature. Every moment, with every single action, this being is seeking to be happy because it is its original nature. Happiness is one thing that was not taught to you.

Philosophies, gods, heavens, hells were taught to you, but nobody taught you how to be happy. Somewhere every being wants to be happy. Happiness is a natural thing within you, this is your nature. So if you go against your own nature, you will never get anywhere. To be happy is not the ultimate aspect of life. To be happy is the fundamental aspect of life. If you are not even happy, what else can you do with your life?

Only if you are happy, some other greater possibilities can arise in your life. People are miserable and they want to meditate. It will never happen. If you are happy, very easily we can make you meditative. If you are a miserable person meditation will never happen, because such a person is always seeking a solution. A miserable person can never pray; he can only beg and complain. He cannot pray. Only because lots of miserable people are praying, prayer has become a kind of begging. Prayer is a quality. If you become prayerful it is very beautiful, but if the prayer becomes begging, it is very pathetic. Unfortunately, most of the prayer in the world has just been reduced to begging.

Questioner: Can we do away with the concept of God? Your talk suggests to me that if we realize ourselves, God can be done away with?

Sadhguru: Now you are talking about realizing yourself as if it is a small thing.

Questioner: Yes, but is it still necessary that I believe in a God of which I do not know, whom I have not seen? In this particular yoga or in this particular way of life, is there a need to belief in God?

Sadhguru: Now, it is not just about this yoga. If you want to go somewhere, really want to go somewhere, you must first understand where you are. Isn't it? The next thing is you must realize what the next step is that you should take. If you sit here thinking about heaven for five minutes if nobody disturbs you, you can imagine that you are in heaven and it feels very good; but, within five minutes reality will catch up with you. Isn't it? The surrounding reality will catch up with you. Some children may come and bother you, a teacher may come and bother you or somebody else might come and torture you. The world will take care of you in some way.

So if you want to go anywhere, the first thing is to accept where you really are right now. Right now, your experience is limited only to the five sense organs. The five sense organs can experience only that which is physical, nothing more than the physical. Anything that is beyond the physical, your sense organs cannot perceive. The only thing that you have known is the physical dimension of life. Everything else is imagination. If you want to go beyond, the only way is to see how to go beyond the physical reality. You have been taught about one kind of God. Others were taught about another God, and somewhere else some other God. This is concerning humans. Suppose there are other creatures on the other planets as people are claiming, and if you tell them "God looks like me, a human being," they will laugh at you. They would believe God looks just like them, however they look. Isn't it so? So tell me, if you want to go somewhere, really want to go somewhere, should you start from reality or from imagination? You had better start from reality if you are serious about going somewhere. If you just want to believe, to belong to a certain group, or a club, or an association, or something, then that is different. You can identify with some belief and be a part of a certain group if that is so, but if you want to truly grow, you must start from reality. Isn't it? And the reality is, right now your experience is limited to the five senses that are physical.

So you just have to see what the next step is to go beyond the physical. To go beyond the physical, to know what is there, you have to experience and see. It doesn't matter if I have experienced and talked to you about that which is beyond. Do not believe me since you do not know. You may have respect for me, you may have reverence for me, you may have many things for me, but still you do not know. Isn't it? The same is true of whatever Krishna said or Jesus said or Buddha said. They said something. You have reverence for them. You have respect for them; but until it becomes true within you, it will not be a reality for you.

Belief will not get you anywhere. Believing means you are not sincere enough to admit, "I don't know." That is the problem. If you want to grow, if you want to know, the first step is to see that you do not know. If you create a big, "I do not know," knowing is not far away. If you become one hundred percent, "I do not know," knowing is just one moment. Right now the problem with your mind is, it can't admit that, "I do not know." It will always make you believe, "I know, I know, I know." As long as you are in, "I know," you will never know. Isn't it?

Questioner: Yes Swamiji, what can we do about it?

Sadhguru: The first step is to see that what I know is only this much: I know my physical body, I know my mind, my emotions, and my energy to some extent. Beyond that what do I know? Nothing. So this, "I do not know," if you come to a big, mammoth, "I do not know," knowing is not far away. You have been told, "The Kingdom of God is within you." If it is within you, how far is it from you? How far is it? If you truly see, "I do not know," only then can you become one hundred percent willing to know, isn't it? If you just believe, you are not willing to know. Without knowing you are pretending to know.

Questioner: Swamiji, what is it that you mean by experience?

Sadhguru: Whatever I may call it; it is bound to be misunderstood. I don't mean to call it anything. That is why we never talk about what is beyond. We only talk about what is binding you here. So let us work on that. See, right now you are tied down to the earth with ropes. Now if I talk about the sky, it is no good for you. I am only talking about how to untie these ropes, that is all. I will never talk about the sky. When you reach the sky you will know what the sky is. How can I tell you what the sky is? I am only talking about how to handle the ropes that are binding you. That is all.

I am not talking about God; I am not talking about enlightenment, I am not talking about anything beyond. I am only talking to you about what is restraining you here and how to get rid of that. That is all. If that goes, I need not tell you what freedom is, isn't it? I can only tell you what is binding you, what bondage is, and how to handle the bondage. Can I say what freedom is? That will be a lie, isn't it? If I tell you what freedom is in words, it is bound to be a lie. If I tell you what God is in words, it is bound to be a lie. When you come to it by yourself, it is different.

Questioner: Then what is the difference between the people who believe there is God and those who don't?

Sadhguru: There is no difference. It is just that people who believe also do not believe in anything. They only believe to a point of convenience. If they really believe, then there is no problem at all in their life. If you believe in God, if you believe God is everywhere, where is the question of fear, where is the question of anxiety, where is the question of unhappiness, where is the question of tension for you? Is it possible? If God is here within you and you are afraid, is this possible? God in this room, and fear in this heart, is it possible? It is not possible, isn't it? So you are just lying to yourself. If God exists in your life, that is the end of fear, that is the end of suffering. If you are such a simple human being that you simply believe absolutely, for such a person, belief is the quickest way. Bhakthi is always the quickest way. Devotion is the quickest path, but only little children, Jesus told you, only little children will pass the gate. All others will get filtered out. Devotion is only for little children; only for those who are childlike.

Questioner: Do we have to be happy always...

Sadhguru: No, there is no rule like that! The worst, the worst imposition that you can put upon people is that everybody must be happy. It is not that there is a rule or there is a law that everybody must be happy. Tell me, how do you want to be as an individual? You want to be happy, isn't it? It is not that somebody is telling you that all of you must be happy. Just look into yourself and see what it is your being longs for – to be happy or unhappy? It wants to be happy. That is true with every individual as an individual, but I can't tell this group, "All of you be happy." If you look into yourself, you know this being is seeking happiness; but if I tell you, "Be happy," then if you try to be happy, it wouldn't work. That is the only reason why people are unhappy, because they are trying to be happy all the time. I'm sorry, continue with your question.

Questioner: I want to be happy always, but things are not happening according to my way.

Sadhguru: You believe in God, isn't it? If things are not happening your way, they are happening God's way. (Laughs) If you really believe in God, why should things happen your way?

Questioner: What if I don't believe in God?

Sadhguru: (Laughs) Then you have to understand the reality. If you don't believe in God then you are coming to your senses, and you want to understand the reality.

Questioner: But I must be happy whichever way?

Sadhguru: You want to be happy, not you must be. You want to be happy. Now if you want to be happy, you have to see what is causing unhappiness to you. If you just sit here by yourself, leaving all your work, your nonsense, your beliefs, your faith and everything and just sit here you will be happy. It is just that in the process of transacting with people and situations, you are becoming unhappy. By your own nature you are happy. Only because you are making something else an investment in your life, you are becoming unhappy. Isn't it? Your work, your family, your ideology, something.

You have invested in something, which is making you unhappy. Suppose you drop all those investments and just be here like a child; you will be happy. So the problem is you got identified in the process of activity. You are becoming that. Now suppose you made this cane basket here next to me, which holds these flowers. Let us say you made this basket. It took you ten days of very good care to make this. Somebody comes here and steps on this basket. Now anger arises within you. That person did not step on your head. He is not walking on your body. Just a cane basket, but so much anger and hatred arises in you. Why?

This is not you. This is just a basket. You are identified with this. Now, are you really the basket? You are not. You are just establishing yourself in untruth, isn't it? You are thinking, "I am the basket." That is why when someone steps it you are getting angry. Even if he steps on your body, you should not get angry, because it is not you. Yes, do not take this literally, but see why this is so. When somebody slapped Jesus, he showed the other cheek. Who can do that? Only somebody who is not identified with the body, isn't it? If he is identified with the body, can he show the other cheek? For one who is identified with the body, this act of Jesus looks ridiculous. Absolutely ridiculous, isn't it? But for one who is not identified with the body, it is the right kind of action. It is the obvious thing that he will do.

Questioner: How can I not hate someone who is a rapist? How can I tolerate such a crime?

Sadhguru: It is not the question of toleration. If you tolerate it you will go crazy. You do not need to tolerate; you can only do what you can about it. You cannot reverse what has already happened.

Now for one thing, you are looking at only the person who is raped as a victim, but the person who is raping is also a victim in so many ways, because in many ways he is degrading himself. The worst thing that any human being can do to himself is to degrade himself like an animal, which he is doing for some reason. Though it may give him some pleasure or joy or power or something at that moment, still in many ways it is a tragedy for him as well. So it is not that one is a victim and the other an assailant. Both are victims. Many things like this happen in society. Many situations are created in this society. It is not just an individual act; it is a complex process of many things that are happening. So should you allow it to happen? No, we are doing whatever we can do to see that those things don't happen.

Yet, those things do happen in the world. So what we can do, we are doing about it, but you cannot change all of it. I want you to understand this. It does not matter what kind of human being you become, even if you become a super human being, you will never have absolute control over the external world. Whether it is your institution, or your family or the world, you will never have total control over the external situation. Isn't it so? But you can have total control over the internal situation. This is always possible. Now if the external has gone out of control, for some reason; people are killing, people are raping, people are doing all kinds of ugly things in the world. Because the external has gone out of control, does it mean to say that you should allow the internal to also go out of control? If your external situations have gone out of control, is it not very important that at least you keep your interiority in control? Now that man has gone insane; he is into that kind of act. If you are also going insane with anger and hatred for that man, what is the difference? He raped, so you want to kill. What is the difference?

Questioner: But shouldn't we do something for the situation?

Sadhguru: Yes, definitely, but without the anger. What you have to do, you do; but when you do it with anger and hatred, it is of no value – whatever you do.

Questioner: But how can a human being not get angry?

Sadhguru: Then it is better not to be a human being. Why you are saying without anger you cannot exist is probably because your anger is the most intense situation you have experienced in your life. It is so, unfortunately, for most people, fear, anger and hatred, are the most intense emotional situations in their lives. Their love is never so intense, their peace is never so intense, their joy is never so intense, but their negativities are intense. So they experience power in negative situations. I want you to understand, as you experience power in anger, the rapist experiences his lust as power. It is the most powerful situation that he experiences in his life, where he physically imposes himself on somebody else.

He feels powerful. That is the most powerful situation that he has experienced. That is why he does it; and that is exactly the justification you are giving to anger. It is not different. It is just that the acts are different. One is socially acceptable and the other is not. That is all. Otherwise both these actions are coming from the same basis. Now you think that you can change the world, or you have the capacity to move yourself only with anger. Why? Why can't you move with love? Why can't you move with compassion? Why can't you move out of your intelligence as to what is needed around you? Okay, not even out of love; at least out of your intelligence, do what is needed for the society around you. The most beautiful things will happen when your actions spring from your intelligence and not from your anger.

In this world, maximum damage has been done with good intentions, not with bad intentions. Many cultures have been destroyed with good intentions, isn't it? Many populations have been massacred with good intentions – good intentions made without awareness. All the people who were killed in North America, all the people who were killed in Australia, those thousands and thousands who were killed in the crusades – they were all killed with good intentions. I want you to know, even Adolph Hitler did whatever he did, killed millions of people, only with good intentions. He wanted to create a super world. This is a very good intention; but just see the pain and misery that he caused.

Questioner: So how do I respond to the situation when I see a woman being victimized? I want to respond to this situation, but how do I do that?

Sadhguru: See, how you respond depends on what kind of situation you are in, who you are, what your capabilities are, what means you have to do that sort of a thing. You cannot respond in the same way to every situation. If you have the power and the means to do something effectively, you can respond in one way. If you do not have the power and the means to respond at that moment, maybe your response is to keep quiet at that moment and see what can be done later, but this is not in vengeance or revenge.

You don't want those things to happen to anyone. Yes? You don't want this to happen, either to a man or a woman, isn't it? Don't single out any one. Both people are in some way being degraded in their life. One is doing it to himself; another is being subjected to it. You don't want this to happen to either of them, not just to one of them. Only then you can say that you are functioning from your love, isn't it? Otherwise, you are functioning only from your identity as a woman, which will not create a healthy world. Since people always act from their identity of belonging to a certain group – religion, race, country or sex – all this misery has happened. If you act without identity, you just function out of your intelligence and see whether you want this or not.

Definitely, you don't want this happening. So how you respond depends on what means you have. All of us cannot respond in the same way to any given situation. It depends on what means we have in our hands at that moment. Out of your emotions if you get into wild reactions you will not bring any justice. You will not bring any well-being to the world. You will just counter one evil with another. That is not a solution. That is definitely not a solution.

Questioner: Why does conflict arise between religions?

Sadhguru: Religion is an inward step, but if religion is only about belonging to this group or that group, it is very unfortunate. That has only brought separation. That has only brought conflict. That has only brought hatred among people. The same people who are together today, the moment they identify with their religions, suddenly they separate. Tomorrow they are burning each other's homes. Ten minutes ago, they would not even think of it.

The moment they become identified as a Hindu, or a Muslim, or a Christian, they are willing to fight. If they did not belong to these groups, at least they would have no reason to fight. Maybe individuals would fight, but the whole group of people, they have no reason to fight. Some individuals will fight for some personal reasons. That's different; but this kind of mass stimulation of animal energy wouldn't happen. So right now religion is about belonging to groups; that is all it is doing to people. Religion should have made them Divine, but it is not even making them human. They are becoming like animals, because, the moment you belong to a group, you want to protect your group. That is a natural reaction within you. Once you are identified with a particular group, you are always a threat for another group. It is a very basic human instinct. The moment you identify yourself with any one particular group, you become an enemy to the other. Maybe you'll talk to each other, you will be okay with each other, but the moment the lines are crossed, it is war. Unfortunately, that is all religion is doing to people right now.

Questioner: It is a reality, isn't it? Hindu, Christian, Muslim, is a reality; but the reason for this is because the religions are based either on myth or mystery. Some religions emphasize that everything is only myth; somebody else says mystery. We were taught not to believe in mystery. We can't do away with the teachings of our religion.

Sadhguru: Why not? Why can't we just become human first?

Questioner: To hear it is very good but…

Sadhguru: Not just to hear; it is a possibility. Maybe right now you can't talk like this to the whole country or the world; but definitely every individual, if you look at him, he truly wants it. Nobody wants this nonsense, but the moment he sits in a group he fights, isn't it? Individually if you talk to him, nobody wants this nonsense; but the moment they are in a group, they lose their individual intelligence, and are fired up with different kinds of things. So why can't we talk about it? It is time we talk about it – it is the new millennium, isn't it? It is time we talk about it, and if we start talking about it today, at least in the next millennium something may happen. If you don't dare talk about it, we will just push the world in this same direction forever. The only reason why they crucified Jesus is because he dared to talk about it, isn't it? Once again the same things will happen with people. So this is not as if once you correct it, it will always remain corrected. No. It needs constant correction all the time. Just one Jesus will not do; one Buddha will not do. Many are needed. Only then there will be a possibility of keeping the world in some state of sanity. Otherwise, people will go to the extremes.

Questioner: But Swamiji, your words resound those of Jesus', and for those words he was crucified.

Sadhguru: No. Jesus did not even question the religion. He did not do anything very revolutionary. He only tried to emphasize the religion, just the spirit of the Jewish religion, by taking away the frills of it.

That is all he did. He did not question their God; he did not question anything; but the culture there was so intolerant and he was persecuted. You see, in India, when Gautama the Buddha came over two thousand years ago, he questioned everything that was Hindu. Their gods – he made fun of them; he made jokes about them. Then the Hindus stepped back and said, "We also know there are not many gods, this is just symbolism. We know there is only one God." Then Gautama laughed and said, "There is no God." Then the Hindus stepped back and said, "Yes, we also know that there is no God, but there is a soul which will unite with the Ultimate Nature." Then Gautama said, "There is no soul. You are a non-soul; you are an *anatma*." He denied everything that this religion believed in and nobody ever threw a stone at him. They called him for a debate; they argued with him, but nobody ever thought of throwing a stone at him because the culture was so mature.

Jesus did not question anything; he was only reestablishing the religion, taking away the frills. He just wanted to throw away the shopkeepers from the temple. He never wanted to demolish the temple itself. Those who were doing business in the temple, he wanted to throw them out, but he never talked about demolishing the temple. Gautama went to the extent of openly saying that all the temples must be razed to the ground. He said, "All these gods must go; all the scriptures must be burnt," however nobody ever did anything to him, because the culture was so mature.

Jesus was not persecuted because he denied the religion. He only reasserted the religion. He talked a little differently. He pointed out the lies that were happening around. They did not like it. That is all. This is the only culture that will accept all kinds of people, because in India, sages and saints have come in different colors, in different dimensions. Each person is different from the other, but all of them have been worshipped and revered. Maybe people did not accept them, but nobody ever persecuted them. That has been the culture always. It doesn't matter in which form he comes in, with what teaching he comes with, the moment he is considered spiritual, he is not touched. Very rarely such things have happened, but not otherwise.

These days the so-called educated, drunk on their own logic, have lost all value and respect for the spiritual dimensions. These ignorant people, who think they are the saviors of the world, tend to become persecutors; but as the culture here has a very deep sense of respect and value for the spiritual, they are still just individuals or small groups. What we saw here was more their personal ego problems, rather than a campaign against what I have to say or do.

Questioner: It is two thousand years since Jesus lived. Has his vision been fulfilled? How are his people carrying his message?

Sadhguru: See one person had a tremendous vision. Because of one person's vision many things have happened. Undeniably things have happened, isn't it? Even today, whether people really understand who Jesus was or not, in his name much is happening for human well-being. Definitely, no doubt about it; nobody can deny that. Even today if you want to send your children to school, you send them to a convent school, isn't it? So a lot has happened because of his vision. If thousands of people carry the same vision, much better things would have happened.

Questioner: But it was not his vision to build convents.

Sadhguru: His vision was to do whatever was needed for the people. Today a school is needed so there is a school. See, it is very easy to comment on everything around you, but it is another thing to create something, something for human well-being. It is very easy to talk from some kind of prejudice that we have. I am not saying everything that is happening in Jesus' name is perfect. No. So much nonsense is happening in his name; but still, many beautiful things are also happening. After two thousand years of one man's vision, still a lot of beautiful things are happening. Two thousand years ago, all the others who lived, where are they? His vision is still working in some way, isn't it? Much well-being has come because of it. Much injustice has also happened, yes, but a lot of well-being has also come from his vision.

So why I am talking to you about vision is just because, one Jesus, one Gautama Buddha, one Vivekananda had vision, that is fine, but it is not sufficient. Only when a large section of the population also has a vision, then things, really beautiful things, will happen in the society. One man had a vision, and all others are working against it, then very little will happen; but if many of them have the same vision, then definitely things will happen. Isn't it? So whether it was Jesus' vision to start a convent school or it was his vision to start a hospital or it was his vision to convert people, that is not the point. The point is to create whatever is needed at that time for the people. In that way much has happened.

It is very easy to talk about whatever is wrong. It is always easy to pick out what's wrong and comment about it. When hundreds and thousands of people are involved, millions of people are involved in a certain activity; many people will do so much nonsense. Now for example, Isha Yoga is going on. In these hundreds of thousands of people, definitely there are a few people who do some nonsense somewhere in the name of yoga. Yes, definitely it happens. Already it is happening while I am living, and I know that much more will happen in the future. I am not a fool to think only good will happen. No. Many things will happen, I know that; but still you can't wipe out the goodness of Isha Yoga because of a little nonsense that happens here and there, isn't it? Similarly, you can't wipe out the greatness of Jesus' work simply because some idiot of a Christian does something stupid. Isn't it so? So some fool of a Hindu does something, does it mean to say everything about Shiva is not okay? Or Krishna is not okay? That is not the point.

Questioner: Swamiji, what is the importance of idol worship in this culture?

Sadhguru: An idol is an image you have created which you think is the image of God. Let us look at a child. When the child is an infant he sleeps with his mother. He knows the comfort of the mother's body. As he grows up you want the child to be separate, which is very essential for the growth of the child in many ways. Suddenly if you put him in a separate bed, he feels uncomfortable. So what do you do? Usually you give him a toy, some kind of a doll to hold onto. These days it has become Mickey Mouse or Barbie. Now he holds on to this toy and he feels comfortable. As he grows up you don't have to tell him to get rid of the toy. As he grows up, this toy which was so precious to him, somewhere down the line goes to the trashcan, isn't it? You don't have to do anything about it. As the child grows, the toy falls away by itself; but when he needs the toy, if you snatch it away, then you will harm the child. You will damage his psyche in a very deep way. Similarly, right now you need an image. You need to hold somebody's hand and walk. You do it. It is perfectly okay as long as you understand that some day you should become free from this also. Then there is no problem. But if you think this is God, then you are in trouble. You only create an image of God because you want to relate to it as long as you need it; you use it. Once you grow out of it, you grow out of it; but the aim is to grow out of it.

This must be understood that in India, temples were not created for worship. Only over a period of time they have become the way they are now. Temple building is a very deep science. The idol, the *parikrama*, the *garbagriha*, everything, if properly matched, will have

163

an energy field of its own. There are five basic aspects – the size of the idol, the shape of the idol, the mudra that the idol holds and the mantras that are used to consecrate this – if these are properly matched, a powerful vortex of energy can be created. A very positive energy is created. It is a system, a mechanism that you are creating. When I say temple, I am talking about the ancient temples. The modern temples are built just the way you build your shopping complexes– for the same purposes, probably. The same purpose that a shopping complex is fulfilling, the temple complex is also fulfilling with its various gods.

Ancient temples were built as a very deep science. Nobody even told you, in the tradition, that if you go to a temple you must worship, you must pay money to the agent or you must ask for something. This is not a part of the tradition. This is something you have started now. They told you that if you go to a temple, you should sit quietly for a while and only then leave. Isn't it? That is the tradition. You must sit there for a while before you leave; but today you just touch your bottom to the floor and run away. That is not the way. You are required to sit there because there is a field of energy that has been created. The practice was, in the morning, before you go out into the world and transact your business, first thing in the morning, you go and sit in the temple for a while and then go. This is a way of recharging yourself with very positive vibrations of life so that you go out into the world with a very different perspective, and temples were advised only for those people who were not on the spiritual path.

In the tradition, it is very clearly said that a person who has started his own spiritual process need not go to the temple every day. Or in other words, the temple is a public charging place, a battery-charging place for you. If you have your own self-charging system, then you don't have to go to the temple. It was not created as a place of God, or a place of prayer. Nobody was ever allowed to lead a prayer. It was created as a place of energy where everybody could go and

Religion and Harmony

make use of it. Everybody contributed to building a temple in the town so that everybody could make use of it, not as a means to send your messages to God. Not as a means of fulfilling your greed. No. Unfortunately, it is being used that way today.

Questioner: Dear Swamiji, we get inner harmony by following yoga. As in religion, yoga is also partitioned as ashtanga yoga, hatha yoga, raja yoga and many other yogas. Are they offshoots of the same yoga or are they different?

Sadhguru: Now, the word 'yoga' literally means 'union'. When you experience everything as one in your consciousness, then you are in yoga. To attain to that unity within you there are many ways. Like for example you mentioned hatha yoga. Hatha yoga means to start with the body. The body itself has its own attitudes, has its own ego, and has its own nature. Apart from your mind, do you see, your body has its own ego? Do you notice this? It has its own attitudes. You have to succumb to it, isn't it? You say, "Starting tomorrow, I want to get up at five in the morning and walk on the beach." You set the alarm. The alarm rings. You want to get up but your body says, "Shut up and sleep." Doesn't it do that? It has its own way. So we start with the body. Hatha yoga is a way of working with the body, disciplining the body, purifying the body, preparing the body for higher levels of energy. All of us are alive; all of us are human beings, sitting here, but all of us do not experience life to the same intensity because our energy levels are not the same. Our pranic energies are not the same. Different people experience life in different levels of intensity.

For example, somebody sees a tree. A tree is just a tree. Most people don't even see it. Somebody sees the tree in more detail. An artist sees every shade of it. Somebody else not only sees the tree but also sees the Divine in it. Everybody sees something, but seeing is not the same

165

because the level of intensity with which you experience life is not the same. So we start with the body because that is something that you know. The whole process of yoga is to take you from something that you know and then to take the next step into the unknown. If you talk about something that you do not know, either you have to believe it or disbelieve it, isn't it? Suppose I start talking about God. You either have to believe my God or disbelieve my God, which will only take you into flights of imagination, not into growth. So now I talk about the body. This is something that you know. You know you have a body. Now you take the body to its peak. Then I talk about the mind. That is also something that you know. Take it to its peak and then take the next step. You can only grow by taking the next step, the next step, and the next step from where you are. Realizing where you are right now and taking the next step is growth. If you talk about something not known to you, you are only going into imagination. Imagination will run wild. Today all that is left in the name of religion is stories, stories and more stories. Now you don't know what is imagination and what is reality. Yes? Many stories — a story inside a story, and you don't know where the beginning is and where the end is.

Yoga starts like this: with the body, then the breath and then the mind. Now we have made this yogic science almost like a physical science. Suppose you mix two parts of hydrogen and one part of oxygen; you get water. When a great scientist puts it together it is water. Even if an idiot puts it together, it is only water. Similarly, in yoga too, if you do this, this, and this, only this will happen. Whether a great yogi does it or an ignorant person does it, it doesn't matter. If he does the practices and sadhana properly, the result is there to be seen.

In yoga, these systems have been identified. To start with, you work with the body, then you move to the breath, then to the mind, then to the inner self. Like this many steps have been created. They are only different aspects. They are not really branches of yoga. In fact, we address all of them at once. It is important that in a very balanced way all of them are addressed at once, as one unit. Otherwise, if you work just with the body, it is only preparatory in nature. There is really no division as such; yoga means union.

Questioner: Sadhguru, what do you have to say on this trend today of believing some so-called holy men who say that they themselves are God? Even very learned and scientifically oriented, intelligent personalities fall terrible prey to this clan. Do you think it is good or do you feel that it is okay since it is giving them some solace? Should it be allowed to stay in the society, or should it be curbed? Isn't it reaching dangerous proportions where many are propagating themselves as an avatar of God? How can we differentiate the genuine from the false? What is your advice to us on this?

Sadhguru: This is not a new trend. This trend has been there for ages where a few men have a need to claim themselves as God, and other men have a need to see them as God. This need is very deep and psychological. The common man wants to see something larger than himself. This is one way of disgracing both the Divine and the human. If God is, He must be everywhere, isn't it? If there is a God – I don't want to start an argument as to whether there is a God or there isn't, whether He is or He is not – if there is one He must be everywhere. If I can lock him up in my closet, He is no good for you. Yes or no? If He is there, He must be everywhere. If He is everywhere, He is here also, within us. The question is just whether we have realized this or not. That is all the question is.

The question or the difference is only in terms of realization. Whether this is God or this is not God is not the question. Anyway, everything that you call as Creation is Divine. If it is not, it cannot create itself. Everything is creating itself and happening by itself. So the Divine is enshrined in itself; that is why it happens. If I say this is God, it is perfectly okay; but if I say, only this one is God, then it is vulgar. Then vulgarity comes in. It is perfectly right and it is the truth to see that which is within as God, but once you see that which is within as God, you cannot help seeing everything as God. You cannot avoid it. Anyway you will see everything as the Divine. Then there is no problem.

God is the greatest business. The most saleable commodity in the world is God because wholesomeness is something that man is seeking all the time, maybe unknowingly. You think you are seeking money, you think you are seeking power or you think you are seeking friendship. It is not so. All you are seeking is to be complete somehow, isn't it? You think if you have one hundred friends you will be complete. You think if you have a million bucks you will be complete. You think if you have a family you are complete. The basic thing is you want to be complete, but somewhere inside we know that unless we know the Ultimate there is no completion, there is no wholeness within us. So the need to find God everywhere around us is essential, and it is a good trend. The only thing is, if you think God can be limited to this person or that person, that is unfortunate. If you can limit the Divine, if you can limit Godliness to this particular idol, or this particular body or this particular being, it is very sad. It is not necessary. Now, how to stop it? You said, "Intelligent and educated people." I would say only the educated people or the so-called intelligent people are going. A truly intelligent person will never go.

Questioner: Can meditation reveal the concept of rebirth?

Sadhguru: I am really not interested in addressing any concepts. If something is true we want to look at it. You don't have to develop any new concepts about life. Whatever concepts you develop about life are just yours. The truth about life is something that you arrive at. Now the question is, to put it simply, is there rebirth or not?

As I mentioned earlier, I really don't wish to talk about anything which is not in your present level of experience. If I talk about anything which is not in your present level of experience, either you must believe me or disbelieve me. If you believe me it will not make any difference to you, and if you disbelieve me also it will not make any difference. If you know it, it will make a tremendous difference to you. If you know there is rebirth, or if you know there is no rebirth, both ways it will make a tremendous difference to you; but if you believe, you will only deceive yourself.

So how to know? Once again the only way to know is to turn inward. What you call as the mind, today, modern psychologists are telling you, you are using only ten to twelve percent of your actual mind. The remaining is just dormant. We have a whole system of meditation which we call Samyama, where a person can go into the deeper layers of his unconscious and bring the unconscious layers into his conscious experience. When a person moves into his unconscious layers, many, many lifetimes will become a living reality within himself. Don't believe this. I am just telling you. Do not believe this. All you have to see is, "Somebody is saying this, let me see." If you have this much openness, something will happen. If you believe, no good – if you disbelieve, no good.

The Way

In every being lies the seed of Divinity. It just requires the molding hands of one who has been there, who knows the path, who lights the way...

The Master at a Sathsang in Nashville, Tennessee, U.S.A

You people have brought the South Indian weather to make me feel at home (laughter). It is so wonderful to be with all of you. Many gurus are called *Koorma* Gurus. Koorma means a turtle, or a tortoise. What a turtle does is, digs up a place, lays the eggs, covers them up, and goes away. It will go away some distance, sit there, and wait for the eggs to hatch, because it knows it's not made like a chicken or something that it can sit on its own eggs and hatch them. It has to stay away. So it stays away and watches with love and with total attention to see whether the eggs hatch. Many Gurus are referred to as Koorma Gurus. They are like turtles. They lay their eggs, go away and watch how many eggs hatch. It's nice to be here with you all.

When you start the spiritual process within yourselves, there will be two things that you need to grapple with. One thing is the heat. And I'm not talking about the weather (laughter). One thing about the heat of the process is that it grips you in such a way that you seem to lose control over everything. Another thing is the mental struggle within yourselves, "Am I really getting somewhere or not getting anywhere?"

Some will struggle with the heat of it because they are unable to grapple with the things that happen with them. Some will struggle because they believe nothing is happening. Now if it happens you struggle; if it doesn't happen you struggle. First of all what should be happening and what should not be happening? This idea that nothing is happening to you comes simply because you compare yourself with somebody else. If you simply look at yourself, definitely something will be happening. The problem is you look at your neighbor who's shaking and jumping and rolling (laughter): "That's not happening to me, so maybe I'm not good enough."

The very word 'spirituality' means, the very fundamentals of it is, you are not trying to be like anybody else. When you follow someone, who ever it is – it doesn't matter what you want to be in the world – in some way you are trying to be like somebody, or in some way you are trying to be better than somebody; whatever you may be doing. When you want to play music, you are thinking of a certain kind of music because you heard somebody. You want to play like Elvis Presley or one-step above him, whatever your standards. Whatever you do externally you are always trying to either be like somebody or trying to be better than somebody.

So the inner journey is to lose that race, to be out of that race within yourself, because you are not trying to be like anybody, nor are you trying to be better than somebody else. You are coming to a state where 'being myself' is more than enough. The very process of spirituality and really the whole of spirituality is to become in such a way like, I am sitting with you here, I am complete by myself. I don't need to become anything; I don't need to make myself into something. If I simply sit here, the entire world is within me. I am so absolute; all existence is within me. So the ultimate goal is also such, and the process is also such, that when you are in the process it is not necessary to be like anybody else. Each individual can be in his own way and still be progressing.

Now the problem is you keep evaluating by your own standards whether you are progressing or not. This evaluation should not be done by you. When you went to school you didn't do the evaluation, isn't it? Though it was quite simple to do it, it was somebody else who did the evaluation for you. You just wrote the exams. Somebody else evaluated you. So even with a simple teaching in school, like a little science or mathematics or whatever, even with that you don't evaluate; somebody else did it for you. When that is so, when you walk on the inner path, why do you struggle with evaluating yourself? There is no need to evaluate yourself. The thing is to simply do what's needed, that's all. The evaluation and what needs to happen will happen in a completely different dimension. You can't 'do' spirituality, you have to allow it. The reason why Isha Yoga is structured the way it is, is to make you understand that these are the very fundamentals. That is, you can't do it. If you allow it, it will happen.

To allow it you need a certain level of maturity within you. Otherwise, all the time you'll want to meddle with it; you can't keep out. So what you are doing in terms of practices is just to mature your energies in such a way that if you sit down you don't need to do anything. You're willing to allow whatever happens. The very fundamentals of Shoonya meditation is just that you are not needed (laughter). If something truly wonderful has to happen you are not needed. If you want small, petty things to happen to you, you can do it, but if you really want something enormous to happen to you, you are not needed. If you know how to keep yourself aside, it will happen.

"How do I do that?" You can't do that; you just have to allow it. So whatever you're doing is just to bring your energies to that level of stability where you can just be. Not trying to do anything, not trying to get somewhere, simply allowing it to happen. See, it doesn't matter how much you aspire, if you don't do the right thing, what has to reach you, will not reach you. It doesn't matter who is around you; even if your Guru is sitting right next to you, your mind can be somewhere else. Somebody else who is sitting a thousand miles away, just a thought, the very thought of the Master can be so powerful that it can burst him, but you may be sitting right next to him and missing the whole point. It's very much possible because it's not a question of distance; it is a question of having the willingness to allow it. Unless you do the right thing, the help will not come.

Once, Shankaran Pillai fell into the septic tank and you know how that would be. He struggled and he was full of filth. He struggled some more and then he started shouting, "Fire! Fire! Fire!" The neighbors heard him and they called 911. Is it the same number here? I hope I got the number right (laughter). Then they all came, screaming sirens and he just kept on shouting, "Fire! Fire!" They saw this man in filth and nobody wanted to touch him, none of the firemen, so they put a hook around his belt and pulled him out and said, "That's okay. Where is the fire?" And, Shankaran Pillai said, "What fire? If I had shouted, 'Shit! Shit!' would you have come?" So, you need to do the right thing otherwise help will not come.

Doing the right thing is just allowing it to happen. This is not a race you've gotten into. This is a way of settling back into yourself. If this has to happen, to move from one dimension to another, you cannot move with understanding. This must be understood clearly. Anything that is not in your experience there is no way for you to understand it and analyze it. This needs to be extremely clear to every individual. People are always trying to understand. I just recently saw a big book, *Understanding God*. I think it's on the popular list? Understanding God. They're even understanding God, that which created you. How did you get to understand that? You cannot understand anything which is in a different dimension than you are right now. The whole effort is to move into a different dimension. If that needs to happen, first you must stop understanding. You have to see "I cannot understand," and there is no need to understand. It is the experience which takes you out of this dimension.

Even for a simple thing. Okay, I'll get you a pickle from India. Try to understand it; you cannot understand. If you put it in your mouth, it will explode. That's different (laughter), but if you sit here and try to understand it, you will not understand it. Try to understand this flower, what will you understand? In your attempt to understand this flower, maybe you will pull it apart petal by petal, but you will understand nothing. Maybe you will know the chemistry of it. Maybe you will analyze everything and then you will conclude everything is proton, neutron and electron. All that is fine, but you will not know anything about the flower.

Now people are trying to deliver spirituality as an understanding. Understanding is needed about how you are bound, that's all. How you are bound to your limitations, that, you need to understand. You cannot understand the other dimension. See, people are always talking about how God is, how heaven is. This will not lead you anywhere except to hallucinations. The only thing that you need to understand is how you are bound to your limitations. If you understand this and free yourself from those bondages, where you have to go you will go anyway. If I talk about the sky, it's of no use. What are the ropes which are tying you down to the earth? That is all that matters. Your business is with the ropes that are tying you down, not with the sky. If you untie these ropes, you will anyway reach the sky. When you reach there, only then will you know what the sky is. Until then, whatever you think about it, whatever understanding, whatever analysis you make, is coming from the limited dimension of where you are right now. There is no way to understand that which is beyond your present level of experience. So the Guru's work is to help you to untie the knots with which you are binding yourself, and to show you where the knots are. If you untie them and you're ready, if you are on the edge, maybe just with one knot left, then he can push you. If he pushes you when you have ten ropes tied down then it will damage you. He can push you only when everything is broken and just one single thread is still hanging. Then he can push you. He can afford to push you because you will not break, only the thread will break, but when you have ropes tied all over, if he pushes you, something of you will break. So the process that we have set in the form of Isha Yoga is just that: to mature the body, to mature the mind, to mature the energies so that slowly, these bondages and ropes that we are tying around us are gradually broken down. A moment comes when all you need is a, "Whoo!" You will go. I want you to speak to me. You can ask questions or you can say anything you want to say.

Questioner: Can you elaborate on what you mean by ropes?

Sadhguru: What do I mean by ropes? What is it that binds you? If you look at it in a very fundamental way, the only two things that bind you are the body and mind. These are the only two limitations you have. These are the only two instruments you have in order to live life here. You are dependent on them in a big way. These are the only two things that you know about yourself, really. So naturally you begin to think, "This is me," because that is all you have experienced, though there may be moments when you think, "This is not me." Most of the time you are experiencing life as a body, as a mind, so naturally you are bound to these two things.

Now we know for a fact that the only two limitations are body and mind, but when we say ropes we are talking about how you are binding yourself to this body and mind. The thing is you get more and more attached to your body simply because of the importance you give it in so many ways. Right now, one simple thing is relationships, which are very important and on top of the American consciousness. Right now for many people the quality of their life is very much dependent upon the kind of relationships that they hold in their life. Is it so? Yes? To a large extent the quality of their life is decided by what kind of relationships they hold. Whatever relationship you may have with anybody, all your relationships, from your mother, to your father, to your lover, to your wife, to your husband, to your child, to your friend, anybody, examine them carefully. Your relationships are very physical. Is it so? When I say physical it is not necessary that you're getting physical with somebody, not in that sense. The relationship and the contact are very, very physical. Or in other words, the only way you can experience the other person is physically. When you develop this you are getting attached to somebody in some way.

Now this attachment to somebody is just a reflection of your attachment to your own body. If there is no attachment to this body you will have no attachment to any-body. I want you to put a hyphen between 'any' and 'body'. If you're really not attached to this body you cannot be attached to any-body. So holding a relationship with somebody is not the real problem but because of your attachment to this body you tend to extend the same attachment to many, many people. If you extend this attachment to a hundred people here, you feel very comfortable and beautiful. You are desperately trying to be spiritual. You want your experience of life to go beyond this body.

Right now sex-based relationships are the most important relationships in the world in many ways; at least in this part of the world they're very, very important, isn't it? The most significant relationship is a sex-based relationship. What is it that you're trying to do? All you're trying to do is extend yourself a little beyond your body; that's all you're trying to do. It's a desperate attempt to be spiritual; but it is just that it's a dead end; you can't go anywhere. You can only go that far and that's it. And repeatedly you get stuck. Then you think there is some problem with this person. "This person would be better, that person would be better, another person may be better," but whatever you do, it's a dead end. All you're trying to do is extend yourself beyond the limited sphere of your body. You want to experience yourself a little more than the way you know yourself. So every attempt, whatever you may be doing, in some way you are trying to extend yourself beyond your limitations. The longing is there, obviously, in every act that you do; it is showing. When you are longing you must also see what is it that is limiting you from really experiencing yourself beyond the limitations of the body?

So fundamentally, because you are experiencing yourself as the body, you are also experiencing every other person as a body. Though you would like to say, "We are soul-mates," naturally you are only body-mates or at the most, mind-mates. Isn't it? Mentally some compatibility has come where friction has been reduced; that's what you're calling 'soul-mate'. Now, the moment you refer to the body or the mind as the deepest core of that person, you are limiting yourself in a big way. You are making sure that you don't seek anything more. And if you want to seek something more you have no means to enter that person and seek his soul. When you have not entered this person (pointing at himself) and sought the deepest core, where is the possibility of you entering the other person and finding the core of that person?

It is pleasant right now; that person's body, that person's emotions, that person's need for you are pleasant; they support you. They keep you going. The physical needs, the mental needs, the emotional needs are fulfilled. And there may be a host of other things, social, financial, other kinds of needs which are all handled. When all this is handled you feel very comfortable, but not liberated. Comfort is there. If the comfort continues, you will see, you will die of boredom! Most of the time a crisis will come so that you don't die of boredom, but if the comfort continues, people will die of boredom. If you die of a disease, if you die in an accident, if you die because of unbearable pain, it's okay. If you die of boredom in such an exuberant world, that would be a real tragedy. Most people don't allow the tragedy to happen to themselves though (laughs).

Now what is binding you is just your identification with your own body, which identifies with every other body. I am just taking a relationship as an example. There are so many other ways. See, you have certain likes and dislikes. This is a deep bondage. We have always believed that, "I like this, and it's my freedom." Like and dislike are the deepest bondages; they don't allow you beyond a certain sphere of experience.

When people come to me and say, "We are serious spiritual seekers. We have come; anything you say we are willing to do." I tell them to do something; I set a process for them. They say, "No, we don't like this." Then I give them a small sheet of paper, telling them, "Okay you write down all the things that you like. Whatever you write down; we will do only that." They usually write down half a dozen things. "What? In this vast existence you just like only half a dozen things?" You excluded everything else in just that one liking and disliking. If you say, "I like only these half a dozen things," you have ensured that you will never go beyond those half a dozen things, isn't it?

Now the very process of Isha Yoga is just this. Do you know this most misunderstood word 'responsibility'? It is not about doing more things in the world. It is just dropping the like and dislike, simply responding to everything as it is needed, responding to every atom in the existence without any like and dislike, simply responding to everything, seeing everything as a part of yourself; it is a very important step. It is not that if you just start to see this mentally and psychologically the removal of barriers for everything else will happen, no, but this condition is very, very essential if one wants to come to some level of experience.

If energy has to expand beyond the limitations of the physical body it's very, very important that the mind has broken its limitations. The mind is a very big limiting factor. It can limit your energy or it can expand your energy. The mind is like a case, the body is a case for your energy; that you understand, isn't it? The body is like a case to contain this energy. The mind is also a case. It is just that it is trickier because it is not physical, but the mind is also a case; it's a glass case. You can't see where it is but it limits you all the time. Isn't it? So the first thing is to drop it. You can't drop it totally but at least stop identifying yourself with it. If you don't identify yourself with the body and the mind, you will see all that can be there. You say, "They are instruments I use in my life but I am not that."

All that is happening with your pranayama and meditation is just this. Deepening this process to make you see, "I am not the body." It doesn't matter how much your ankles are paining. You continue to do the pranayama, slowly it will give you the feeling, "I am not the body." If you handle your energies in a certain way as we are doing – see, there are other ways I can blow you into a different level of experience, but most people will not be able to sustain that level of experience. Unless the basis is created, unless a proper foundation is created within themselves, just building a huge superstructure would be foolish because it will collapse. When it collapses nobody can save that person. You have my word on it.

So that is why we are going through a process, though it is slow, we are just trying to create the necessary foundation on which something else can be built. Later something else will happen by itself. If we want to create big experiences then we need a safe house, like a *Bhava Spandana* program. A Bhava Spandana program is a place where we have created enough cushioning. People can shoot up and fall down, it's safe; but if they do it by themselves, somewhere else, then they get badly damaged in so many ways. The experiences that some people are touching during this program are quite enormous. They're really touching the peaks in many ways but they are not able to sustain it all the time. They fall down to a certain level of experience, maybe not totally down, but they fall down to wherever their energies are established.

So the whole thing is to establish a foundation which will sustain a higher level of consciousness and a higher level of energy. See, if you sit here, if your energies are beyond this body, you may not know how to retain this body. If your energy is raised to a certain pitch, a certain level of intensity, you cannot stay in the body any more. This is the reason why the moment of enlightenment and the moment of leaving the body are the same for most people. Ninety percent of people leave their body at the moment of enlightenment because their energies reach a certain pitch; after that they cannot retain their body nor do they care to retain it. Unless the necessary foundation is created with the proper work, you can't just do something.

The work that you're doing is just that right now, to build the necessary foundation so that slowly you will see you are not so much of a body. Many of you are already experiencing food and other things are not so important anymore as they used to be. Is that noticeable? Small, small physical things which were very important for you are not so important for you now. This is because – you may not be doing it consciously – energy-wise you are becoming less of a body. So the whole process is to make you less and less of a body and a mind.

As you become less of a body and a mind you can use your body and mind in a much, much better way. That is also possible. Whether you're going to use it or not use it, that is your discretion, but the important thing is you are becoming less of a body. Hunger comes, a little hunger, people cannot bear it; they'll go mad. If they can't drink water they'll go mad. If you don't allow them to use the restroom for half an hour they'll go mad. You will see all these things are receding as you do the practice. You are hungry, it doesn't seem to matter. You're thirsty, it doesn't seem to matter. You can wait another hour; it doesn't matter, because you are becoming less of a body.

This is a constant progression. It is happening. Why all the time, for ages we have been insisting that practice should happen whether you understand or don't understand is for this reason. It doesn't matter even if you don't understand, just stick to the practice. As you move into the practice, things that your mind cannot do, slowly your energy will do. These four things are complementary – your body, your mind, your emotions and your energy. If you handle all of them properly, your growth is very quick. If you handle all four dimensions properly, your growth will be very quick, but above all, handling your energy properly is the most important thing, because if you transform the body you can reverse it in no time.

See, let us say for the next two months you practice hatha yoga. You'll feel very good in the body. For another week you just party every night, drink and go crazy and you will see, after a week's time, the body will be beaten. Two months of work is lost in one week of doing whatever you did. Similarly with the mind, you can cultivate the mind with lots of care, but very easily you can go out and reverse the whole process very quickly; but when you cultivate the energy, it is not so quick. Once you cultivate the energy it doesn't matter where you go or what you do. It gives you a certain sense of freedom that situations don't overpower you, don't overtake you. They don't decide your quality. Wherever you go, you still maintain your quality.

So this is the reason why there has always been so much stress on practice. It doesn't matter whether you understand or you don't understand, whether what you are doing fits into your analytical way of looking at things or not. Just stick to the practice and see. Gradually there will be a transformation. "No, I am still getting angry! I am still getting frustrated, I am getting this, I am getting that!" All that is okay, but the important thing is, you are becoming less of a body, less of a mind. That is the most significant thing. That is the direction in which the practice is taking you.

So the four ropes, if you look at it, are: your attachment to your body, your attachment to your mind and your attachment to your emotions. With your energy you don't have much attachment, but there is bondage there. So these are the four ropes we are trying to release. If you untie these four then there is nothing to hold you down.

Questioner: You've been talking about this person or thing or energy that is beyond the body and mind, something that exists beyond. That's well and good, but don't we need to be a physical person to live in this world?

Sadhguru: Is it necessary you've got to be something? Is it essential that you have to be something? Maybe you're not a thing.

Questioner: But isn't that what you say?

Sadhguru: It's not that I say, you tell me. Before I went through this body and mind, before I cleared this up for you, if I talk about something that is not in your experience it is just a waste of time because you will either believe me or disbelieve me. Both ways it's of no use. It's of no use believing me; it's of no use disbelieving me. Only if you come to the experience then you know it. So before getting there you want to know. It will not help; it will only help you to hallucinate.

All your analysis belongs to the dimension in which you exist right now. It doesn't even touch anything that is beyond. So whatever projections you have about the beyond are simply false. They are just falsehood, but you like to feed yourselves with that, and that is the way you increase your attachment to the mind. Understand, you like your ideas too much. You are getting more and more attached to the mind. Your philosophies, your ideologies, your beliefs, they mean so much to you! That is the way you are increasing your attachment to the mind.

So now you know God, you know the soul, you know what's beyond also, in your mind. So when your mind is such a wonderful instrument that it can even grasp the Creator, naturally you will get attached to the mind, not to God. So your mind is even bigger than Him, isn't it? Yes? If you can contain your God in your mind, your mind is even bigger than God, isn't it? So you're deeply attached to your mind, unconsciously there is a very deep attachment.

Questioner: How can I quieten my mind? It seems like the longer I do my practices, the mind seems to be telling me that I have more important things to do even though I know I want to do my practices (laughter).

Sadhguru: The very first step in Isha Yoga is to see that whatever is happening in me is my responsibility. Now it is not that you have become dis-identified with the mind right now, but at the same time you are talking as if you are dis-identified with the mind. Now you are blaming the mind. "It's not me. I want to do my practices but my mind, you know?" If you had a mother-in-law in the house, you would have chosen the mother-in-law, but you don't have one and so you are choosing your mind; somebody to pass the buck to. So your mind is chattering. Whether your body is well, your body is ill, or whatever, the first thing is to see it's my responsibility. Then everything gets centered in one place. Otherwise your life is scattered. If I think, "My mind is like this, so my practices are like this; my mind is responsible. My career is like this; my boss is responsible. Something is like that, somebody else is responsible," now, your life is scattered, isn't it? The first thing is to get it centered so then you see, it's *me*, nothing else but *me*. Whatever may be happening, or whatever may not be happening it's just *me*.

Now you have become straight with life. This is not spirituality; this is just learning to be absolutely straight. That's the first step, the most important step. In the name of religion you have lost your basic ability to be straight. Unfortunately, if you look carefully at all kinds of minds you will see a criminal's mind is more straight than the so-called religious people's minds. Really; at least their values are quite straightforward, you know? They know what they want. And they pursue that irrespective of the risks involved, isn't it? But in the name of religion we make the mind so devious. See, this is a simple fact. Everybody's saying, "I love God, I love Jesus," whichever form they might have told you about. Here you say Jesus; there they say something else.

Where did this love come from, for a man you have not met, when you have no love for people that are sitting right next to you! You can't say hello to them. From where do you get all this love for a man who lived two thousand years ago? Now, suppose they told you right from your childhood, if you love God your life would be absolutely miserable. Would you love God? Would you seek God? They have told you if you seek God your life will become beautiful. Everything will work. Your career will bloom. Your bank balance will increase. Your relationships will be wonderful and you will go to heaven and have eternal pleasure. Yes?

All you're seeking is candy, not God. You make it so devious, as if you are actually seeking God, but what you're seeking is a cheaper currency than the dollar. To get what you want through the dollar is difficult; you have to work. This is a cheaper currency, you know. If they told you that if you worship God you will lose everything, would you worship Him? No, isn't it? This is the reason why a whole culture was created. In India we were always told that if you seek Shiva he will destroy you. He will devastate your life. So all the ancient prayers in India are, the devotees are praying, "Please destroy me. Take away everything. I shouldn't even get a morsel of food in my life. Make it like that."

That seems to be crazy, isn't it? And that's how all prayers are. Now, this man is seeking, "Please destroy me the way I am." He's not saying, "Save me," he's saying, "Destroy me." Now please see what you're seeking is not God; what you're seeking is not heaven. What you're seeking is free happiness all the time, isn't it so? If they told you that if you seek God you will be miserable, you would not seek Him. You would avoid Him. Only because they told you that if you seek Him everything will happen well for you, you are seeking Him. So what you want is well-being and you are not willing to admit it. You better admit it. Be straight with life – that's the first step. If you are straight with it then we can see what else. Then you know that even if everything is there, even when your life is well, it's still very limited! Then we can see how to cross the threshold of those limitations. If you're not even straight with yourself, how can you get anywhere? If you can't afford to be straight with everybody in the world, at least be with yourself.

People who believe that they're devotees, they're almost there but they'll never be there. Almost there means, it's like this: once a school kid came home and immediately, as usual, went straight for play. His mother caught hold of him and asked, "What happened? What happened to your math test? Hmmm?"

"Oh, Mom, I nearly got 100."

"Really? That's wonderful. How much? Did you get 98?"

"No, I got two zeros."

You're nearly there, almost, but until that *one* happens the two zeros are meaningless, isn't it? So, until this *one* is sufficiently baked, those two zeros don't mean anything. So first thing, right now see what you call as 'myself' is not yourself. It is a lot of nonsense that you gathered from situations in which you have lived. So much cultural bondage is there. Why this bondage is there is, who you think you are, is not really who you are. Everything that you are has been made by somebody else. So if this *one* happens then a million zeros will follow; no problem; but if this one doesn't happen, you go on adding zeros, nothing has changed.

Your education definitely came to you from outside, isn't it? If you had sixteen fingers your arithmetic would have been different. So that has come to you from outside, your whole education, whatever you know. Your language has come to you from outside. Everything that you believe as your religion has come to you from outside. Your gods and demons have come to you from outside. What you believe as right and wrong has come to you from outside. Your whole morality has come to you from outside. Yes?

Like this you go on discarding everything that has come from outside and create a distance between you and that. You don't have to drop it. You still live in this society and so you need some of that stuff, but create a clear space between you and that. "That's not me," then you will see everything you are doing in the form of practice will go much, much faster. Right now you don't have one spiritual path. You have five going because today people are reading about everything; there are people writing spiritual paths in books. So they have a hundred books in their house and they've read everything. They've picked up a little bit of here, there, there, and they're trying to assimilate their own path.

In the neighborhood one woman delivered. She's been delivering for the last ten years once every nine months. Just yesterday she delivered the kidneys. Last year she delivered the heart, the year before last the lungs. It's almost complete now. Next year she'll deliver the toes and it will be a complete baby. So, it comes as a whole, isn't it? If you are picking up bits and pieces, it will not become a whole; it will not. Unfortunately that is what is being pursued now as a spiritual path.

I was recently reading something, some group of a hundred scholars went to Israel and they did a lot of research about Jesus' life. They are saying – I don't know how accurate it is – that only sixteen percent of whatever is held as the Bible or Christian teaching is said by Jesus. The rest of it has been made up by all kinds of fools along the way. Only sixteen percent! That sixteen percent is so deeply garbled, lost in all the other stuff that it is mixed up with, that Jesus' words are somewhere in the back seat.

So if you wanted a spiritual path you should have just followed what he said, isn't it? Maybe then there would be a way. And his teaching is very simple. His teaching is just, "Come, follow me." If you're not an innocent being, you cannot follow him. You cannot, isn't it? This is because now you're a mess of things in your mind. You cannot follow Jesus, and he made it very clear to you only children will get across this because he knew thinking minds could never follow him. The thinkers of that society, the scholars of that society, the so-called religious people of that society never took a step behind him. In fact they worked to persecute him, isn't it?

Today after two thousand years you think it was a great injustice that was done to him. "What happened? How could they have done it?" I want you to understand, the people that did it were just people like you, ordinary people. This man was talking so much nonsense against everything that they believed in. What else to do with him? And you're not able to ignore him because he made sense. If he talked total nonsense you could have ignored him. He made sense but he makes you feel like nonsense! So the best thing was to crucify him. Isn't it? They did the best thing they could do to him. That is the best thing this mind could do, unfortunately.

Once you believe in something, once you identify yourself with something that you think is right, this is all you can do, crucifixion. Maybe you will not actually take nails and put them into somebody, but you will crucify them in your mind in so many ways because you are identified with what you think is right, yes? The moment you're identified with what you think is right, if somebody else is saying something totally opposite of that and it becomes overpowering, you will want to do something to him. You've felt that way the second day of the class, didn't you (laughs)?

So you are responsible for your practice. If you're not doing it, you're not doing it. "No, my mind is chattering!" Let it chatter. Did we say your mind should stop chattering? See, that is a mistake lots of people have made. They always told you your mind should be serene. I'm telling you let it chatter, because people who are talking about a pure mind, those people have never looked at themselves. A great deception is going on. There is no such thing as a pure mind on this planet. The mind is just a garbage bin – anybody's mind. It is just how much distance you have kept with it, that's all the difference is. You can be a pure being. You can't be a pure mind, isn't it? If you purify your mind, your mind should become empty, absolutely. That's not possible, but you can make an inner space. You can dis-identify yourself with the mind. Is there a pure mind in the world? Do you believe it? People who are talking about pure minds have never looked at themselves.

Questioner: I have heard about systems in Eastern cultures, in India especially, where couples separate after they complete their worldly responsibilities and they have an option to work on their inner selves. It is accepted. It seems in the West, we are constantly expected to be busy, to be productive, to do, do, do. I am wondering what are our options if we want to withdraw.

Sadhguru: There is something called *Varnashrama dharma*. Varnashrama dharma means life is segmented into different stages. Varnashrama dharma says from the moment of birth until twelve years of age is called *Balavastha*. That means it's a child state; until twelve years of age it is only play, nothing else but play. In India this is how it is classified. Up to twelve years of age only play. So when the child reaches twelve years of age there is a certain process which is called *brahmopadesham*. Brahmopadesham means that the basic mantra which is taught to him is, "*ahum brahmasmi*." Ahum brahmasmi means, "I am the *Brahman*." Brahman means, "I am the Divine." Those days, it used to happen experientially for a twelve year-old boy, when he's just on the verge of becoming an adult, and a little thought is evolving in him. They would make him go through an experience where he realizes, "I am the Divine." Only after this process he's allowed education, because education was seen as a tremendous power. So this power should not be handed over to a limited person. This power should be given only to that person who sees himself as really responsible for everything. Only that person should be educated. Otherwise he should not receive education, because education is seen as a great tool.

Today it is because all kinds of people have gotten educated and the power of science and technology has come into their hands; just see how wantonly we have destroyed this planet, isn't it? Living in a Nashville suburb, the comfort of being here, you may not realize what's coming up, but environmentalists are measuring this and desperately they're appealing to everybody that there are certain things happening on the planet which you cannot ignore, which can mean a great calamity for the human race. There are certain things which are advancing at an alarming pace that, if you don't take care for them now, they will mean total calamity, a very large calamity.

This is happening simply because people who have no sense of really feeling the world as part of themselves are educated and empowered with science and technology. They will do anything for their profit. They will do anything. At no point did these people think that there are other creatures on this planet who have as much right to live as they do. Yes, to live you have to kill, you have to eat; you have to do certain things which everybody does, which all animals do. To that extent you can also do, but now you have crossed all limits where you somehow believe that every creature on this planet is only there to serve your lives. Once you get into this attitude you are inviting a calamity; it is just a question of time. Today we know a lot of scientists and others are getting alarmed and they're giving warnings, but those voices go unheard because you are splurging on your comfort right now. You are not willing to look at it, but some day nature will force you to. It will not necessarily happen to those people who abused it; it will happen to everybody. It's not just going to happen to one person or to a million people who abused it. It is just going to happen to everybody. So that's a common karma you are performing right now on this planet.

This is why the first step was to make a person realize that he is the Divine. When he says he's the Divine he is saying, "I am the existence. Everything is a part of me." Only after that he is educated. So from the age of twelve until twenty-four, the next twelve-year phase is for education. This is called *bhramhacharya*. At this time a person maintains absolute celibacy and pursues whatever he has chosen to study. So his life is dedicated to study, where study means – normally, in the Western sense you're always thinking educating yourself is to make yourself into somebody, yes? But in the Eastern sense education always meant it is a method to become a nobody. Education is a process of dis-identifying yourself with everything and just becoming available to everybody and everything. That's what is meant by education.

There is a certain way we go through teaching. For example, when people come to teacher training, or even in the Isha Yoga program when I am repeatedly telling people, "Don't write anything down," they just don't understand. They think they must. When I am not looking they think they can write down a few sentences (crowd laughs). You know it has happened! Because they have a whole training, right from childhood: gather! Gather everything that you can get. They think gathering is education. The very nature of your mind is to gather; all the time it wants to gather. Now people are busy gathering spiritual teachings. They've gotten half a dozen Gurus in their handbag. In your life, in your many lifetimes, if you meet one live Guru you are fortunate, but today people have half a dozen Gurus in their handbags.

See, somebody may be a Guru to somebody else, but he may not be a Guru to you as yet, because he becomes a Guru to you only when you begin to experience him beyond his person. As long as you're just looking at him as a person and thinking you will receive some teaching, maybe he's a guide to you, but not yet a Guru. He will become your Guru when you become open enough and he can touch you in a way that nobody else can touch you. No individual in your life could have touched you that way. He will touch you that way; only then he's your Guru. Until then he's your friend, he's your guide, but he's not your Guru yet.

So this education is a process of dissolution. When he reaches twenty-four years of age he completes his education. This education happens in a completely different way. For example, people come to train themselves as teachers for Isha Yoga. One simple thing that we do with them is – for Americans just the Guru Pooja will do – you have to learn the Guru pooja. That will destroy who you are. It will twist your tongue out and destroy you (laughs).

Now, what we do is, we have some forty pages of notes for pranayama as to what is pranayama, how it happens, and everything else. These notes have been carefully crafted. It is not just instruction; it is the way your body actually moves. If you sit and close your eyes and write pranayama notes, that's how it will come out. It's written in such a way that it makes a deeper contact than just memory. So now these forty pages are required to be learned word by word. You're not supposed to say it any other way than the way it has been written. Just by learning this, you will see; you will see education is a process of dissolution, not a process of making yourself into a somebody. Once you become a somebody and become powerful, you're dangerous in many ways. If you're a nobody and powerful, you're useful to existence, but if you become a somebody and powerful, you're dangerous.

So education is over at the age of twenty-four. So now people choose. Generally in ancient India about seventy percent of the people chose family life. At the age of twenty-four they got married. Thirty percent of the people chose the ascetic life; they went into monastic life. Seventy percent chose family situations. That was a good proportion, but today whether they want to or not, society is channeling them in such a way that if they don't go for the opposite sex there is something weird about them! Everybody must go, whether they have it or they don't have it, whether they really want it or they don't want it, they must just run after the opposite sex either in the form of marriage or whatever. Some relationship they must have. They have got to run whether they like it or not, because otherwise they are weird. Thirty percent of the people chose not to even look in that direction because, if you sincerely look into yourself, many of you may not have such needs. You're doing it simply because everybody else is doing it, and you don't know what else to do with yourself.

So at the age of twenty-four those who went into monastic life continued with that; their life was different. People who went into the family life from the age of twenty-four to forty-eight, that is twenty-four years – these are called two spans; one span is twelve years – two spans of life you spend with the family. Generally if you have children, twenty-four years of marriage means your children have reached somewhere around twenty years of age. When they reach twenty it is time for you to leave. It's time for you to dissolve the family and leave. So husband and wife live together for twenty-four years. See, in this culture, once you're married there is no question of choosing something else. It's a choice for life. For a thinking, logical mind this may look like bondage but it gives such stability to them. Maybe pleasure-wise it may not be much, but it gives such stability to their lives that though people are much poorer, even though they don't have the basics of life, you will find they are still stable. You will not see the kind of insecurity that you see here in the United States, with all the affluence. Here there is a tremendous sense of insecurity. You will not see that insecurity on the face of a beggar in India. He is okay even at that level. In comfort he may not be there, in food he may not be there, in nutrition he may not be there, but when it comes to security, he has his own sense of security, because everything was structured to bring stability into his life. This stability is essential if you want to pursue higher levels of who you are. For twenty-four years husband and wife lived like each other's shadows. There is no question at all of looking another way.

Now in modern India, slowly the question is arising in people's minds, "Is this the right man for me? Is this the right woman for me? Should I choose another woman, another man?" This is happening. Otherwise in the tradition it was fixed in such a way that it was a sacred relationship. It is not for you to make it or break it. It is made by somebody else, and it cannot be broken by you.

So when you complete forty-eight years of life, you dissolve the marriage, and for the next twelve years you go into what is called *sanyas*. That means you become a monk. In those days there were arrangements for men and women to pursue this separately; they would part and pursue their own spiritual path. See, when you are young you have energies; you know, you have your hormones, you have struggles going on in your body, in your mind, longing for this, longing for that. All this has been settled. You have pursued your career, your business, whatever. Twenty-four years you have made yourself into something. Then at the time when you're really hitting the peak of attachment, you dissolve. You dissolve this marriage and go into monastic life for twelve years.

At sixty years of age, after completing the next span, the husband and wife come back together and remarry. Even today, even though people live together continuously, at the age of sixty most couples are remarried once again. Are you aware of this? No? In India there's a tradition that at sixty they will get remarried; the same couple, get married again. Now the first time when they married, it was a fire in their body which brought them together. Now they have left those fires behind. They're marrying in a completely different way. This second marriage is not conducted by a priest. A Guru usually conducts this marriage so that these two beings will become partners on a spiritual path, so that they can grow together. Now their bondage is not of the body anymore. Their bondage is of a much deeper dimension so that they can use each other as a support to go on the journey of spirituality. This is called *vanaprastha*.

So once they remarry like this at the age of sixty they will not come back into the city or town. They will go into the forest or into a hermitage and live there as an old couple until they die. So those twelve years of sadhana from forty-eight to sixty meant if somebody truly gave themselves, in twelve years they could attain. So they have attained to their peak. Once again they're together. This is different. When people come together like this, not because they have needs to fulfill, simply because they want to share their blissfulness with another person, now this marriage is tremendously significant.

This is how life was fragmented. This comes from a tremendous wisdom, but today, as you said, you are entangled in so many things. "So where do I go?" You can just go. There are places to go. Isha is always open. Maybe if many of you want to go we can set up one in the Nashville suburbs (laughs). Now, one problem is, people have become absolutely logical thinking and nothing else, to a large extent, and their emotions are always spilling around them most of the time. What I see is, with the smallest provocation, people here in the United States, with the littlest provocation become emotionally charged, hysterical, wherever they may be, yes? Do you see this happening with the slightest provocation? Such things wouldn't bother anybody, but here, even with little things, people just become hysterical.

Once you start arranging your whole life logically, you will become more and more desperate because a logical mind expects your whole life should be in a perfect line, and it will never be in a perfect line. You will become more and more frustrated. The frustration rises in such a way that the emotions will spill all the time wherever you are. It should be really difficult to live with people like that! Whoever is living with you must be having a hard time. If you're so emotional, if your emotions are so fragile, it would be very hard for anybody to live with you. No wonder every two years people want to change their partners and try out somebody else! It must be quite difficult.

Once you think only logically, there is no other value to life except logic. You cannot remain anywhere for too long. You want to shift all the time. I don't know how much this is true, but they say an average American never stays in any job for more than three years.

Is that so? Is it a reality? Some people say that; maybe they must have just surveyed a certain segment of society probably, I don't know. Some reports say it is like that, that they never remain in any job for more than three years; they keep shifting. The same could be happening with the relationships for lots of people. They never remain for more than three years or whatever number of years. This need to shift comes because there is a feeling of insecurity all the time.

So the first thing is to stabilize life; it's very important. You can't settle the whole society for your sake. It's not going to happen in a day's time, or we don't know, in a century's time, it still may not happen. So the first thing is to stabilize your system, your energies, your emotions and your mind. If you stabilize these, irrespective of what's happening around you, you pursue your goal; and society will change only when hundreds of people become stable within themselves. You can't stabilize the society without stabilizing people, isn't it?

So Patty, if you want to go, it's all right (laughs).

Questioner: The other day I heard a speaker say that high experiences and low experiences in life come and go. He says that we should not attach importance to them, but should practice a state of constant gratitude. That when all else is gone, gratitude remains; it is all that matters.

Sadhguru: See if you want to hold a flood with a band-aid, it's up to you. You will know after some time it will not hold. Okay, you can go on practicing. See they have taught you this earlier; they taught you kindness. You went on being kind to everybody and in the end you were so frustrated that the next person who comes along you want to murder. Why they're talking kindness is because they don't know how to be loving. All they are doing is talking kindness, gratitude and things like this as a substitute because they don't know how to be joyous and loving. I would like to see a world where nobody needs anybody's kindness.

They told you, "Forgive everybody," and they're blaming Jesus because he forgave everybody. Repeatedly he told you, "It's not me, it's you. And you're already forgiven." Yes? But now, you're blaming that man because He forgave everybody. If I have to forgive you, the first thing is, I have to make you into a sinner in my mind, isn't it? I have to make you not okay. Only then can I forgive you. If you're okay with me, how do I forgive you? If I see you as a part of myself I don't have any gratitude for you. I want you to understand this. I have no kindness in me. I have no gratitude for anybody. Do you have gratitude for your hand, which made you eat lunch today, this afternoon? Do you feel gratitude for this hand? It would be stupid, isn't it?

Now stability will not come by playing tricks with your mind. It will hold you for a while, definitely. It will hold you. It is just that a flood will build up and burst in a bigger way. This so-called practice of kindness, forgiveness, has driven people to madness. For no reason people are just pulling out guns and shooting at anybody and everybody. Isn't it? They're just fed up with being kind and forgiving, yes (laughs)? You're only suppressing. Instead of understanding, you're suppressing. If you suppress, for how long can you do it? See, initially you try to control people with fear, "God is watching you. If you do this... you know in hell they've got all those torture instruments? Do you know what all he will do to you?" Fear!

When people grew up and they started questioning that, they went into more subtle tricks, "Don't worry, God will forgive you." Now, for all the nonsense that I have done God is going to forgive me? You have gratitude. They're trying to bind you with gratitude, with kindness, with other things; fundamentally suppressing. This suppression will not release you. It will help you to avoid certain things for a certain period of time. Afterwards you will burst. Why should you practice kindness? Only because somewhere inside you have a tremendous cruelty within you. Isn't it? Yes? Otherwise where is the need to practice kindness? Now if there is an animal in you which growls and wants to bite, you better handle that animal rather than trying to clothe it with kindness. If I sugarcoat the poison pill, it won't be bitter in your mouth. It will be sweet, and it will make you feel good for some time, but once it goes in, and digestion begins, once again it poisons you, isn't it? So, don't try to sugarcoat that which is within you. It is better you address the basic root of where it's springing from.

Now, you are unkind to somebody. Why? You are cruel towards somebody. Why? What is it that allows you to be cruel to somebody? What is it?

Questioner: Is it because I do not see him as a part of myself?

Sadhguru: Yes! "This is not me," isn't it? "I don't see this as life. Only *this* is real life (pointing at himself). Everything else is there only for my well-being." And I will use you and also express my gratitude to you and say, "Thank you." If you see this as a part of yourself whatever you do is not a question of using somebody; it's just being together and sharing. It can be very different. So instead of changing the root of your experience which is bringing all this, you are trying to fix it in subtle ways. You're pruning the tree.

You can prune this tree into many shapes. You know people are pruning trees into the form of Mickey Mouse? Children will enjoy it. If there was a tree in the shape of Mickey Mouse in Nashville, kids would gather around it. They would really enjoy it; they would like to see that tree every day. How wonderful it would be! But this tree, which is being pruned like this every day, will never see any fruit. Yes? If you want it to bear fruit you have to allow it to express itself for what it is. You want to make a Mickey Mouse out of a tree then no fruit or flower will ever come out of it. Isn't it? So right now it's just that you are trying to make a Mickey Mouse out of yourself. No, maybe not such a funny thing; you're trying to make a Jesus out of yourself, a Krishna out of yourself, somebody out of yourself. It is not going to work. Unless you find your original nature, it's not going to work.

Finding your original nature is not far away from you. You are just identified with the wrong things. Dis-identify yourself from that, it is there! Isn't it? Who you are is definitely within you, isn't it? So, you're just identified with so many things. If you dis-identify yourself from that – it is called, "*nethi, nethi, nethi,*" one of the most ancient spiritual processes. To go on saying, "I am not this. I am not this." See right now, suppose, not your body, let's say your clothes are lying there, if I step on them and go, it may bring anger in you. They are pieces of cloth, but you are identified with them, "This is my dress," and it can bring so much anger in you, isn't it? Because you're so deeply identified with it. Even if I walk upon your body there is no need to be angry if you are not identified with it, but now you're identified with it. If I step on your clothes it actually hurts you. It's reality, isn't it? Yes or no? It actually hurts you. You definitely know, even with your logical mind, that this cloth is not *me*, but 'it is my cloth', you are identified with it, and it hurts.

Like this, see in how many ways you have spread yourself. And this spreading yourself; I'm not saying it's wrong; it is the right longing, you want to expand; but I'm telling you that way you will not get anywhere, that's all. The longing is right, you want to expand but that's not the way. Physically you can never become unbounded. You will always be limited, isn't it?

Questioner: I recently had a car accident, I crashed into another car and my car was spun around on its side and the driver's door was crushed in. I was not hurt, but they took me to the hospital to take x-rays just in case. I just had some bruising on my leg, but no real trauma at all to the body. The nurses kept telling me I would be very sore the next day, but I wasn't sore. I think maybe I am experiencing some looseness in the body because of my yoga practices.

Sadhguru: Less of a body. Whether you can observe it or not, whether you put it to the test or not, if you are sticking to your practices you have definitely become less of a body than what you were. Definitely you are much less of a body than what you were. One example like this makes you see it. Every day if you are sitting there and doing the practice, you are becoming a little less of a body. The day will come, if you sit here, your body is here but you are totally loose from it.

Experiences like this might have happened to people in Samyama or even in Shoonya meditation; but the problem is again when they get involved with life, they seem to be stuck with it, the body. It doesn't matter. As your energies mature, you will see, a clearer space will arise between you and the body. Once there is a clear space between you and your body, if you're not attached to your body you will not be attached to anything. All your attachment just springs from that one connection. Then when the moment comes, you're going to shed everything and walk away from the body.

Don't look for drama in life. When this building is being built, brick by brick, there is nothing dramatic about it, but when it stands up it's a big thing. So don't look for dramatic things to happen. It's not necessary. We create some drama for you just to inspire you sufficiently. That's it (laughs). Just to keep you inspired enough to continue. Otherwise no drama is needed. Very gently, slowly one can progress.

Especially in this society you need some drama; otherwise you will give up your sadhana. So once in a while I will come and create a little drama for you, but at other times just work.

Questioner: I am noticing a lessening of my obsession with exercise. Could this be because I am less of a body due to the practice?

Sadhguru: There is no need to be obsessed about your exercise. Your body needs exercise, all right, and that much exercise you can give to the body in so many ways. Being obsessed with exercise usually comes with a certain age in your life because you fear old age so much. When you're identified with the body, youth is the most important aspect of your life, naturally, because when you're youthful, your body is at its best. If you're identified with the body, as you age you will become more and more unstable. Only a person who is not identified with the body can grow old gracefully and beautifully. Old age can be as beautiful as any other part of your life, in fact more beautiful because you have a whole lifetime of experience behind you.

Youth is beautiful, but you know you're so confused, you don't know what the hell you're doing most of the time, yes? So old age can be even more beautiful because you have a whole life's experience lying behind you. That is, if you have become wise with the process of life; but if you have become wounded with the process of life then old age is a great misery.

Now, there is definitely no need to be obsessed with food either, for eating food or not eating food. You know both ways people are obsessed. Some are obsessed about simply eating; some are obsessed about not eating because – this thing is a little different. So similarly with exercise, no need to be obsessed about yourself, isn't it? If you are obsessed with exercise you may be manufacturing diseases in your body. It is very much possible. Not necessarily, but very much possible. Don't be obsessed with exercise. It is nice and necessary to keep this body well, isn't it? It's your business to keep this body. So for keeping it well, whatever you have to do, do it joyfully. There is no need to be obsessed about exercise. With obsession, you may have hard muscles but cancer inside. You will manufacture this in your body; it is very much possible. So, any kind of obsession is not a good thing, isn't it? You should be obsessed to break your limitations (laughs).

At the Master's Feet

The Master-disciple relationship: very intimate, very subtle.

A three-month intensive wholeness program took place in 1994, the first ever in-house program to be conducted at the newly formed Isha Yoga Center. Amidst the fury of the rain and winds, in a temporary thatched structure and the barest of necessities, disciples encountered the Master in all his compassion and fierceness.

I really want to do some big energy experiments with you, but I don't know if we sufficiently impressed upon you sixty to ninety days ago that the physical body has to be in a good shape. I don't know if it has been sufficiently impressed upon you. The whole purpose of why we want to go on a high-energy trip is because only when your energies are really high, you have total control over your needs. All the petty needs, which are important now, do not matter anymore when your energy is high. You are sitting here now and there is a strong need to stretch your legs. If you don't fulfill this need life becomes a misery. This is a very, very small need, this wanting to stretch your legs. It is such a small thing in your life, but it can change the very way you experience your life today. When the energy is high enough, these small needs like food, sleep, eating, standing, do not matter; they are not important anymore. Only when a person is able to transcend these small needs, then we can look at something else, something totally different. When I say different, I am not saying something different from the reality. Reality is something different from the illusions that you have woven around yourselves. You have built a whole cocoon of illusory experiences around yourselves. Using the sense organs and the mind, you have built a very nice coating around yourselves, which makes you believe that nonsense because it is experientially true. Your hunger is experientially true, but that is not the truth. To break the whole cocoon that you have woven around yourself, to transcend that – one of the very first steps of sadhana is to transcend the sense organs themselves, not using the sense organs and the motor organs. There are five for each of these two. The sense organs are the eyes, ears, nose, mouth and skin. The motor organs involve movement: the legs, the hands, speech and all the other movements in the body.

The first step to transcend these illusory experiences is to limit these ten organs – both sensory and motor – that is the whole purpose of sitting. For someone who is not aware, sitting down simply for hours together during meditation may seem boring and dull, but once you stop these ten functions totally, then the reality opens up. Once this opens up, the person is in a totally different level of consciousness where there is no comfort or discomfort. That is the first goal or the first step that you have to take. Now if you want to limit the functions of your sense organs and motor organs, one thing is the body has to be fit and another thing is your energy has to be sufficiently high.

Why a triangle within a circle has been chosen as the symbol for Isha is because this is the most fundamental yantra. Yantra means a certain form, which has a certain vibration. A fundamental yantra means the basic yantra. In both the tantric and the yogic cultures it is said that the whole existence is created out of this yantra. First it was nothingness. This nothingness became sound. The first form that was created was this, and from this all beings and all existence were created. There is a scientific basis for why it is so, but right now let us look at it symbolically. Let us look at it as a symbol.

What is this yantra? This yantra describes you; in the center there is a small dot. This is supposed to be your being, whatever you call it. In some schools of philosophy, they call it a being and in some others they call it a non-being. They call it the atma, soul or whatever you want to call it. That is the basis, it is emptiness, but because people won't be able to see it, we have put a dot. I thought it would be better to put a small circle; it suggests a little emptiness. And inside there is a triangle. In the triangle, the left side of the triangle, the slanting line is the body. The one on the right is mind. The bottom line is the prana. Now that segment of the circle which is in correspondence to the bodyline is your physical activity which includes the sense organs and the motor organs. The segment of the circle which is in correspondence with the mind line is the thought process, the whole range of mental activity. The bottom segment is the life process or the pranic activity within the system. This yantra or this symbolism is supposed to represent a whole human being.

We first start our work with the body and the body's activity, then the mind and the mind's activity and lastly the prana and the pranic activity. If we have some amount of mastery over these three aspects of activity, the body's activity, the thought process and the pranic activity – to some extent if you have some mastery over them – then the gates will open to the inner dimension. If you know a little bit of engineering, then you will know that the triangle is the most stable form. Of all the forms that you can create, the triangle is the strongest form. If you build an aircraft, everything is a triangle inside it, the structural part of it. It is understood that the triangle is the hardest structure even by your engineers. So the fundamental yantra is a triangle. The way your body, mind and pranic system are made comes from that. It is very firm and tremendously strong. If you use it properly, you can do incredible things with it.

Now with the asanas and the simple stretching stuff that we are doing here, the body seems to struggle. You will see after a week's time that the body is capable of coping with not only this but a little more and more and more. Once a person stretches this body there is no limit to it; he can go on stretching it.

One example that I would like to talk about is Malladi Halli Swami from whom I first learned my yogic practices. In his sadhana he used to do four thousand and one surya namaskars every morning. The body can be pushed like this! When he was at his peak, he was doing these four thousand and one effortlessly. He could have done more but only for lack of time he was stopping there. Otherwise, he would have stretched himself to ten thousand also. Just because it took too much time, he stopped at four thousand and one.

All the chakras, the pranic chakras are all triangles. We call them chakras because it symbolizes movement, growth, but it is actually a triangle. Now we must start with the body. In the morning you have done your asanas with the body. The right way to go if you go according to the natural progression, is the mind, but we will go with the pranayama, simply because the nature of the mind is such. The mind is a very cunning person by himself; whatever you try to do with him he will do something else. This is simply because your dependence on the mind is such that the whole process of growing up, the social exposure, everything is such that you become too dependent on the mind. If you simply live in the forest, you wouldn't use your mind so much, and you would still be very intelligent.

If you have been into a forest with a tribal, the way he uses his body and his intelligence is tremendous. You will feel like a fool. The city man feels like an idiot in front of a tribal who sees and hears so many things that he is not even aware of. He sees everything but you don't see anything. Even if there is an animal nearby and this man points his finger in that direction, the city man would still be searching. The tribal's eyes and body have become like that; he senses everything. The animals are much deeper into this. Their bodies are so extremely sensitive that an elephant can hear sounds across three hundred to four hundred miles. They communicate three hundred to four hundred miles with subsonic sounds. You cannot hear those sounds. Whales communicate over ten thousand miles across the oceans. Their bodies have become the main instruments in their lives.

With man, the mind has developed to a certain extent, and this mind is such that it can either go this way or that way. It can be developed in a very lopsided way. The mind has a certain fluidity which the body does not have. You can only develop the body in a particular way, in terms of strength and flexibility. You cannot develop the body in terms of some lopsided development. Maybe you can to some extent, but it is not really much; however, with the mind you can deviate very far from the natural path. The body keeps you rooted to nature. The body is nature; the mind takes you far away from nature. So this aspect is the main barrier between you and what reality is because the mind is a great divergence. It can go anywhere. You can train it to go anywhere. You can take it in any direction, far away from Truth. The body does not go, whatever you do, after sometime it wants to come down and sit on the ground. You may be jumping up but you always come down. The body is always very close to nature because it is nature. The mind is capable of diverging. So the mental attitude is something we want to tune in to for the first thirty days, so that it doesn't go away, but it comes as close as possible.

Questioner: How does one do it?

Sadhguru: We will create many devices on the way. The next thing is the prana. We will be doing many things with the prana. This is the quickest way to develop; at the same time it has risks involved which means it needs a lot of care and preparation. Let us do this session of pranayama now and after that I want to check each one of you and decide who is going to do what here. I will be asking a few people to do certain sadhana and others not to. This does not mean the people I have asked to do those things are one step higher than the rest. It is not so. You are no less than them. Don't try to do what I have asked you not to do in secrecy. Do not attempt such things. There is no such thing as grades. We are just seeing what is more suitable for you. If you do something which is not suitable for you, it can very easily cause damage.

Questioner: Dear Jaggi, how do I become aware? What support can I seek for this?

Sadhguru: Unfortunately, most people are still lame. They always need a stick to walk. Without a crutch they cannot walk. Support, once again, is at many different levels. If you are physically lame, you need a physical support. If you are psychologically weak, you need a psychological support; if emotionally imbalanced, emotional support. On a different level, if you are financially weak, you need financial support; if socially weak, social support. These are different aspects. When I say support in relation to your growth spiritually, it was connected to all these things in a way. Some people need some psychological support; some people need a physical atmosphere support. Physical support is needed for a few people. When they come to a particular program, they meditate well, they do their pranayama well, but if they sit at home alone, they can't keep their eyes closed and do any sadhana even for ten minutes. They need support. Physical atmosphere is very important for them. Without support, outside support, for a lot of people, not only their way of being, their awareness, even their sadhana disappears; yes, it is happening.

Awareness is hard to keep. You should be able to keep at least the sadhana. When I say hard, I am not saying it is difficult; I am only saying that it needs application; it needs awareness. It just needs awareness. When it isn't there, to be aware or to make an attempt to be aware is hard. Awareness is not something that you have to learn or cultivate. The innermost core of your being is awareness. It is just that when people are living on the surface of their life, they are only experiencing the surface of what they are, just the body and the mind. Then awareness seems to be the most impossible thing, so difficult; but the innermost core is simply awareness. There is nothing to be done, whichever way you are, you are aware anyway.

Now this Wholeness program, why we have come here is just to create an opportunity for a person so that slowly he can drop his crutch. It may not happen immediately. Still many people, even after ninety days of this program will need outside help. We are taking at least one step in this direction in this program, this is our idea.

Questioner: Jaggi, What is a whole person?

Sadhguru: Who do you think is a whole person? What kind of a person would you call a whole being? What are the qualities for a whole being?

Questioner: Jaggi, you are a whole person to me.

Sadhguru: I am asking about quality, not about a particular individual.

Questioner: A steady person is a whole person.

Sadhguru: I am not discarding this quality, but let us look at the different kinds of steadiness that people have. For example, a person who is really fired with some idea or some ideology is extremely steady on his path. A fanatic is very, very steady; you can't get him off his path. Whatever you say to dissuade him doesn't get across. He is very steady. I am not totally negating this steadiness, but when you think of a quality and say this is it, when you want to make it happen in your lives, you may end up with that quality but still not with wholeness. You may be extremely steady. People who are running after money, food, drink, are very steadily going after it. Nobody can get them off that. Can you get them off their track? They are extremely steady; there is no second thought in their mind. We will keep steadiness aside and look at it later.

Questioner: Is somebody with a clear mind or rather clear thinking a whole person?

Sadhguru: Once again, a fanatic has very clear thinking because it is of a single track. A single-track mind is very clear thinking. There are no contradictions in his mind. Now if you believe your Bhagavad Gita is right, that's it. Your mind is clear thinking. This is how people fool themselves. By reading a book or believing in an ideology or believing in a teaching, he feels his thinking has become clear. All he has developed is a single-track mind. That's all. When you become a linear mind, you are only one track. It seems to be clear because there are no opposing thoughts, but this is not the clarity we are looking for. Let any input come from any direction and you can still be clear and receptive. By being receptive to everything you are totally open, but you are still very clear. You allow everything and anything to enter you from any direction and you are still clear. Otherwise that clarity becomes meaningless. Generally, people attain clarity. It is not attainment itself. People think they are clear, but they are just making themselves linear, making themselves single tracked.

Questioner: Is it somebody who is at peace within himself?

Sadhguru: It's yes and no. Let us look at the no side of it, why there could be no peace. Once again peace is achieved in so many different ways. You eat, get a full stomach and lie down. See how peaceful you are, – at least most of you are. Somebody drinks alcohol and is very peaceful. Whenever your ego is satisfied, you are very peaceful. Wherever you go, in a place, if people are willing to support and boost your ego, in that place you are very peaceful. Only in those places where your ego takes a thrashing, that's where you are not peaceful, isn't it?

Generally, in the world, when people talk about peace of mind, it is only about somehow making their ego comfortable. Instead of being in a disturbed state, they should be comfortable; but the very process of trying to make your ego comfortable is the whole process of discomfort also. The more and more a person tries to be peaceful, he only loses his peace and goes off somewhere else. A person who is trying to be peaceful will never be peaceful. Just the reverse of the process will happen.

Peace means nothingness. Peace is not something that you create. Peace is not something that happens. Peace is something that always is. Peace is the fundamental existence. What happens on the surface is disturbance. This is just like the ocean. On the surface of the ocean you will see waves, tremendous turbulence, and tremendous turmoil going on, but if you go deep down, it is perfectly peaceful. The fundamental quality of existence is always peace. If you are in tune with that quality, then yes, it is, but generally the peace that you achieve is only making yourself comfortable. Now when you are here looking at the mountains, you are peaceful. Peacefully, you are enjoying the mountains and suddenly an elephant rushes out of the forest, straight towards you and all peace disappears.

So this peace is of no great significance. It is just okay. At least for some time, on and off you are able to experience a little bit of peace; but it is better to be disturbed, because if you are disturbed you at least search. If you become peaceful, you only become complacent. Complacence is the greatest enemy. Disturbance is not your enemy. Your complacence is the greatest enemy, and this kind of peace will create only complacence. Complacence, the so-called well-settled family, when I say a well-settled family, everything is right for them. Your bank balance is right, your business is going well, your children are healthy, the wife does what is needed and the husband does what is expected out of him. Everything is right. In this family, generally one person will be terribly disturbed; another person will be complacent. Look at your own family or all the families you know that are perfectly matched in every way. You will see one person is mostly disturbed and another person will be complacent. This is the nature. Just look into your mind for a few examples. One person is aggressive, angry, restless and another will be complacent. Maybe in some cases, both are disturbed or both are complacent. But, if what you thought as the best kind of life, ideal life, if it has happened to you, then this is the nature.

You have not achieved anything, it is just that the balance is hit. This person becomes complacent while that person is disturbed and vice versa. It just alternates between the two like this.

Peace comes out of a certain complacence also. Peace also comes out of achievement. When you have achieved something you feel very satisfied. You feel like you are a whole being, but it is just for a moment. That wholeness is not wholeness. You achieved peace out of this also but this is not peace. When your wishes are fulfilled, when your ambitions are fulfilled, or when everything is right for you, when the situation around you is comfortable for your ego and your body, these are the times when you feel peaceful, generally. So this peace is no peace. This is not peace.

Questioner: Jaggi, can a person who enjoys everything within himself be termed as a whole person?

Sadhguru: Someone just said that being whole is when a person enjoys everything within himself. Then he has to keep his eyes closed always. Only then can he enjoy everything within himself. If he opens his eyes, then his enjoyment comes from outside.

Questioner: Jaggi, is it being free from bondage?

Sadhguru: It is to be free from all bondage. Once again, yes and no. Generally people think freedom is always physical. For most people freedom is always physical. What freedom means for most people is, "If I become free from my work, from my family, from all restrictions," – all that he thinks are restrictions – "if all these restrictions on me go, I am free," but wanting to become free also becomes bondage. The very desire is bondage. The moment you have a desire there is bondage. This desire; why does this desire come? Thoughts are there. Everything that you see, everything that you perceive through these five sense organs, one way or the other ends up as a thought process within yourself.

Suppose you see something beautiful, let us say a beautiful car; "Oh! How beautiful it is," is the thought. Between this and before it becomes a desire, like, "Oh! I wish I had it," there is a certain space. A thought is simply a natural process because the five sense organs are functioning, perceiving things constantly, and it ends up as a thought process; but it is us who unconsciously make it into a desire. Once the desire comes, there is a drive; there is a sense of incompleteness. A desire means that you are incomplete. A desire means, "I am here; something is here. If I reach this, or get this, I am going to be total. When I reach the goal, I am going to be total." That is the basis of a desire.

At every step, desire creates this illusion: "If I get this; that is it." Whether you really thought about it that way or not, that is the fundamental quality of the desire. The thought is a deception. You cannot go on desiring for your whole life. People go on desiring even on their deathbed. They go on desiring because the deception of desire is such that it literally seduces you into believing that the moment your desire is fulfilled everything is going to be okay. That's the feeling it gives you at every step, isn't it? With this deception it just keeps you going all the time, but between desire and thought there is a certain space. If one becomes aware of this space, the desire completely evaporates. Now you are sitting there. If you want to move from this place you have to consciously create a desire in your mind. "Let me go," must be forced upon the mind. Otherwise there is no urge to do anything. Just being here is enough, because it is really enough. It is really sufficient to be here. There is no need to go anywhere.

Questioner: What is the fundamental goal of yoga and the spiritual path? At times I get very confused as to why I am here and what I am doing here.

Sadhguru: This whole confusion about what is what – not being able to see what is what – is simply because of the discriminating character of the mind, wanting, not wanting. So the first step is to bring down or scale down likes and dislikes, *kama* and *krodha*. If you bring that down, slowly things start fusing and merging. At least when you sit and meditate, when meditation happens, nothing else exists. Once you open your eyes again, everything is real. At least in those few moments, nothing else exists. There is just a being; nothing else is there.

Questioner: But Jaggi, how can you say there is nothing? The plants are growing; the dogs, the cows, they are still there.

Sadhguru: Yes, it is really hard to believe! There is so much happening in the existence: the mountains, the trees, the animals and the breeze. How can you say this is not real? It is very hard to believe, isn't it? It is not that it is not real. It is just that your mind is not real. Everything that you look at through your mind becomes unreal and what you call a reality right now, or the current reality, is not so. Let us look at it this way, the current reality and the Ultimate Reality. So when I say the former is not real, it is not that it doesn't exist at all. It does, but its nature is so transient; the next moment, if the existence wishes, the whole game will evaporate like it was never there.

I think you can look at it this way. Let us say you went to a cinema theatre to watch your favorite film star and the movie turned out to be a good one. You got involved, you cried with your hero or heroine, you laughed with them, you fought with them, you did everything, and everything was so real; it was life. Most people live their life only through the cinema. Where do they live their lives really? They have lived their lives only through the cinema; it is so real. Now in the end, at least they mention, "The End"; it's over. That is it; it is over. Some people are so involved in the movie, it is hard for them to believe it is over. They just sit in their seats in disbelief and there it is, over.

Have you seen this? They don't want to get up and move. They still cannot believe it is over. They just cannot believe it. It is the same here also. The whole thing is a game of light.

Another way of saying it is, everything is ultimately just light. Your aura is more real than this body; it is so. Right now, what you are seeing is a lesser reality than what you are not seeing. That is the truth. Your aura has more reality than your body. Even if the body disintegrates, the aura stays. You can say ultimately all physical matter becomes light. This is physics. First it becomes sound, then it becomes light, then it becomes nothingness. See the progression of existence: from nothingness to light, light to sound, sound to what looks physical now and once again the reverse process goes on everywhere.

So the fundamental goal of the spiritual path is, when a person experientially realizes that everything is so transient, he becomes loose within himself. He is not stuck to anything. When he is not stuck to anything, if he wishes, he can withdraw from everything; and if he wishes, he can enjoy everything, but there is no suffering. If he wishes, he can suffer also. Sometimes, even that is good; that suffering is not a suffering anymore. You can allow yourself to melt and fuse with somebody. You can cry with somebody if you want to, but it is no longer suffering. After the crying is over you are a new being.

Questioner: Jaggi, I don't understand; it goes over my head.

Sadhguru: There is nothing to go over you. Let us start with what you know right now, what is real for you. What I am saying is, this much you know, that today you are here; tomorrow morning, you may not be. I am not saying you will not be. You *may not* be. It is very much possible, isn't it? Tomorrow morning you may not be. Maybe not because of the wind, maybe not because of this thatched hall; the mountain may fall on you. We don't know. Things have happened like this. [For most of the duration of the program, there was a very heavy storm and the temporary thatched structure in which the program was being conducted shook precariously, due to the heavy winds. A big tree got uprooted and fell on one of the Master's disciples, who miraculously got away with only a minor injury].

Now the tree fell; next the mountain itself may fall for some reason. And don't think that it will happen only because you are at the foothills of the mountain. Something may fall on Coimbatore or wherever you may be. It can fall anywhere. Yes? And nothing need to fall, you may just drop dead. So that much you know, isn't it? This much reality you understand; this much everybody understands.

Today you are here, where everything is so real, you, your wife, your child, your property, your work, your ideas, your ego; everything is so real. Tomorrow morning if you are dead, what will happen to all this? Where will it go? Do you see that much? Today you are here appearing so real. Tomorrow morning if you are dead, what will happen to you? Where are you? Where did you go? Your body is a nuisance. Once you are dead, nobody wants your body. Yes? Even the most loved ones in your family, if he or she dies will you keep the body in your bedroom? Like Shankara says, "Bharya bibyathi thasmin kaye." This means, tomorrow if you die, that person who loved you very much or who seemed to love you, even she will be scared of this body. The wife who loved you so much – loved you means she only loved the body. If you come with a different body she will not love you.

This is only a body, so don't get attached to it. Somebody who loves you today, tomorrow morning if you are dead, will they keep your body and be very happy with it? They are afraid of it and want to get rid of it, yes or no? You do know if we bury you here, you will become earth. If we burn you immediately the results are there for you to see.

If we bury you, it takes a little longer, but what happens to *you*? So it needs probing sometimes. It needs looking at. Definitely, it needs to be looked at, isn't it? This man who is here today, so real, tomorrow if he can suddenly evaporate and disappear, it is your business to know, because it is going to happen to you also. Definitely, it is everybody's business to know, isn't it? So, that's where the first step is.

The first step is, for you to start looking at death; then you become spiritual. Don't look at the gods. Don't think by going to temples you will become spiritual. By looking at gods you will only hallucinate; you will only create more and more stories. You know how many gods you have created, and you can go on. When you sing a bhajan you can add another ten names, *Visalakshi*, this akshi, that akshi, akshi, akshi, you can go on like this! Every time you sing a bhajan, you can add one more name. One is *Kailasa vasa* another is *Kashmir vasa*, another may be, *Coimbatore vasa*; you can always say that also. You are only singing the address, after all.

By looking at gods you only hallucinate more. You don't come to reality. You go away from it; but when you look at death, when you think of death – there is no point thinking; thinking is meaningless. Start looking at your own death. You will definitely become spiritual; there is no other way. Unfortunately, today in society, you avoid the word death itself. Even children cannot use that word. You've made sure that nothing ever happens in their life, that there is no possibility of growth. You say "Rama, Shiva," but the word *savu* or death is banned at home, because you are scared. Just the word, the reminder, scares you. Many people are scared to even see a funeral passing by on their streets, because it reminds them of their own death. Whatever you may shut yourself off from, are you really going to shut yourself off from death?

Now when you walk the path of spirituality, we will teach you how to even fool Yama, the Lord of Death. Sometimes you can do that also.

You can't do it forever – even that, they say there are people who do it forever – but we can definitely trick him. We can misplace his appointment book.

Questioner: Are you saying death of the body?

Sadhguru: Death is only about the body.

Questioner: So death can be fixed by you...

Sadhguru: It is not that you fix it or they fix it. There is no question of you and them. First of all, there is no such thing as you and God. Both are the same. When you have seen that both are the same, there are only certain laws. This is known as *Sanathana Dharma*. We have a culture, we have a tradition, we have a lineage of people whose maturity is such, it cannot be matched with anybody, because it comes from inner realization, not from thinking.

Understanding life from within and understanding life from outside are two different things. They can never be compared. It doesn't matter how much you think and how much you propound theories about it. Simply one vision – in India, philosophy was not *tathvam* it was known as *darshana,* meaning a vision, to simply look at something. That's all. That is the only way to know the existence. You can never know the existence; you can never know the reality with any tathva. You can only know it by a vision. That is known as darshana. So all Indian philosophies were known as darshanas, not as tathvas. Tathvas were created by scholars. Scholars took over later. The earlier part of the civilization was pure consciousness. It is only somewhere on the way scholars took over and they made philosophies out of everything.

Questioner: Jaggi, how can one trick Yama? How can one decide the time of one's death? How is it in your case?

Sadhguru: It is not that you decide or somebody else decides, because there is no somebody else. There is no such thing as *somebody else*. It is all you. There are not two realities; there is only one. Everything is expanding from that one reality. This existence today is expanding infinitely. Cosmologists are propounding theories – they cannot actually see it, but they are propounding theories – that the existence is expanding infinitely. It is not of the same size. Endlessly it is expanding.

Yes, it is true, but it is expanding from the same being. It is always expanding, but there is only one reality which you can call yourself, or God, or with whatever name you want. There is only one reality, so there is no question of you and them. Once you are in a physical form, there are certain laws, because the whole physical matter has to be under a certain law. The very creation happens with a certain basis. See, if you want to create something, even if you want to build this building, there is a certain law. To make this building stand like this there is a law, which you call engineering or whatever. So whether the man has gone to an engineering college and learned this or he has learned it in his own way, it doesn't matter, but some engineering is used, without it the building won't stand.

Similarly, for this body to be here now, a tremendous amount of engineering has taken place. So all the laws together create matter. Without it, it cannot go on, unless it is re-created once again. Generally to re-create means, you drop this body and take on another one. That is how the cycle is happening. This is rebirth happening. Another way of doing it is going into long samadhis where it is like hibernation and life is extended. Now let us say this body has to end tomorrow morning at eight o'clock. Now tonight at eight o'clock this body goes into a samadhi state, where he is unapproachable, where he is as good as dead. He limits everything to the minimum; life is just at the minimum. His heart has stopped, his liver has stopped, his kidneys have stopped; it is just kept alive at the most minimum level. Now the life of the body gets extended. By remaining in the samadhi for a period of six months, this man may be alive for another six months or even one year. It depends on many factors. There are so many karmic factors; there are physical factors and there are energy factors as such; and there is another thing, the ultimate thing: the time is over. There is no business for that being to be here anymore. It is finished. If you ask me personally, why it is so. First of all, me coming here itself was not necessary – as far as I am concerned. It should have ended the last time. Simply because of a few people, their love was such that I decided, okay, once again.

Questioner: Dear Jaggi, what is the price I should pay to know myself?

Sadhguru: To get to your own Divinity, what is the price? If you want to become God, what is the price you are willing to pay? Any price is meaningless, isn't it? There is really no price. Whatever price you pay, that is too little. That's all I can say. Whatever you pay, even if you pay with your life it is too little. It is not too much; it is too little, but people think it is too much. Coming for thirteen days, three hours each day is too much. They say, "I came for thirteen days and nothing happened!"

There was a great swordsman. He was one of the Samurai clan of the Far Eastern culture. They are warriors and their weapon is the sword. They are proud of being good swordsmen. There was a great swordsman. His name was Nikichi and he had a son who was also known as Nikichi. Now this Nikichi II is a hapless person. He is not skilled in anything. So the father got frustrated with this boy, his son that he is not going to become a great swordsman. It is unbearable for him. So he disowned him saying, "You are not my son; get out.

You are unfit to be a swordsman." Suppose you try to make Somu a warrior (pointing towards a tall, lanky bhramhachari who takes care of the accounts department, whom Sadhguru is very fond of)! It is not possible, you know. He can calculate interest. He can take care of accounts. He can do all that, but if you ask him to go and fight a war, he is not the man. So this Nikichi II is that kind of a man. He is not made to be a swordsman and so his father disowned him. The shame of being disowned by his father fired him up so much that he went in search of another swordsman who was the greatest of all. He lived up in the mountains. His name was Bansu.

These swordsmen were also Zen masters. He was a great master. Nikichi II went up to him, fell at his feet and said, "I want to become a swordsman; my father has disowned me." So Bansu said, "Take three steps. Let me see." He took three steps. Bansu said, "There is no way you can become a swordsman. Go back." By the very way a man walks, Bansu knew that this man could never be a swordsman. Nikichi II said, "Nothing doing, you have to do something, you are my last resort. How long will it take?" Bansu said, "It will take a lifetime." Nikichi II said, "That's too long. By that time my father will be dead. I want to go and prove to him that I can be a swordsman." After a lot of coaxing, Bansu said, "Okay, ten years." They came to an agreement. Then Bansu said, "You must never talk about a sword here. Now, starting today, you cook, wash the dishes and be here."

One year passed; two years passed. Every day Nikichi II is dying to know something of the sword. He is not allowed to even touch a sword. He is only given dishes to wash, to cook and sweep. Everything he does, but no sword business. Three, four years pass away, but Nikichi II did everything sincerely, waiting, hoping that someday the master is going to teach him something. One day Nikichi II was sitting and washing vessels. Bansu came. For training they use wooden swords. He came up with a wooden sword and whacked Nikichi II on the back. Then Nikichi II leaped up. You know when somebody hits you, you develop a different kind of reflex. Your whole body becomes different. He jumped up and went in another direction. Bansu attacked him. Furiously, he attacked him. Nikichi II did everything possible and escaped. He was badly injured.

Whenever Nikichi II was cooking, or washing, or doing something, at any time of the day, without warning, Bansu would attack him. This kept Nikichi II always on his toes, so alert, that within a few weeks he was learning all the things that a swordsman needs to learn. He learned it so quickly that it really brought a smile to Bansu, who was always dead serious. It brought a smile to Bansu's face to see how quickly this man was learning. Within about six to seven years Nikichi II became the greatest swordsman. He came back and proved to his father that he had become the greatest swordsman.

So the process of learning will be different for different people. A way to bring out the best in a person need not be the same for everybody. Maybe I will not come and whack you on the back with a sword. Life will do it; life will do it by itself. Our methods are not this crude, but sometimes even that may be needed; you never know!

Questioner: Many holy men suggest bhakthi yoga. Only very few people like you suggest this type of yoga where it is a mix of different things.

Sadhguru: Now these *margas*, or paths, that you have heard of, bhakthi, gnana and karma, if anybody separates these things, that person doesn't know what it is all about. You are here as a human being. Gnana means to use your head and realize. Bhakthi means to use your heart and realize. Karma means to use your hands and legs – meaning through your actions – and realize. If you were only heart, or only head, or only hands and legs, realization would be very difficult.

Do you understand? If these three things are not put in proper proportion, the question of realization for many of you will be very difficult. You will only hallucinate at the most.

Questioner: Dear Jaggi, if we do not attain in this life would all this sadhana that we are doing be carried forward to the next birth?

Sadhguru: *"Chesina karmamu chedani padharthamu,"* they say. This means, karma is a non-perishable item. It is never lost; but don't understand karma in these terms, "I left my meditation here. Can I start my meditation from there?" No, it is not like that. See, the action itself is not the karma; it is the volition that is the karma. Volition means *nokam*, or intention. Volition is the right word. It is the intention, or with what volition you are doing the action, that matters. That is what decides your karma. Now, suppose you are a butcher. Everyday you chop animals to feed other people. You are not killing these animals with any vengeance; it is just your job. Like everybody is doing something, you too are doing something; that's all. Maybe because your father was a butcher you are also a butcher. So you don't have the karma of killing. You only have the karma of unawareness. That's all; but if you kill that animal with vengeance, with anger, or just for the sake of killing, of enjoying the pain of the animal, then it is a different karma.

Unfortunately, somebody's pain is a pleasure for somebody else. People go and hunt animals. They don't even eat them; they just shoot and kill. They don't even bother to cut the animal, take the meat and eat it. At least, if it is for eating, it is okay. After all, you have to eat something. It is your choice to eat an animal. It is okay. It is your problem; but people hunt not for eating. They hunt simply for the pleasure of killing. That karma is different from the karma of killing to eat.

To sustain this life you have to kill something, maybe a carrot, maybe a chicken, maybe a deer; you don't know what you have to kill, but you have to kill something. Everyday here at Isha when you put these soaked peanuts in your mouth, just chew with your eyes closed and meditate upon them. They are full of life, and when you notice they are full of life, if you are immature you will vomit. When you begin to notice every time you chew the groundnuts that so much life is struggling to live and you are causing their death, you will throw up everything. If you are immature, you won't be able to eat the food anymore. If you are mature enough you will eat it with a tremendous amount of gratitude. Recognizing that this one peanut gives you life, with much gratitude you eat it. Normally, at least in some moment in your life, you may have tremendous gratitude for your mother. That's the kind of gratitude you need to have for this peanut, but if you are on the level of thinking, it will just make you puke. So the karma is not in the action itself, it is in the volition.

Now you are on the spiritual path. Next life when you are born, it is not that you are going to sit up and meditate as soon as you come out of the womb. That's not the point. You will be like any other fool, but something will fall into place in such a way that slowly, somewhere life provides opportunities here and there. Above all, definitely the other aspects of life like food, clothing and shelter fall into place. Generally, a person who goes into the spiritual path gets well placed in life, so that he doesn't have to worry about the basic necessities. The existence placed you comfortable enough in life that you don't have to worry about the basics for survival. You can focus yourself on something better, but again, because of your unawareness, you may get so caught up with your comforts and position that you may just sink into that itself. So once again, the struggle begins somewhere else. Otherwise for the person who makes use of life's opportunities, it definitely starts off from where he left off. I can clearly show examples here among you like that of people who are starting from where they left off.

Questioner: Dear Jaggi, what will happen to the chakras after death?

Sadhguru: The chakra is not a physical wheel or something, which is there in your body. It is just a certain energy center. Now you've seen the whirlwinds. Have you seen it? When it is there it is so real, isn't it? The next moment it disintegrates and it is not there. So where did it go? Its existence itself was just a happening. Just like the waves in the ocean. Such a huge wave, but where does it go the next moment? It just goes back, and nothing is there, isn't it? It is the same with chakras also. When the whole existence is energy, there are some points where there is something like a whirlwind. It is there for a while and then it disappears. It need not go anywhere. It just disappears, that's all. This going and coming is all your idea. The logical mind is always thinking that if something is there it must go somewhere. If something is gone it must come back. It is not so.

There was a Zen Master who was on his death bed. Death is very important in Zen. They have to die in total awareness. Now another Zen Master came to see him off. He was Chang Tzu. It was just at the last moment. So Chang Tzu asked, "Do you need my help? Can I help you across?" So this Zen Master who was dying said, "What can you do? This one just comes and it goes. It comes by itself and goes by itself. What can you do about it?" So Chang Tzu said, "If that is your problem, if this coming and going is your problem, then I have to tell you there is a way, a way where there is no coming and no going." That man got the point, smiled and died.

Yes, because really there is no coming and going. The coming and going itself is an illusion. This coming and going business itself is a great, big *thamasha* that is going on, which seems to be there but is not there. Once you attach so much importance to coming and going, there is no way you cannot be attached to what is there now. Do you understand? If you attach too much importance to coming and going, staying becomes equally important, isn't it? Naturally you get attached. So where it goes, what happens, leave all that nonsense. There is nowhere to go. Just dissolve here. There is nothing to be done. Just be here.

Questioner: When there is nothing to be done, why are we doing this sadhana? Why are you driving us like this?

Sadhguru: When nothing is there to be done, why are you torturing us from morning to night? Now, 'nothing to be done' is an idea. It is the way you are; because you are not in that state of simply *nothing to be done* but always in *something to be done*, we thought it would be better at least if we do this rather than something else. It is a question of choosing action. Anyway you are going to be active. Wherever you are left, whether you are left in the Himalayas or Madras or here at Isha, you are going to be active if not physically, at least mentally. So at least let us create that kind of activity, which leads you to growth. That's the idea. Otherwise, the activity itself has no meaning. It is just choosing the activity which brings you the closest to what is true. Other kinds of activities may take you away elsewhere. At least this activity brings you closer. That is the whole purpose of yoga. The whole system of yoga is just built on this principle, about creating the right kind of activity.

Questioner: Dear Jaggi, I very much want to be here at your feet and grow within, but sometimes my mind's chatter wouldn't let me be.

Sadhguru: When I give you an instruction, if you make that instruction your whole life, where can the mind be? There will be no mind. Now, you are still cautious. I told you, "You just dissolve, you just die." It is okay. Probably it is wrong to say this as far as your language and your sensibilities are concerned. Somebody saying, "You just die."

The word die might not sound right to you but I don't find anything wrong with that. It is perfectly okay. It is not something that I think is wrong. It is actually a bigger step than life itself. Death is a much bigger step than life. If you can take it, it is beautiful, if you can take it. If it is forced upon you, then it is ugly and painful, and you will be full of fear. Die, die the way you are right now then maybe something wonderful will surface.

Now, when I instruct you to be in silence, if you really take the essence of it into you, you will become silent. Then food, bathing and all the other things will not be important to you. A stage will come where somebody has to remind you about these things. Otherwise, you will simply *be* if you have taken the instruction into you. Even if you have heard the instructions, you are all very smart. You have to do all the things required to look nice; it is necessary for you. It is not that you have not taken the instruction to heart. It is just that you do it to the extent that is convenient for you. Yes, you are being silent only to the extent that is convenient for you. If it goes beyond your convenience, you will break it.

The whole purpose of being here is to go beyond these comforts and discomforts. One early morning, a few days ago, when I came and wrote for all of you to see, "To be spiritual is to go beyond nature," it was simply to support you towards that. Yet you don't even go beyond your nature's calls, forget about going beyond nature. This is simply because you take things for granted. The first two days you were conscious about making yourself silent. After that you thought it would be okay and you laughed and you rolled around. You thought it was all right. See, with this attitude nobody grows, not only in spirituality, but in any field. If you want to set up a business, if you want to run an industry, if you want to do anything in this life, if you are slack like this you will not make it big.

Let us say you want to compete in athletics. If you are slack like this, after two days of training, you will just be walking instead of running. You think you are going to make it big in athletics by being slack? Even for simple physical achievements that you have to do in the world, some commitment and grit are needed, isn't it? Now if you have to conquer your consciousness, if you want to grow to reach your very source, it needs a tremendous amount of grit. Not ordinary grit; it needs courage. It takes extreme courage or it needs tremendous love. Either this must be there or that must be there. If both these things are not there, there will be no growth. You will remain mediocre all your life.

If you can't do all this nonsense – I call this nonsense because it is really a non-sense – if you can't do sadhana or your practices, then just hand over your will to me. In one stroke, in just one stroke, I will dissolve all the karma for you. If you hand over your will to me totally, not holding on to one end and giving me the other end so that when it becomes uncomfortable, you pull it back – no, not that kind of giving. If you hand over your life to me then there is no sadhana for you, no meditation for you, no pranayama for you. You enjoy yourself; I'll strike it off in one stroke, okay? See if you can do that. If it is easier, you do that, otherwise, stick to your sadhana. Both ways are available to you. Whichever is easier for you, you do that. You're not willing to do the first one, is it? Probably you are thinking, "At least we will sit here and slowly grind ourselves, but handing over ourselves to you totally?"

Questioner: Jaggi, we are willing, but we don't know what or how to give. It is not that we don't want to.

Sadhguru: Nachiketha, the first seeker; he is supposed to have been the first seeker in the world, maybe the first significant one. One of the Upanishads starts with him. Nachiketha was a small boy. His father took a certain vow to perform a yaga, a sacred ritual where all the material possessions that you have – including your wife, your children, your house, your everything – you have to give it away as dana to all the rishis, the brahmins and the other people. Then you'll attain to spiritual bliss. This is a device somebody has set up in the tradition.

So a few people take this vow for spiritual attainment. Nachiketha's father took this vow and he gave away all the sick cows, the useless property and everything that he didn't want, which was a burden in one way or another, and made a big show of it, but he kept everything else that he really needed, including his two wives and children. Nachiketha saw this and he was very hurt. He saw that his father was not being sincere. His father made a vow that he will give away everything and attain spiritual bliss, but that man is playing tricks like everybody else. So Nachiketha went to his father and started talking about this to him. A small boy about five years of age, physically he was five years of age, but the boy had tremendous maturity.

Nachiketha told his father, "What you have done is not right. If you didn't want to give away everything, you shouldn't have taken the vow. Once you took the vow, you better give it away. You have to give away everything. You tell me to whom are you going to give me?" His father got angery. Fathers always get mad when you point out things like this, and he said, "I am going to give you to Yama." Yama is the Lord of Death. So the boy took it very seriously and he prepared himself to go to Yama, and he went. Don't start thinking in terms of, "How could he have gone, with the body or without the body?" That's not the point. He went. Yama was not there. He had gone visiting. He makes house calls. So he had gone visiting. For three days Nachiketha waited. A small boy, without food, without water; he waited at Yama's doorstep. After three days Yama came back and he saw this little boy totally famished and tired, but fully determined. He was just sitting there not moving. He had not even gone searching for food here or there. He was just sitting there waiting for him. So Yama was very moved by this boy's determination, waiting for three days without anything. So he said, "It is great you've been waiting for three days. What do you want? I'll grant you three boons. What do you want?"

The first thing Nachiketha said was, "My father is in extreme greed. He wants material possessions right now. So you bless him with all the material possessions that he can have. Let him become a king." Okay, it was granted. The second boon he asked for was, "I want to know what kind of karmas, what kind of yagas I have to do to attain." The Vedic literature always talks in terms of yagnas and yagas. The whole literature is like that; everything is in terms of yagas and yagnas. So Yama taught him what he had to do. Then Nachiketha asked him, "What is the secret of death? What happens after death?" So Yama said, "No, this question you take back. You can ask me anything you want. You ask me for a kingdom, if you want. I'll give it to you. Riches if you want, I'll give you. All the pleasures in the world, I'll give you." He goes on offering, "What do you want, you tell me; all the pleasures in the world, I'll give you. You take them but this one question, you withdraw." Nachiketha says, "What will I do with all of them? You've already told me, all these things are transient. I have already understood that all activity, everything people are involved in, is meaningless. Simply it seems to be there. It is not the reality. So what is the point in you giving me more riches? It will just be a trap for me. I don't want anything, you just answer my question."

In many ways Yama tried to avoid this question. He said, "Even the gods do not know the answer for this question. I cannot give it to you." Nachiketha said, "If that is so, if the gods do not know this answer and only you know, then you must definitely give me the answer." He wouldn't leave him. So once again Yama left him there and went visiting for months. He just wanted to avoid this boy somehow.

He wanted to get rid of him, but the boy just stuck around for many, many months; and they say, right on the doorstep of Yama's domain, he attained to his full enlightenment. He got the answers for everything he had to know in the existence and dissolved himself. He was the first seeker. And he is always used as the best example. A five-year-old boy with that kind of determination, who didn't fall for a chocolate or a visit to Disneyland or anything. He wanted that and that's all it is.

When a person is like that there is no need for a path for him because the end is here itself. It is not on the top of Velliangiri Hills. Only when it is not here, it is on Velliangiri Hills and we have to slowly climb it. When you are like Nachiketha, there is no need for a path for you. It is already here. There is nowhere to go. It is very much here. Now the whole purpose of doing everything that we are doing here is to create the intensity. That craving should become so strong, so powerful, that God cannot stay away, and the Divine cannot avoid you anymore. It is not that the Divine tries to avoid you, but this mind and ego tries to screen the reality from your eyes in so many millions of ways. Millions of tricks are played.

Questioner: Walking the spiritual path by itself is difficult enough, and on top of it, Jaggi, sometimes it hurts when you use harsh words.

Sadhguru: Oh! A Guru should not use harsh words! Why should he not use them? Many people think, except for those who have been on the spiritual path, the whole world generally thinks that all these so-called spiritual people are good-for-nothing. They think, "Those people who cannot do anything else in the world are going to the ashrams and doing some nonsense. They don't even earn their own living. They are eating off society." This is the attitude; this is the general opinion because that is how most of the people have become.

That's what I was trying to tell you the other day. If you are here just to laze around and do stupid things, naturally what they are saying is right! You are proving them right. If you are doing something a lot more intensely than what they are doing in their life, they will value what is happening here and think, "Whether we understand or not, they are doing something which we cannot do in our lives. We cannot even think of sitting like this, doing these practices, so let us do something for them." It is only out of this that spirituality gains support from society; but whenever lethargy came into the spiritual circles, then naturally the whole society thought, "These are good-for-nothing people. When they have nothing to do, when people are incapable of making their lives in the society, in the world, they will go and join an ashram." This is the only conclusion they can come to. Definitely, at least as long as I live, Isha will never be that kind of an ashram where all the lazy people can come and settle down and do nonsense. Never!

You just feel and see how the world feels. If the world feels insulted then society will also feel insulted. The other day, a boy shared during one of the programs that every time he sees some Swamiji, some ashram, he gets angry. He said, "We are working like dogs out here to just run our lives. This man just sits in one place and eats well and goes about in a car. When I see this I feel like going and killing this man, but now I see, after going through the yoga program, something which we do not know, something which we are not aware of, that something is here."

And he is right! He is absolutely right! If somebody is just going to sit here and live off somebody and enjoy his life, then definitely people are going to be angry and after some time become vicious. Only when your very presence shows that feeding you does not go waste, then they will respect you for what you are. If anybody feels that feeding this person is a waste, you think they are going to give you that food?

They would rather give the food to the dogs than feed you. At least the dog will bark. This is how it is going to be seen tomorrow. If you are not intense enough, that is how everybody is going to see you; it is pathetic. If such a thing happens to your life, it is really pathetic. You better be a beggar on the street rather than being spiritual. It is not worth being spiritual. It is not spirituality; it is just an excuse for laziness.

So a spiritual person should be one hundred times more intense than the most ambitious person in the world. You must be one hundred times more intense than Alexander the Great. Only then can you conquer the inner nature. To conquer the outside world that man was so tremendously intense, he slept for only one to two hours a day. So it was with Napoleon Bonaparte. They were so intense just to conquer the physical world.

Now if you want to conquer that which you have not seen – he was trying to conquer that which he could see; you are trying to conquer that which you cannot see – how intensity should be! Otherwise there is no chance, really. Whether you walk the path of karma, gnana, kriya or bhakthi, whichever spiritual path you walk, without intensity there is no path. Whichever path it is, it is the intensity which keeps you going, not the path itself. Any amount of sadhana, any number of kriyas, do you think it is going to do something? It is just going to be a lot of nonsense. Sitting like this, sitting like that, focusing on this, focusing on that, all of this is just going to be sheer nonsense if there is going to be no intensity. When there is intensity, every practice will move you into a different dimension. It has the power to do it. The practices are designed in such a way that they will not work for a fool. The way they are taught is such that they will never work for a fool.

I am telling you, kriya by itself is not going to do anything. It is not the kriya which is going to transform you. It is the intensity.

Only when you are intense the kriya is a tremendous support. It intensifies you more and more. That is the whole purpose of doing the practices. The practices themselves do not do anything except give some physical and psychological well-being. They are not going to make any person realize anything unless he has intensity, whichever path it might be.

If you love somebody half-heartedly, you will never know love. There is no love. It is either one hundred percent or zero. Isn't it so? Can you love someone ninety-nine percent? Then you have not known love at all. So it is with all this. It is the same with action. If you don't perform your action one hundred percent, then action is useless. It is better you sit and rot. It is not going to produce anything great. Maybe at the most, it will earn food for you. That is all it will do; it will not transform you in any way. It cannot transform you, unless the action is one hundred percent, it cannot transform you. Unless the kriya is one hundred percent, that kriya cannot transform you and unless your love is one hundred percent, that love cannot transform you. It may be just a device to get something. The barter system; something may happen, but in real terms, in existential terms, nothing happens.

Once, in a village, in a certain place, there was a certain snake, a serpent which was very vicious. It would not allow anybody to walk on a particular path. Many people had paid with their lives. The villagers were terrified to use that path because the serpent was always waiting to strike. Once, a certain Master, a holy man, came there. When he wanted to use that path people warned him against that saying, "There is a wicked serpent there waiting to strike you and it might kill you." He said, "It doesn't matter," and he went on. As usual the serpent was waiting and he wanted to strike this man, but his presence was such that the serpent cooled off, melted down. Then the holy man initiated the serpent onto the spiritual path. "Why are you wasting your life being so wicked? It is a waste. You are not going to achieve anything by becoming a great bandit. You are just going to run like a dog all the time. Maybe you are not caught, but you are still running like a dog, endlessly. So what is the point? You just do this." From that day the serpent began meditating. After some time the boys in the village thought that the serpent had either lost its teeth or he was not willing to bite anymore. So, slowly they became bolder and started going closer to the serpent, throwing stones. When he didn't react, they started using sticks, beating him. People poked at him when he was lying in his cave. They did all kinds of things to the serpent.

After one year this holy man came that way again. The serpent was excited because the Guru had come and he went and fell at his feet. The yogi saw that the serpent was in a miserable state; he had not eaten for many days. He could not come out, for if he did people stoned him and tortured him in many ways. So he just stayed inside his cave. On top of it, his body was also damaged in so many ways. So the yogi asked, "What happened to you?" The serpent just said, "It is nothing. I just did not eat." He did not even complain. He had reached a stage, that level of acceptance where he didn't even complain that people were beating him. He just said that because of not eating he had become weak. The yogi, after seeing all the wounds on his body said, "Not eating will not do this to you. What happened, tell me." Then the serpent told him, "The local boys want to come and play with me and they just poke at me and have fun and go." The yogi said, "I told you not to bite anybody. I never told you not to hiss! You could have hissed. That much you could have done. This is not spirituality. You have missed the point. You will have to at least hiss when you have to hiss. If you don't hiss, they will forget that you are a snake and do all kinds of things to harm you."

So sometimes we have to hiss and one important factor, one important quality that is very essential is to develop acceptance or at least tolerance.

If you are accepting, we don't have to talk tolerance. Until now I have not uttered this word tolerance anywhere, not in any class. I don't like it. I don't want tolerance. If a man can accept, acceptance is far better than tolerance, but if acceptance doesn't come to a person, then we teach that person tolerance. Do you know the difference? Acceptance is the highest; it will release you from everything. That is the path; but for people who are not aware, who are not in any level of acceptance and who get irritated for every small thing, such people should at least develop tolerance. I am stepping down and I don't like this. Until now I have never talked about tolerance but you see, even after three to four years of this yoga, many of you still get irritated with small things and react in so many small ways. You may not actually go and beat them or poke them in any way but it is happening in so many ways. I must also get your undivided attention or else you will miss it.

Once it so happened. Shankaran Pillai bought a donkey, a work donkey, you know, for work. The previous owner who was selling the donkey to Shankaran Pillai said, "This is a very sensitive donkey. You should not abuse this donkey. You should not use bad words. You should never beat him. He is very sensitive." So Shankaran Pillai said, "I am also very happy to have a donkey like this. Everyday in the morning I have to do *sahasranama* and then beat it. I am fed up with these donkeys. If there is a sensitive donkey like this it makes me very happy." The next morning Shankaran Pillai got up, went and invited the donkey, "Let us go." Nothing happened. He pleaded; nothing happened. Prayed; nothing happened. Begged; nothing happened. Then he didn't know what to do because he is not supposed to use the usual technology: no screaming, no abusing and no beating. He didn't know what to do next. So he went to the previous owner and he told him, "I did everything. I requested, I pleaded, I begged, I prayed, but nothing happened. What should I do next? I am scared to fall at his feet." That may be a wrong thing to do with a donkey;

you can get kicked. "Is that so?" the previous owner said and he came to the place where the donkey was. He picked up a thick stick and one hefty whack on the head, *paddaarr* he gave and then he said, "Let us go," and the donkey moved. Then Shankaran Pillai became furious. He said, "You fool. You told me you should not beat the donkey, and in my whole life I have never beaten a donkey like this. You are using such a thick stick and you are hitting it on its head. What is this nonsense you told me that it is very sensitive?" So that man said, "No, no! No beating is needed. It is really very sensitive. The only thing is that first you have to get his attention." You see, I do not wish to use thick sticks.

Questioner: Dear Jaggi, after going through the program I do have some idea as to what yoga is …

Sadhguru: So by now you have enough ideas about yoga, too! That shuts you off to yoga. See, the process of going through any program, any teaching itself is a barrier. Do you understand what I am saying? The process of going through anything, whether yoga or whatever, itself is a barrier because it leads to more ideas. As far as possible I have always been seeing how not to allow you to get any ideas about anything, but the mind makes its own ideas about everything in no time. It cannot remain without a conclusion. An idea means a conclusion that you have formed in your mind. The ego cannot remain for a moment without a conclusion. When a real 'I do not know' comes, when you really come to a big 'I do not know' in your life, your ego dissolves. Isn't it? 'I know, I know, I know' is how the ego grows. A big 'I do not know' means there is no support for the ego. All your ideas, whatever kind of ideas you had formed, you gave them up and you are now forming new ideas. These new ideas are also simply supports for the ego. It is just that the whole process of what we call growth is to remove all those sturdy supports that you have built for the ego. There are some supports for the ego, which are very sturdy. It is hard to remove them, so we remove those slowly and give a more fragile support. Earlier it was like a solid concrete building. Now you make it like a pack of cards, but still it is supported. If this pack of cards has to collapse, even this support has to be removed. The supports are a little more fragile now. The kind of sturdy supports you had created in your life before and the kind of support that is there now, is it more fragile or is it sturdier?

Questioner: But Jaggi, this path is everything for me now. My very life is dependent on it. Do you also call this an ego support?

Sadhguru: Spirituality can become the greatest support. From being an ordinary fool if you become Swami Ananda Moorthy it may be the greatest support for your ego that you always wanted. That may be a better support than what you had. Now, you do not worry about what purity is, what truth is, what God is. Do not worry about these things. Just search for the supports you have created and see with how much little support you can be. You cannot go totally without support right now.

The whole process is to slowly cut off the support as much as possible and keep the minimum possible support and be. A day will come when even that can be removed; but right now, it cannot be removed. "No, no I have removed all my supports." That itself is the support. Do you understand? Everything has become a part of you, including your deceptions. All these parts, if you remove them, only then there is wholeness. Only then there is a meaning to this Wholeness program you are going through. Part by part, part by part you have to remove these ego supports. These few days, do you feel at least some of it has been removed? Have some parts been removed? Have they? Or are you now, 'Wholeness'? Is it so? Is that the badge that you are going to wear from now on among the yoga circles? Already I see some of the volunteers outside are feeling lost. They are asking when the next wholeness program will be. When I tell them that I do not know, they sigh and say, "Oh! these forty-eight fortunate people," you know, like those twelve who were with Jesus. It is like that. For the people who are outside right now, it is like, "These forty-eight people made it!" Now will this, 'Wholeness' also become another great support for your ego? Will it?

Questioner: Jaggi, with your guidance it should not happen.

Sadhguru: So you *are* seeking my guidance. There is one Swami Vedhabharathi; somebody asked Vedhabharathi the process of his growth since he has been on the spiritual path for about forty years. He is an old man now, about sixty years old. He said, "What was the process of my growth? What is the process I have been using? It is not that I used any process. It is just that I have a Guru who always had a pin in his hand and he went on pricking the balloon. He never allowed it to blow up. The moment it blows up a little, he just went on pricking it all the time. This is the only method used for my growth; but it hurts." When somebody pricks it, it really hurts. You need to understand that.

If at any time you say, "I completed the Wholeness program." if you say this, it is finished. You cannot complete the Wholeness program. The first step has been taken and it should go on with life. It all depends on how much intensity you put into your sadhana and the effort you put in for being aware. When you are fully aware for all twenty-four hours of the day, in your speech, in your actions, in your work, in everything that you do, then extending it into your sleep will naturally come. Then extending it into death will also naturally come.

Questioner: How can we control the thought process?

Sadhguru: "I want to control the thought," this itself is a thought. Once you get into this trying to control the thought process, there is no end to it. It is an endless fight. One way is, the way of Isha Yoga; just let it be. Don't bother about it. Let it go on by itself. You be aware of it. Slowly it loses its momentum and it falls away. That's one way.

Another way is what we are doing now. You control your prana. Ultimately, whether it is your thought or your heart or the cellular activity, whatever it is that is happening in the body and within you is primarily supported by the prana. If you control the prana, there is no more thought. If you have sufficient mastery over your prana, you have mastery over your thought, your body and all the organic functions of the body. It is so.

The control will not come because you try to control your thirst or try to control your hunger. It will simply happen because the prana is in control. Similarly with the thought process also. If your prana is in control, your thought process will naturally be in control. You must have noticed that when you hold *kumbhaka* and *shoonyaka*, generally there is no thought. Unless you think with effort, it is usually not there. Otherwise, once you hold kumbhaka, there is no thought. That's how it is.

So as the energy level rises a little bit and the flow is steady and there is a control over it, thought is not there. See, if I sit like this for hours together, I sit without a thought. I am not meditating. I am not doing anything. Simply I just sit there. I thought I would read a book, but generally these days, in the last three or four years, every time I pick up a book, I just read a few sentences or maybe one or two pages. After that I just sit, but that one sentence is enough to convey everything about the mind of the writer. It can be simply seen without the thought process. I've always been talking about this, the difference between looking, simply seeing and thinking. Just looking does not need the thought process. Looking does not mean only with physical eyes. Even with eyes closed you can look. So once you develop awareness, you start looking, not thinking. When you are in full awareness, there is no thought process. The moment you are aware there is no thought. The moment the thought is there, your awareness has gone, generally. Maybe in meditation you are aware of the thought process, but otherwise it is generally so – unless you walk in the knack of Samyama, where you can be in the thought process and still be fully aware, which I doubt. I doubt if there is anybody here who has the hang of Samyama yet! Are you able to really do Samyama properly, effortlessly, talking to people and do Samyama, listening to people and still do Samyama?

It needs application and I find application is lacking, because we still think spirituality is a side business. Life is elsewhere and spirituality is just on the side. It is not so. It is okay, right now you have structured your lives like that, but if you really want to see the end of it, if you really want to see how big the inner world is, it needs more application. If you are just happy with little highs, if you are willing to settle for a little happiness, all you are looking for is a drink without spending on it, without hangovers. In short, you want a small trip. You come to the yoga class, you feel a little nice and that is it. That is like going on a small high, a trip with a little drink, or some drug; it is just like that. If you are happy with that much, okay. That is your karma right now.

Now if you want to go all the way, then it needs more application. It has to be your top priority. Only then things begin to open up for you. You can literally peel yourself like the petals of a flower. Step by step, every day you can peel yourself off. Everything disappears, and what is perfectly real, only that stays. Everything that can fall off, let it fall off. You are spending so much of your life just to hold onto those things which are about to fall off. You are spending all your life just trying to support things which are always trying to fall. What is going to fall, let it fall, let everything fall down. There is something which cannot fall down. You will approach that very quickly when you allow these things to fall.

Questioner: Why do people on the spiritual path use the color orange?

Sadhguru: Why orange, or why people who walk the spiritual path choose orange as their color, at least in this country, is because orange suggests so many things. As we go into the pranayama, the Kundalini pranayams, you will see that each chakra has its own color. Orange and black are the colors of *Agna.* So when a person is moving towards Agna it can be very visibly noticed that the color of Agna is orange. This Agna is also known as 'the third eye' because it gives you vision. So the color of the Agna is orange. It is organically and naturally so. If you go into certain meditations, you will clearly see that Agna is orange. It is either orange or black; it turns both ways. So orange symbolizes that. Right now a person might not have reached that, but it is symbolism. When you wear orange clothes, the darker shades in the aura get purified. Another aspect of orange is that orange suggests something new; it is like the rising sun, which is orange, a new *udaya* in your life. A new sun is beginning to rise within you. You are making a new beginning in your life. That's what it means.

Normally a person who switches to orange drops everything that was old – his name, his identity, his family, his looks, his everything – and shifts into a different life. That means he is making a new beginning, a new sun has risen in his life. A certain realization has come where he is willing to shed everything and walk into another dimension of life or another possibility. Orange also suggests ripening. In nature, anything which ripens, normally turns orange. You know ripeness is always indicated by orange. So when a person has reached a certain level of maturity or ripeness, it means he turns orange. It suggests a new beginning, a ripeness and it is also connected with your aura and your Agna chakra. It also suggests gnana and vision. A person has developed a new vision; that's what it means. Either he has developed, and that's why he is going into it or he wants to develop, that's why he is going into it. For both people it is good to wear orange.

The next best color for a sanyasi to wear would be black, but generally we have identified black with so many negative aspects; so black is avoided. Yet it has been in the tradition that the Christian monks always use black or close to black. Even if they use brown outside, the inner cloth is always black. For Christian nuns and monks, the head cloth is always black. It is only the outer cloth that is some other color. Now, because there are so many congregations, just to identify themselves they are changing it to gray or some other color. Otherwise fundamentally the Catholics used black for their head, the rest dark brown, and the heart is white. That is the symbolism. You know the breast is covered with the white cloth, the head is covered with the black cloth, the rest of the body with brown cloth because the heart is pure, and the head is in gnana. The rest is brown which is a very steady and uninvolved color. Brown is one color that doesn't involve itself. Brown is one color that your eyes can easily miss. So it suggests non-involvement in the external world.

Wearing orange definitely has a certain impact on a person. Now many of you have started to wear orange, but maybe after a few months or years, we will see how things pass. Then people will wear orange with a different significance, with a totally different significance.

I think Kusum has some idea or some vision about what orange does to your aura. Yes, it definitely changes the quality around you. Just by changing the color it helps.

Questioner: What about the significance of the color white, Jaggi?

Sadhguru: White or *aatvarang* means the eighth color. There are seven colors; white is the eighth color. This eighth color or aatvarang means that dimension of life which is beyond. White is not really a color. When there is no color, only white is there. It is the absence of color that makes it white. At the same time, white has all colors in it. It is all-inclusive. The white light that you see contains all of the seven colors. You can refract those colors and separate all seven of them. So white includes everything; it is all-inclusive. White has a good impact on you. Especially when you live in a tropical country, white is the best color to wear. It is comfortable weather-wise.

Traditionally, a person who wears orange cuts himself off from family and social situations. The one who chooses white walks the spiritual path, but is still involved in the other aspects of life or he may be in a preparatory stage. That has been the tradition. It is a way of setting them apart, some demarcation to show this is this man and that is another. For a man on the spiritual path, changing the dress, changing the name and appearance is all to break the identity. When you take sanyas, normally in any sampradaya, if you go and take sanyas, one thing is, they take away your name, your appearance, your hairstyle. You are removed from your parents, your children, your wife, your husband, and everything you are identified with. You will even perform *karmas* or the last rites for your parents and everybody. Do you understand? When you want to take sanyas, you perform karmas for them.

Do you know what is a *karma*? It is the last rites you do for the dead. Why you perform the last rites or rituals is because once you are a sanyasi you cannot do it for them, also it means the relationship is over between you and everyone else. It is over. You are making a completely new beginning. A complete new beginning, like you are born once again into a new life. For most people this is very essential. They are not able to drag the old and still be new. For most people it is like that. They are unable to carry the old burden without any attachment and still be fresh moment to moment. They need to be completely cut off from the old and made new. That is why the procedure is like that.

There are different methods of initiation. Different traditions are there in India, which follow different methods, but people who go in search of Gurus and spiritual paths, they are always in trouble. If you want to find a spiritual path, don't go looking for it. You just be sincere and desire for it. The Guru will always come to you. If you go looking, it may become like this man, Shankaran Pillai, who wanted to take sanyas, wanted to turn spiritual. Normally when you want to turn spiritual, you want to go to the best. Naturally you want to go to the best Guru, definitely. So who is the best Guru in your mind? The most famous is the best Guru in the country! The biggest cult, the most famous is the best! Isn't it so? So at that time, in India, one of the most popular cults of sanyasis was the Goraknath. So he went to the Goraknath cult and asked for sanyas and they agreed. They shaved his head. Goraknath people always wear a big glass or ivory bangle, mind you, not a ring, literally a big bangle in their ears, a huge one. They pierced a huge hole in his ear and they put that bangle in, shaved his head and put that orange dress on him. He stayed there for one month. He was not satisfied so again he went and continued his search.

He was going about in search, seriously searching, while walking in a forest he met a fakir. So he asked the fakir to initiate him and make him a sanyasi. The fakir asked him to remove the orange robes and donned him with a green one and then said that he also had to be circumcised, and that was also done. It was not done by a doctor and it was in a deep forest, too. So whichever way they knew best, they did it that way. Still the wound has not healed for Shankaran Pillai!

The fakir said a shaved head would not do and he must let his hair grow, not only on his head but also his beard! So it started growing. That was done and he stayed there for a couple of months and he was still not satisfied. He was very dissatisfied. He left and then he came across the Kanphats. The Kanphats are another culture, which is a very dominant sanyas cult. Goraknath people wear a bangle on their right ear. Kanphats wear one in their left ear. They said this is wrong and made another big hole, this time in the left ear, and put the bangle there!

Like this it will go on, do you understand? Everybody will make a hole in you somewhere. When a person sincerely seeks, it always happens to him. He need not go running after it. It always comes. For many of you, even Isha Yoga came at a crucial moment in your life. Is it not so? Somehow things were reaching a boiling point or breaking point; that's when it came. And that's how it always comes. If it has not reached that point for a person, it is just another fad.

Questioner: Why do some yogis have long hair and beards and others shave their heads?

Sadhguru: Some have hair. Some are bald. There are two kinds of paths. One path is the hard path. For example, Mahavir's path is a hard path. Here you don't shave your head, you pluck your hair out. That is Mahavir's path. Everything that he did was hard. That's why he said, "There is no possibility of mukthi for a woman." He taught practices for women in order that they would come in their next life as a man because that is the path he knew and that path was impossible for a woman. It was very hard. So he decided mukthi itself was not possible for women.

There is another path, which is going in tune with the existence. Not pushing the river, but flowing with it. People who are on that path, they normally don't shave their head. The significance of shaving your head is once again to change your appearance, to change your identity. You have a certain hairstyle. If you go and look in the mirror you know you are Muthuswamy because of your moustache. We can't make you grow a beard all of a sudden. It takes time. Everyday you look into the mirror and get identified with your appearance. So one thing is to suddenly change your appearance. Though your name is changed, if you still see the same face in the mirror, that name just becomes superficial. The name will be wasted on you. So, somehow to change the appearance the tonsure is done. That's one aspect.

Another aspect is, initially, the first few years of sanyas, the sanyasi is supposed to live as a Parivrajaka, a wandering monk. He has to remain a wandering monk, without any support from any organization or anyone. He has to just live, beg for his food and live. This is the tradition. Different schools and different traditions fix different durations.

The Nagas, Goraknaths and Kanphats live as wandering monks for twelve years. There are systems where they live like this for one year, two years and so forth. Some time, some duration is fixed depending upon the aspirant. During that time he keeps his head shaved. The idea is to make you look like a clown, so that you don't look smart any more.

You just look like a fool. Let the whole world think that you are a fool and it should still be okay with you. Do you understand? Right now what people think about you decides everything about you. When you are like that there is no sanyas. Now if you look like a clown but it makes no difference for you and you carry your appearance of a clown everywhere with no problem, without any problem inside, one aspect of life is handled. Appearance is such a small thing, but it is so big and important in peoples' minds, isn't it? Did you look in the mirror in the last few days? There are no mirrors? Then you must be looking at your face in your stainless steel dinner plates after washing them!

Questioner: Actually I've forgotten my face, Jaggi.

Sadhguru: It's okay, you haven't forgotten anything worthwhile. It is all right if you forgot your face. The idea is to change the appearance so that when we change the name and other aspects of your life, everything is changed, so that you don't still stick onto some aspect of yourself. Generally hairstyles are very important for people. We don't want you to go to the extent of cutting your nose or something because you cannot grow it back. If that were possible, they would have done that also. The idea is to change the appearance. Whatever could be done to change your appearance so that your identification with the body becomes less, without actually disfiguring you, is done. Cutting a nose or an ear is too violent and you cannot replace those things. The hair is okay. So it gets removed.

Questioner: So Jaggi, every time the hair grows do they have to shave? Will it be like this at Isha?

Sadhguru: Yes, every month we shave; and once a person reaches a point in his life where it doesn't matter to him anyway, whichever way it doesn't matter to him, then it is okay. It can grow and you don't disturb anything which is not necessary. Once your life is turned inward, you are not really concerned about another person's opinion about you, about how you look, how you are. Then it doesn't matter. Then it is better not to disturb nature. Just leave it as it is. By disturbing the hair, or by cutting or by trimming the hair, definitely you disturb some aspect of yourself. It is just that in society everybody is doing it, so you are also doing it. It is not that a shaved face looks more beautiful. It is not at all true. It is just because everybody is doing that in society, so you have also started doing it. Especially for a meditator, if they really gather some meditation around themselves that is there with them all the time, then without a beard they look like something less; really. That's how it is. A person looks more matured, more subdued with a beard.

When people are aggressive they want to cut something. If they don't find anything, they cut something of their own. Generally in India, nobody ever shaved their face. Only after the Muslim and the English culture came in, men started shaving their faces. Otherwise every Indian had a beard earlier. It is not that only Indians have a beard. Every man all over the world has a beard; and these fashions of shaving this and leaving that, this may look nice for a while, but after some time these fashions look stupid. Maybe it looks nice when you are young. When you grow old, in great desperation you have to keep that style, though it doesn't fit your face any more. This is simply because you can't change your style. Just like the hair on the head, the moustache becomes your ego, isn't it? Veerappan, the most sought after man by the police, all he has to do is shave off his moustache and come and live in Coimbatore. Nobody will ever find him, but it is not possible for him to do that. Even if his life goes he will not remove his moustache because his entire ego is in it. Just a little bit of hair, but that's where it is. So slowly man gets identified like this and becomes limited. He just becomes a bunch of hair or no hair, whichever way. Once you don't care, it doesn't matter whichever way it is.

Whichever way God has made you, let it be that way. What is the hassle? Women have fewer problems, at least in this regard.

There is also a science behind this. Have you heard that some women, who have never cut their long tresses, if they suddenly tonsure their heads, they will become mentally imbalanced? This is happening as the shaving of hair makes your energy surge upward. If the person is unprepared, it may lead to imbalance. So every fourteenth day of the month — that is one day before the new moon day, which is known as Shivarathri — when the energies naturally tend to swivel upward, people on the spiritual path shave their heads, as their whole life is to allow the upward movement of energy and they have already put in the necessary amount of sadhana.

Questioner: Dear Jaggi, we all love you and trust you. You have left a few of us behind and taught a select few some higher practices which are a lot more intense. Very unknowingly we could have broken the silence by saying one word when absolutely necessary or just by a hand gesture. This was done only because of either the snake or some sickness. Instead of segregating us from those chosen few, you could have thrashed us with a stick. We feel ditched. Why are you so ruthless, Jaggi?

Sadhguru: Many times people who have been around, I've been telling them, if you don't wake up I will use a stick. Maybe I'll have to use a stick. In ancient times the Gurus used to use a stick, simply because there was no receptivity. It was not for any other reason. And you thought that I am so crude that I'll pull up a bamboo stick and beat you. The stick has to be used the way it has to be used depending upon who is in front of me. If there is a donkey in front of me, yes, I'll take the bamboo stick, but for these donkeys that stick won't work. That will only close off things for you.

You felt ditched, but sincerely look at it and see, who ditched whom? Just look at it and see who ditched whom? Some of you are telling me the instructions were not clear. If they were not clear, it was your business to get clarification. Repeatedly it has been told to you – hundreds of times I said, "If something is not clear, please ask." Don't just sit there like a stupid person. Just stand up and ask. What's the problem? Hundreds of times it has been said, isn't it? After everything is over, after thirty days you tell me the instructions were not clear. What nonsense is that? You have to grow out of this kind of nonsense at least. I don't know whether you'll get enlightened or not, but at least you should grow out of this kind of nonsense. I think the instructions were very clear. I made it very, very clear that this silence is extremely important. I said even if you die it is okay; be silent. What more is to be said? I said it does not matter; even if you have to skip your practices, even if you have to forget your practices, your bath, your food, it is okay. Just melt, dissolve into this; but I saw everybody, at the right time, going to the bathroom, doing this, doing that, washing their clothes; all the nonsense possible. If it is necessary, you do it, but don't make that the most important thing. That's not the important thing, whether you have a bath, whether you eat, whether you do the pranayama, that's not the important thing. The important thing was just becoming silent.

I definitely knew, even before I started that about twelve or thirteen people here would break the silence for one reason or another. They are here with grace marks. I know those people. It is okay with me. Those people are okay, but people who are capable of doing things, when they don't do things, I think they have to be beaten one way or another.

If you are not capable, I have all the compassion that's needed for you. I'll sit with you for the rest of my life and see what I can do with you, if you are not capable. If you are capable and still don't walk, you have to be kicked. Otherwise, when will you stand up and walk?

If you do not have legs, I'll never kick you. When you have legs and you don't walk, you have to be kicked. There is no other way. Now the moment you love anyone, you have big expectations about them and in my case expectations are something I will never fulfill. It is so for you also. Love has come into your heart and you have big expectations about me. I am not going to fulfill these. Probably if there is another program like this, if the same group of people come, I really want to do something very drastic. I have been too soft.

Now trust; if you have trust, what is the problem? Whichever way it is, it should be okay, isn't it? Without trust, on this path, you will never go anywhere. If there is no trust you'll never progress even an inch; it doesn't matter what is poured over you. It is not a question of opportunity; it is not a question of teaching. It is just a question of your own receptivity. That's all it is. The opportunity is one hundred percent here all the time. Every moment it is there. You may take the opportunity if you want or take nothing; it is up to you. If somebody doesn't kick you once in a while, I see most of you will never take the opportunity. During the silence, many of you were laughing at the others for your own stupid reasons...

Questioner: But Jaggi, we were just laughing to ourselves!

Sadhguru: I am not against laughter. I love laughter. I really like to hear that lilting sound of laughter. If it is there all the time it's beautiful, but that laughter has to be spontaneous. When it bursts forth from your belly, it is beautiful, but if you laugh at somebody, it is a sickness. It is not out of joy. When you are laughing, if you are pointing at somebody, ridiculing them, there is no joy in your heart. Sincerely look at it. You were perversely doing it. It became a preoccupation for most of you; and when a person seeks support for his laughter, you need to look at what it really is. You are asking for a support, isn't it? Not only are you laughing, but you are also looking at others, seeking support. If you feel like laughing, laugh as much as you want, but why are you asking for support from others? You instigate other people to laugh. Why? Because the ego always needs a support. It cannot exist without support. It is always seeking support in every action that it does. Whatever you do, another ten people should also be doing it, only then you feel okay. Isn't it? This is the nature of the ego; and this laughter is a sickness. It is not joyousness. If laughter is coming out of your ecstasies, it is truly fantastic. I want to hear that laughter. That's the laughter we want. Not this sick, cynical laughter. Like Somu said, a moment came when he and a few others were afraid to even utter the prayer because whatever they said others were going to laugh and make them feel totally lost. Are we here to support each other to grow, or are we here just to pull each other and do some nonsense and go?

The thing is just this. There are two paths. In the Upanishads they say there are two paths in life, only two paths. One is *Shreya* and the other is *Preya*. Shreya means that which is good. Preya means that which is pleasant. So these are the choices you always have in your life about everything. Either you take that path which leads you to the ultimate good, or you take that path which is pleasant right now. It is up to you. Whichever you chose, you tell me. You need to choose between Shreya and Preya, accordingly we will be here.

Questioner: Jaggi, everything has gotten a little heavy on my head. So ...

Sadhguru: If this is too burdensome, go outside and relax. If you want to eat, go to a hotel and eat and then come back. Go trekking, enjoy yourself; if that's all you have come here for, do that. I am not against enjoyment. I am definitely not against enjoyment. I like to enjoy everything. I want everybody to enjoy everything, but tell me, if you go on trekking everyday, if you go on laughing everyday, if you go on cracking the same stupid jokes everyday, can you enjoy them? With the same old jokes making the rounds, after some time you'll quarrel, I am telling you. If you allow this to go too far, with the same jokes somebody will get irritated and he will shout at you. And you'll shout back at him and you'll fight. It is bound to happen, that's where every step is leading you. If you know it is leading the right way, go all the way; but if you know it is not for your well-being or the well-being of another, what is the point in taking that step? What is the point?

Questioner: But Jaggi, a snake came into the toilet and a few participants got very scared.

Sadhguru: Snakes came, scorpions came; now you must understand that snakes and scorpions have not just appeared. They have always been here. You are the one who just came here. You are the intruder, not them. If you have not understood that much as a meditator, it is simply very sad. Why shouldn't a scorpion come? It is his home. You are the person who is destroying his home and doing all this nonsense to him. Haven't you understood that much? Should you scream and yell every time a snake appears? What is it doing to you? Is it attacking you?

Questioner: I have to take action to avoid that. Don't I, Jaggi?

Sadhguru: What action? No action is needed. If you just move, the snake will go away. It will take its own time and go. It is not going to come and jump on you. Don't think any wild animal is going to jump on you. They are not going to. The moment an animal feels your presence, it is going to go away. It will not come towards you. All you have to do is just wait. In five minutes he will go away. They have told you this in the tradition, isn't it? If a snake crosses your path, wait for ten minutes and then go.

Questioner: What if we are not aware of it and in the night we may step on it?

Sadhguru: Yes, you have to be aware of it. If you step on him he will bite you. That's why we have told you to bring a torchlight. If there is a snake inside the toilet what will you do? Tell me.

Questioner: I called you and you took it in your hand and let it go somewhere outside.

Sadhguru: Even that was not necessary. Only because I thought all these people were going to break their silence and also for the sake of the snake, I had to pick him up and I left him a little distance away in the forest. It was simply not necessary. If you had let it, it would have gone away. It will not come where a person is. It will try to avoid you. It is not coming in search of you. All you had to do was just let it pass. We are the intruders, not them. The sounds from the microphone, the noises we make are disturbing them badly. You may not know this, but I really feel that we are disturbing all of them. They may be so confused by all these noises, suddenly there are people; their whole life has become upset. On top of it, you even considered beating the snake. Beating the snake; such a thing should never happen here. Do you understand? Such a thing will never happen here. Don't even get the idea in your mind. You will suffer for it. If people who are around me kill any snake they will suffer. The people around me will suffer if you harm a snake.

Questioner: We just got a little perturbed.

Sadhguru: Okay, but for that, why did you have to break your silence? Why did you have to go there and make sure he was gone? Anyway he will go. I walk without a torch at night. I walk on the path. If there is a snake, if I step on it – it will not happen, but if I step on it and it bites me, it is okay with me. I do have a torch in my room and I even have one here on the dais, but whenever I walk around; I purposely don't take it. If that is how it has to be, let it be. It will not happen. We have enough trust that it will not happen. That is what meditation means. That is what spirituality means. If you are going to flash torches, use your searchlights in order to beat this and that, that's not the way. You have no trust in anything.

How many snakes are there on this ashram land right now? Can you tell me? How many could be there in your imagination? Are they crawling everywhere? Is it so? Some snakes are just passing through; they are not even living here anymore. Since we've started construction, we are hardly seeing any because they have all moved out. Once in a while they pass through, yet even then you want to make a big fuss. Let them come.

If you find a snake under your bed, all you have to do is roll up your bed and wait for him to go. He will go. If he wants to snuggle next to you, he will do that also. Just leave it, nothing is going to happen. Ninety percent of the Indian snakes are not poisonous anyway. Only the cobras, vipers and the banded kraits are poisonous, nothing else, really. All other snakes are not really poisonous. They won't even bite you, but even if they do, nothing will happen. It will feel like an ant or a mosquito bite. It probably won't cause that much pain. You need to see this much, it is not about the snake. It is about your fear of the snake. And why is there so much fear? You tell me. Look into yourself and see why there is fear? If a snake comes, what is the fear? You are the people who are saying you want to dissolve. You say, "We want to melt into the existence; the body is not important, nothing is important." If a snake bites, it is good. In full awareness you can go. In one stroke, your sadhana is over! You are talking about dissolving yourself, you want to make it this time, and you don't want to be reborn again. You want mukthi; that means this body is not important. You want to transcend this body as quickly as possible. So what is the problem?

Questioner: Jaggi, you have been telling us that if we go unaware, we will take one more birth.

Sadhguru: Yes, why should you be unaware? Walk with awareness. That's what silence is about. You have been into about nine days of meditation, everyday about six or seven hours of intense meditation. After that, if you go into silence and then you say, "We did not know that we had to be aware. You did not instruct us." What does it mean to you? You tell me, what does it mean to you? Should it be spelled out? "You must meditate. You must do Samyama. You must watch your breath. You must do this," and on top of it I must tell you, you must be aware as well. Is it so? The thing is not about making somebody feel guilty. The thing is not about punishing somebody. Who am I to punish anybody? I will never punish anybody. I have never felt that way in my life about anybody and I will never punish anybody for anything. It is just that some things need to be done. If it has to be done and if it goes undone, it is a sin. When you have to give something to somebody, whether it is hard or soft, pleasant or unpleasant, if you don't give the right response at the right moment, that is the sin that one commits.

There is one doctor, Patch. He is causing some kind of minor revolution in the medical fraternity in the U.S. He is bringing back what is known as *friendship medicine*. He calls his medicine friendship medicine. He is a doctor and a very wonderful personality. He is six feet-four inches tall and has waist-length hair. He is such a joyous being. You just have to look at him to know what a joyous being he is. Now, they've been running an institute – you can call it a hospital – which is run only by dedicated volunteers. All of them live there. The doctors and all the medical personnel live there. They are not paid anything. All of them work and with whatever donations they get, they live. That's all. There is no salary as such. He is bringing back the whole system of a doctor making house calls. He visits your house. He takes care of you. He gets friendly with you. He will play with the children. He will do many things. The whole thing is to get friendly with people.

He says love is of two kinds: hard love and soft love. He says hard love is needed more than soft love. So hard love is needed. Soft love doesn't always work. Don't think love is always soft. Love can be very ruthless. Just because somebody is ruthless, don't think that there is no love in him. It is not true. A person who doesn't know how to cut off his own arm if it develops gangrene, if he doesn't know how to chop off his own arm without any sense of feeling about it, that man definitely doesn't know what love is.

When you love somebody you will have to do so many things, sometimes very harsh, very, very harsh things! If you don't do that, that person will never grow. That person will never flower. At that moment if you start reacting, it turns negative. The whole situation becomes negative, but if you have known that somebody really has love, that somebody has love and compassion within him, how can you suddenly think that it has left him this moment? Can it go? No. If somebody at any moment has felt a certain person to be truly loving, if it is true, it is not just about a situation. Let's look at it. If you have felt that a certain person is very loving and you have really felt this love at a particular moment, how can you feel that in some other situation this love has gone? How can it go? Where can it go? It is just that it has changed its color because it is needed. You can't just play the same tune all your life and it is not going to work either. It is just not going to work.

I had a similar experience almost fifteen years ago when I started my farm. The bullocks needed to have their hoofs shoed, or what you call ladams fixed. It is done in a very crude way. Sometimes their feet start bleeding. They have such pain. The way they are tied up, put down and the way it is done is too much. Once I did it and I just did not like it. Everybody does it, but it is okay with them. It is their problem, but for the bullocks that were on my farm, I thought this was not needed and they could manage without it. The shoes got worn out and I refused to call the man who fixes these hoof shoes, but he knew when the shoes would wear out and he kept calling me asking for the job. I said no more ladams for my bullocks. The man kept saying it was wrong to leave them without shoes, but I asked him to leave. I found that after eight months my bullocks were suffering very badly. Their feet were all split up. They were in such great pain, and ultimately they couldn't do any work; they were finished. One bullock was finished. The other one, I fixed the ladam and set it right, but the first one was totally finished, just because I hesitated to put on the ladam. Even the nailing bit was okay. As long as they nail on the surface, it is okay. Only if they go deeper it causes pain; but making those bullocks lie upside down, and the sad face they make when they lie down like that – I just could not take that. I realized after eight months that I had ruined them. Even if these bullocks were sold they would only be taken to a butcher because their legs had become useless, and they could not be used for any work. So, that is the difference. If you are always soft, you will ruin many things. You may ruin it totally. If it has to be nailed or not, things will go totally wrong.

Those people, who cannot be sincere about something that they are doing for their own well-being, can never, never be sincere about something that they will do for someone else. If you cannot be sincere for something that you are doing for your well-being, will you do it sincerely for somebody else's well-being? It is impossible because you cannot love anybody more than you love yourself. It is just not possible. You only love people to the extent that you love yourself and respect yourself. If you don't love yourself, if you don't respect yourself, you cannot love others either. If it is just a pretension because everybody has told you that you must be loving, you must be kind. Things will catch up with you, overtake you and you will suffer for this kind of false love. You will pay the price. You will pay a very big price for that. In just imagining that you are loving toward all these people around you, all that you are doing is extracting. They are trying to extract things from you and you are trying to extract things from them. Everybody involved in this game pays a price. Whether it is now or later, they will pay.

So, coming back to Shreya and Preya, whether you want the good path or the pleasant path, whether you want to reach a place which leads to ultimate illumination of your being or you just want to have fun and go, it is up to you. I am not against fun. Fun is perfectly okay, but once the urge has come to reach the highest, settling for second-best is stupid; that's all I can say. For the person for whom the urge has not come, there is no point talking to him about anything else. When you are with him just play, laugh and crack jokes. That's all I do with most people. If I go to Mysore, if I meet my friends, do you think I talk to them about the highest goal in life? I just crack jokes with them. That's all. If I talk about enlightenment, mukthi, do you think it is going to make any sense to them? But once the urge has come into you, you should have enough sense to keep yourself on the track all the time; otherwise, if you are just lukewarm, when?

Anyway, there is no hurry. There is a whole eternity ahead. Don't think the world is going to stop. "But, Nostradamus has said so." So what? Even if the world ends, you will create another one for yourselves. So there is no hurry; but if the urge has come to you that you must get it, don't waste it on stupid things. Make use of it. Use me now, right now. I might not be here tomorrow.

I am telling you, compared to what a person who walks the spiritual path normally goes through, you are going through a deluxe path.

If you don't know this, go and visit ashrams, visit the mountains, see the sadhus and sanyasins. Have a look. Then you will know you are in a deluxe vehicle. I am telling you that in sixteen days, whatever has happened here is quite incredible. It is incredible. Nowhere else have these kinds of things happened in such a short time. Definitely, I am saying that nowhere else will things happen so fast. What is happening right now is just fantastic, but I am not willing to settle only for the fantastic. For what was possible in the last fifteen days, and what we have made possible, it has fallen badly short. Do you understand what I am saying? What has happened is really great, but what is possible in this hall, and to what extent we are making use of it, it badly falls short. Why?

If you go anywhere else you have to put in twelve years of sadhana into asanas and pranayams before you get initiated into meditation. If asanas, pranayams and other practices are sincerely practiced, only then that man is initiated. This is the normal course. Before *kumbhaka* is taught, you must do *nadishuddhi* for six months. This is how it is taught. From day one of you coming here, you are on a certain energy high, simply because of the atmosphere that is created around you. Otherwise it is impossible. See what's happening in the hall. I don't know how many of you are aware of it. If you just go out, stand there for ten minutes and walk back into the hall you will see the difference. Do not waste my time and energy. There was no need for me to have come once again; do not miss this opportunity.

You don't have an idea; you still don't have any idea as to who you are with. You know Jaggi through his speech, you know Jaggi in the classes but you don't know Jaggi, the being. Not yet. When are you going to know? Twelve years from now? In twelve years will you know? It is very sad to know that you can't shut up for just eight to ten days. It is okay if you are not able to do asanas, if you can't bend your body, if you can't hold your breath, but can't you at least shut up?

That's the simplest thing I can ask of you, isn't it? You broke the silence not out of some great emergency or necessity. It is not so. It is just that the mind, the ego, needed an excuse and in so many cunning ways your ego will find a way of establishing itself.

Look at it sincerely. If you become silent, your ego will disappear, but your mind will not allow that to happen. So, that is where the sadhana fits in. That is where the whole point of sadhana is, not falling prey to these tricks. If you are not able to do it by yourself, just stick to the instructions, that's all. They are very simple. It is not that everything is lost. There is still time enough that we can do things if you are really sincere. Even now, I will leave it open, the first fifteen days we've driven you and maybe you feel it is hard, though I feel it is not hard enough; but I am being careful. Many people, either physically, mentally or emotionally, are not capable of taking any more pushing. So, I am treading softly with them but I would like to push much harder. Really, I would like to push everyone much harder.

If you want to walk the pleasant path, we will walk that. For fifteen days we will have real fun; the time of your lives you will have before you go, okay? If you want we'll even get samaras or whatever and just enjoy ourselves. There is nothing wrong. If you have come for that, let us at least fulfill that properly and go. If you have come to enjoy, let us enjoy and go. What is the problem? I am not against it, but I think choosing the second best is stupid and stupidity is not a crime. I accept it. Stupidity is definitely not a crime. It is okay; but when a person says, "I want to grow," and still he sits not doing anything about it, then something has to be done about him. If you clearly express that, "We will grow at our own pace; don't push us," we will go at that pace. That is also perfectly okay with me, but there is something else as to why we are going on like mad people. All those beings who have been in touch with us here or somewhere else, one way or another, I want to see if I can pack all of them up and go.

Not leaving even one person behind, I want to see if that is possible. The opportunity is definitely here.

Do not miss the bus. Personally there was no need for me to have come once again. Even now if I just sit back with either my eyes open or closed, I am complete. Once you come to a certain level of awareness, once you do certain practices, it is very important for that person not to physically drive himself too much. Every yoga *shasthra* says that once you are into certain intense sadhana, not to put in too much work, too much activity and not do things that involve too much movement. When you want to go about doing things actively, it is better to stop your practices. Too much physical and mental activity is not good for a person who is meditative. That's the reason why people, once they reach a certain level, they settle down in one place. It is against my nature to do that. For that, definitely I paid a price, physically and in so many ways. Definitely the body paid a price and I am not saying this is a big price that I have to pay, but it reduces the effectiveness. If I am weak, if I become physically weak, maybe I don't care if I have to die tomorrow morning, but what is the point if it reduces my effectiveness? If whatever I am doing is less effective than what it could be, then the purpose itself is defeated. The very purpose of donning this body is defeated, really. That's the reason I want to slow down. I really want to slow down my pace. It is becoming too much. Right now, my condition is like a large building without a foundation. How long the air is going to hold it up is very hard to say. Something has to be done. Too much running around has to be settled to some extent; otherwise, we'll pay a big price.

There will be no meaning in life for me, if I have to just be here physically and not be capable of doing anything. There will be no point in living. I am not living because I want to live or I like to live, nor is it because of a choice. It is simply because there is something to be finished.

Questioner: Dear Jaggi, the games this mind plays can be very deceptive. How do I get out of them?

Sadhguru: A certain incident happened in Germany a few years ago. There was an accident where a man was hurt. His leg, especially the big toe was totally crushed, and the leg was smashed up a little bit. That toe was causing him terrible pain. He had crashed somewhere on a country road and could not be found for two days. He was just lying there by himself in terrible pain. Eventually, someone found him and took him to the hospital. Only after he arrived at the hospital did the real pain start for him. The doctors and nurses started handling the wounded part and began moving that leg a bit, maybe to check where the exact injury was. As long as a person who has hurt himself stays put, without moving, the pain is very minimal, but once people start meddling with them, the pain becomes multi-fold. This man could no longer bear it and he fainted. He lost his consciousness.

They found that the leg had developed gangrene and they had to remove the foot. They had to remove the whole foot, but when the man regained consciousness, he began to complain of terrible pain in the toe. The nurse first thought that the man was hallucinating as the foot itself had been removed but the man kept repeating that he could not bear it any longer. So the nurse apprised him of his situation and explained that he no longer had that foot, but the man kept saying that his toe was hurting very badly, even though they tried to convince him in many ways. Just try and tell a man who is in severe pain that this is not your body or you are not the body and that all this is maya; he will kick you in the face. When the man kept insisting about the pain in the big toe, the doctors scanned every part of his body to find the source of the pain, and they found it; a nerve which carries impulses from the brain to the toe was still vibrating the same way, even after the toe was gone. The man was actually experiencing pain.

The brain does not really know; whatever the nervous syste. ... ys, it believes. It understands only what the nervous system signals and accordingly it creates the sensation of pain or pleasure. So his nervous system was signaling that the big toe had been hurt and it was sending those messages to the brain. The man was really experiencing pain! This can be done to you.

It is not the mind, but it is the brain that responds to all these things. There is actually no pain it is only because it is connected with the brain that there is pain. If you just cut one nerve, there will be no pain there. If you pinch, burn or cut, do whatever you want, but there will be no pain when you cut off the connecting nerve. A man afflicted with paralysis will never know what you are doing to the affected part. There will be absolutely no feeling. The leg is still very much alive, blood is there, life is there; everything is there. It is just that the connection has been cut. So the pain is not in the leg; the brain creates it.

Pain is just a protective mechanism. If there were no pain in the body you wouldn't have lived this long. You wouldn't know how to protect yourself. It is only because there is pain you become alert when danger is nearby. If there were no pain, you would have destroyed yourself in no time. So pain is there to remind you when something goes wrong, so you can protect yourself. It is simply so because you are not sensitive enough. Unless you are poked, unless pain is created, you won't wake up. So it creates pain.

If the nervous system can do this – where there is no toe it can create pain for you – it can also play a lot more tricks with you right now. It could be, and it is. I am telling you it is very much so. There are so many things here, which you do not sense, that even an animal senses. Suddenly, some of you started noticing these sounds like never before. Somebody walking on this floor that is not paved – a paved floor has more vibrations – it is normally never noticed. Unless a person is running, one never notices it, but now even a gentle walk is reverberating in your ears, isn't it? Even the thumping of the heart, it is going like a big drum beat sometimes. It has always been there, the drum has always been pounding away, but you never heard it before. There must be a lot of discrepancies like this, isn't it? Within yourself you are beginning to feel so many things now that have always been there. This is not happening because you came to the Wholeness program; it has always been there. It is just that you have started noticing them now. You may not be noticing many things that exist and you may be creating so many things that don't exist. That is the truth. You have created much nonsense that does not exist and you have missed much that actually exists. If one has to transcend this, you have to stop relying on these five messengers. Only then will you start seeing something. Silence was just an effort towards that. You keep these five messengers to the minimum. You can't totally cut them off now, but you keep them to the minimum.

When you sit in meditation, you have your hands locked one way or another, you have your eyes shut and to a large extent the function of your ears is also kept to the bare minimum. You don't hear many things and if you hear, somehow it is never absorbed. So like this, one by one, you shut them off and see how you can be without them. The first thing is the eyes, because the eyes play a very important role in doing all kinds of mischief with you. Have you heard about optical illusions, mirages? Sometimes when you are walking on the road you see water gleaming on the surface of the road, at a distance, but when you get closer, it is not there. When you were far away and you noticed that there was water there, could you say there was not? Especially if you were thirsty! You are not dreaming, hallucinating. You are very much alive and awake but you are seeing water with your eyes and when you reach it it is not there. So what do you say for this?

This is the truth with the whole world. It seems to be there but when you really reach out, it is not there. There is something else which is always there, but you have never reached out for it. You are trying to reach out for that which does not exist and make a mess out of your life; but that which is there, nobody is reaching out for that. *"Parame brahmani kopina shaktaha,"* Shankara said. Nobody is reaching out for it. You have to wear your night vision glasses. Just remove these tinted glasses and wear night vision glasses, then you can see something more, a little more; at least what the animals and insects are seeing, you will begin to see. It is time you started seeing something other than what you've been settling down for all your life. Are you beginning to see something else? If you are beginning to see, you know there is something else. Is it for sure or do you think it could still be your imagination?

Questioner: Jaggi, there is something very wonderful happening here. Many things that I did not know existed, I am able to notice very clearly.

Sadhguru: Are you sure? Definitely is there something here which you have not felt before? Definitely is there something? Is it true? Be sure about it. Don't imagine; don't think it could be like this, or like that. Is it definitely, experientially true? So, if you are beginning to see it, is it not worth seeing it totally? Is it worth seeing? If it is worth seeing, we have to go, isn't it? We have to go and see it. Actually, there is nowhere to go. It is not that you have to go anywhere, it is here itself. Because your minds are in such a mess you have to take a walk, you have to go all around just by sitting here you are unable to see it.

Everyday the sun sets and rises the next morning. If it were here all the time you wouldn't have seen it. The sun is so big and shining, but if it were there all the time you wouldn't have seen it. Because it goes down and comes up in the morning you see it. If it were here all the time, you would never have noticed it. That's why you have never seen God, because he is always here. If he had appeared and disappeared, you would have seen him. The problem is, he is always here. That's why you have missed him. So if you want that which is always here now, the mind and senses just will not do. You have to develop a new kind of vision. A blunt knife will not cut through this; a razor sharp mind is needed. It is not that the mind is not needed; the mind is still needed. Don't think ahead of yourself. It will not lead to growth; it only pulls you down. Never think ahead of your own step. It is not going to work.

Let us just look at it this way. Now you are here but you want to reach the Himalayas. Don't start thinking in terms of how to climb the mountain and all that you should do there. First see how to wear your boots. If you start hallucinating or dreaming right now, I can tell you, people are not going to go anywhere. I have always been impulsive, if that is the word I can use for my nature. Around midnight if I felt like going to Goa, within ten to fifteen minutes I would have packed my bags and started off on my bike!

There were times when I used to call my friends. They would all agree to go but then they start planning the event. When to go, what to take, how long to stay and all the other details. Discussions would go on for hours. Someone would come up with excuses like, today there is an examination, a sick mother, some engagement, and so on. They would keep altering the dates. I just used to sit listening to them and at the end of it I would just tell them, "It is fine to go during the summer holidays or whenever, but I am going now. Maybe, if you really go during summer vacation, I will join you, but anyway I am going today." Let me tell you, these people will never go, whether they are going to some place or seeking a spiritual path. There are millions of people who are talking spiritual, thinking spiritual, but never take a single step in their life. There are millions like that. Do you want to be one of them?

Once the ego settles into pleasure and comfort, it doesn't move out of it. Whatever you try to do, it just comes back and settles there. You just give your body one kind of comfort just for fifteen days and see how it will demand that comfort again and again! During meditation, just because you complained of back pain I said you could use a backrest. See how difficult it becomes to take away that backrest after that. It is not just the body discomfort; the ego is like that. It is always like that. If you give it any comfort, it will not budge. In so many cunning ways it will try to demand that and get that, unless you really stand up and cut it down, or if somebody else cuts it down for you. We are building the meditation hall without walls. When Spanda Hall comes, there will be no walls, no backrests!

The ego is like that. You give it anything and it will use it as a support and bloat. That is its nature. Either it has to be brutally cut down or you have to bypass it totally. Right now, this path of doing sadhana is to brutally chop it off; you can't chop it off once and for all. You have to chop it step by step. If you want to bypass it, you hand over your will to me. Then there will be no problem. It will be solved in one stroke. It is not like the will you make where you bequeath your belongings to someone. Here is my will, take it; that is not the way. Then how to do it? That is the problem. When you want to walk this path, there is no *how*. Come, let us eat.

Unmaking

Those who feed upon the written word
Claim to know the limits of the boundless beyond

In the realm of the beyond
Clueless is the scholarly dud

The gloriousness of the written word
Is but the excreta of the deluded mind

If in you a raging longing I have made
Don't you quench it with the delusions of the mind

Allow yourself to be unmade
Into the vastness of the beyond you will be made

– Sadhguru

Isha Foundation

Isha Foundation, founded by Sadhguru Jaggi Vasudev, is a charitable trust registered in India and a non-profit, tax-exempt corporation established in the USA. This 100% voluntary organization has over 100 centers in India, the United States and other parts of the world.

Isha Foundation practices the ancient principle that the body is the temple of the spirit and that good health is fundamental to spiritual development. Yoga is communicated on an experiential level and encourages an opening of the heart and consciousness to new dimensions of feeling, thinking and living. Isha Yoga programs provide a supportive atmosphere in which people can make the change to a healthier lifestyle and learn how to improve their relationships and level of self-fulfillment.

Specialized yoga programs are conducted for schools, hospitals, government offices, corporations, and sports organizations such as the Indian national hockey team. After a pioneering program for life-termers at the Coimbatore Central Prison, Isha Yoga programs were conducted in several central prisons of South India at the request of the Inspector General of Prisons. For the first time ever in the United States prisons, Sadhguru conducted Isha Yoga programs in several state prisons of Pennsylvania. Working mostly with life-termers, this program, **"Inner Transformation for the Imprisoned"**, has transformed many hardcore criminals into sage-like beings.

Isha Foundation renders community health services for the regional population in coordination with hospitals, colleges and social organizations. On a regular basis, the foundation conducts medical camps to provide general health checkups, and eye camps for the economically disadvantaged. Isha Foundation also operates a yogic hospital at the Isha Yoga Center to treat chronic ailments using yogic and natural methods.

Sadhguru's unique program, **"Action for Rural Rejuvenation"**, networks like-minded individuals and organizations with the villages to revitalize the rural society, thereby strengthening the very roots of the nation. This program aims at rekindling the spirit of the rural population by establishing a library, computer center, *yogashala*, gymnasium and a herbal garden in every village. Restoring indigenous and local healthcare traditions, afforestation and empowerment of women also form an integral part of this program.

Universality has been the bedrock of Isha Foundation. **Sadhguru Jaggi Vasudev** works among the world's pre-eminent spiritual leaders and institutions to foster peace, global understanding and international cooperation. As a delegate to the **United Nations Millennium Peace Summit** and a member of the **World Council of Religious Leaders,** Sadhguru works tirelessly to impart the goals established therein through his grass-root level activities and speaking engagements around the world.

Isha Foundation administers the Isha Yoga Center, located on 50 acres at the foothills of the Velliangiri Mountains. Surrounded by thick forests, it is a part of the Nilgiri Biosphere, a reserve forest with abundant wildlife. Isha Yoga Center is a powerful spiritual *sthana,* offering all aspects of yoga - *bhakti, jnana, karma* and *kriya* - under one roof and re-establishes the Guru-shishya paramparya (Master-disciple relationship) in the true lineage of legendary masters.

The Yoga Center also houses a large residential facility, the **Dhyanalinga** - a Multi-Religious Temple and the **Spanda Hall** - a 64,000 sq. ft. meditation hall and program facility. The Center provides a supportive environment in which people can shift to healthier lifestyles, improve their relationships, seek a higher level of self-fulfillment, and realize their full potential. The **Yogic Hospital** of the Center employs the powerful practices taught in the Isha Yoga programs and other yogic and natural methods to provide relief to chronic ailments like cancer, heart, nervous diseases, spinal and other disorders which are beyond the scope of modern medicine.

Financial contributions towards the activities of the Foundation may be made in favor of **Isha Foundation**. Such donations are exempt from income tax under section 80(G) of Income Tax Act.

How to Get There

Isha Yoga Center is located 30 kms west of Coimbatore at the foothills of Velliangiri Mountains, part of the Nilgiris Biosphere. Coimbatore, a major industrial city in South India, is well connected by air, rail and road. All major airlines operate regular flights into Coimbatore from Chennai, Delhi, Mumbai and Bangalore. Train services are available from all the major cities in India. Regular bus and taxi services are also available from Coimbatore to Isha Yoga Center.

Limited accommodation is available and visitors may contact Isha Yoga Center for availability.

Isha Foundation

15, Govindasamy Naidu Layout, Singanallur,
Coimbatore - 641 005, INDIA
Telephone: 091-422-2319655   **Telefax:** 091-422-2319654
Email: yogacentre@ishafoundation.org

Isha Yoga Center

Velliangiri Foothills, Semmedu (P.O.), Coimbatore - 641 114, INDIA
Telephone: 091-422-2651298/141
Email: ishayoga@eth.net

Isha Foundation, Inc.

10 Belcaro Circle, Nashville, Tennessee - 37215, USA
Telephone: 1-615-665-3812   **Telefax:** 1-615-665-8326
Email: info@ishafoundation.org

For worldwide program information: **www.ishafoundation.org**

Other Isha Publications

☞ Dhyanalinga - The Silent Revolution
This richly illustrated book presents a deeper definition of yoga and its metaphysical essence. It culminates in the presentation of the Dhyanalinga, the pinnacle of a yogi's journey.

☞ Encounter the Enlightened - Conversations with the Master
This book is also available in Tamil, Telugu and French.

☞ Dhyanalinga Temple - The distilled essence of yogic science
An overall view about the Dhyanalinga Multi Religious temple. This book provides a look at the science of its making and the tremendous possibility it presents to all spiritual seekers. Also available in Tamil.

☞ Eternal Echoes - The Sacred sounds through the mystic
A compelling and provocative collection of poetry by mystic, master, and yogi, Sadhguru Jaggi Vasudev. The Master's mystical experiences form the bedrock from which spring forth these divine verse of bliss, playfulness and the boundless possibility of inner experience. As is his life, these poems are an offering in an attempt to help us find our way.

☞ **Mystic's Musings**
This is a book for the thirsty. It is a glimpse of an oasis for someone willing to rise above the intellect and move towards the fountainhead of knowing through the wisdom of an enlightened master.

Here, Sadhguru Jaggi Vasudev, a mystic of unfathomable proportions, intrigues the reader as he dwells upon life, death, rebirth, suffering, karma and the journey of the Self.

☞ Uyirrenum Poo Malarum
This book is a biographical account of Sadhguru's life and works. Available only in Tamil.

☞ Forest Flower
A bilingual (English-Tamil) quaterly newsletter featuring the Masters discourses and contributions from meditators worldwide.

Glossary

Aatvarang   Lit. *white, the eigth color.*

Advaitha   Lit. *nonduality.* Referring to the interconnectedness of everything.

Agna chakra   Lit. command center. The sixth of the seven major energy centers of the human body. Physically, located between the eyebrows, it is also known as the 'third eye'. Derives its name from the fact that it is an able receiver of the Guru. Hence, it is also called Guru-chakra.

Aham Bhramhasmi   Lit. *I am the Bhramhan.* The basic tenet of Vedanta.

Aham   Lit. *'I'.* Referring to the conditional ego.

Amavasya   The new moon – the darkest night of the month. The planetary positions of the earth and moon have long been made use of by spiritual seekers in India for special spiritual practices.

Anatma   Lit. the soul-less one.

Anithya   Lit. *impermanent.*

Appa   father

Arjuna   Great epic hero to whom Krishna delivered the Divine message of the Bhagavad Gita.

Asana   Lit. *physical posture.* Generally referring to yoga postures, or postures that lead one's energies to liberation. The third of the eight limbs of yoga.

Ashtanga   Lit. *eight limbs.*

Atma   Individual spirit, the supreme soul or *Bhrahman.*

Bhagavad Gita	A dialogue between Lord Krishna and his chief disciple Arjuna, on the battlefield of the Mahabharatha. One of the most sacred teachings of the Hindus.
Bhajan	Devotional song. Individual or group singing of devotional songs, hymns and chants.
Bhaktha	A devotee, one who has surrendered to the Divine.
Bhakthi	Lit. *devotion.* Refers to the spiritual path of self-realization through love and devotion. Intense desire and will for union with one's chosen deity.
Bhava	Sensation or feeling.
Bhava Spandana program	Bhava means sensation or feeling, Spandana means to resonate, emphatic vibration. This four day high intensity residential program is offered as a part of Isha Yoga programs. It is an opportunity to raise one's energy to a higher pitch in the presence of Sadhguru, where participants have the possibility to experience Einstein's theory of relativity: $E=mc^2$, higher levels of consciousness that take one to an experience beyond the limitations of body and mind.
Bhramha	The creator in the classic trinity of Hinduism, the other two gods being Vishnu and Shiva.
Bhramhachari	Lit. *bhramhan* means Divine and *charya* means path. One who is on the path of the Divine, who has realized that the source of joy is within. Usually refers to one who has formally been initiated into monkhood through a certain energy process.
Bhramhacharya	The path of the divine. A life of celibacy and studentship on the path of spirituality; the first of four stages of life as per the *Varnashrama Dharma.*

Bhramhin	Member of the priestly Hindu caste, which is the highest in the Indian caste system.
Bhramhopadesham	The traditional initiation of young Bhramin boys into the spiritual path
Bodhidharma	One of the disciples of Buddha.
Buddhi	Faculty of discrimination, analysis, logical and rational thought; intellect.
Chakra	Lit. *wheel.* One hundred and twelve plus two points in the energy body where the pranic bodies or channels meet in triangular configuration. Of these, seven are considered foundational. They are main points or junctions of confluence of the pranic nadis or channels in the energy body. Each chakra has a distinct color, form, sound and quality.
Charwaka	Atheist.
Coimbatore	Closest major city to Isha Yoga Center, in Tamil Nadu, a South Indian state.
Dana	Lit. *generosity, giving;* a gift
Darshana	Lit. *vision.*
Dharana	Maintaining mental focus. The fifth of the eight limbs of yoga.
Dhyana	Meditative state. The sixth of the eight limbs of Yoga.
Dhyanalinga	A powerful energy form consecrated exclusively for the purpose of meditation at Isha Yoga Center.
Garbagriha	The innermost chamber, or sanctum sanctorum of a Hindu temple. It is usually a small room, usually made of granite stone, that only priests can enter. Esoterically it represents the cranial chamber
Gautama	Referring to the Buddha.

Gnana	Knowledge, perception, discrimination. One of the four kinds of yogas - Bhakthi, Gnana, Karma and Kriya. Mere accumulation of learning is not gnana.
Goa	An Indian state on the western coast known for its pristine beaches.
Goraknath	A great spiritual Master.
Grihastha	A householder, the second of the four stages of life as per varnashrama classification of the stages of life.
Guru-Shishya paramparya	Master-disciple relationship
Hatha yoga	Physical form of yoga involving different bodily postures and practices. Used as both a purificatory and preparatory step for meditation and higher dimensions of spiritual experience. 'Ha' is sun or heat; 'tha' is moon or cool. Hatha is to balance the positive and negative energies within the energy body.
Isha	Formless Divine energy. Also the name chosen by Sadhguru for the foundation created to offer a spiritual possibility to humankind.
Janaka	An ancient Indian King and an enlightened disciple of Sage Ashtavakra, Janaka was known for his extraordinary wisdom.
Jilebi	Popular Indian sweet soaked in sugar syrup.
Kailasa	Lit. crystalline or abode of bliss. Here referring to the four-faced Himalayan peak in Western Tibet; the earthly abode of Lord Siva. It is an important pilgrimage destination for all Hindus, as well as for Tibetan Buddhists.
Kama	Lit. *desire.*

Kanphat	A spiritual sect in Northern India, who are so called because of their tradition of piercing their ears.
Koorma	Lit. *complete*
Kosha	Lit. *sheath;* vessel, layer.
Kriya	Lit. *act, rite.* Refers to certain class of yogic practices. Inward action as opposed to karma external action.
Krodha	Lit. *aversion.*
Kumbhaka	Breath retention during yogic practice, especially in the practice of pranayama.
Kundalini	Lit. *serpent power.* Cosmic energy which is depicted as a snake coiled at the base of the spine (Muladhara chakra) and that eventually, through the practice of yoga, rises up the sushumna nadi. As it rises, the kundalini awakens each successive chakra, until it reaches the Sahasrar. The manifested Kundalini becomes Kula, the all-transcending light of consciousness.
Kurukshetra	An extensive plain near Delhi, scene of the great war between the Kauravas and Pandavas, as it took place in the Mahabharatha.
Linga	Lit. *the first form, the primordial form.* An energy form consecrated for worship, generally associated with Lord Shiva.
Mahavir	Considered as the founder of the Jaina religion, he lived in the fifth century BC. A contemporary of Gautama Buddha.
Maitreyi	An accomplished vedic scholar and one of the few women spiritual Masters during the times of King Janaka.
Mala	Garland or necklace.

Marga	Lit. *way or path.*
Maya	Delusion, the veil of illusion which conceals one's true nature, or conceals reality. It is used in contrast with the absolute reality, which is dondual.
Mudra	Lit. *seal.* Referring to certain hand gestures or positions used during yogic practices to direct the prana through the body.
Mukthi	Release, liberation, final absolution of the Self from the chain of death and rebirth.
Mysore	South Indian city where Sadhguru was born.
Nadi	Channel through which the life force or prana flows through in the energy body. It is said there are 72,000 nadis interconnecting the chakras. The three main nadis are named Ida, Pingala and Sushumna.
Naga	Lit. *serpent.* Symbol of the kundalini coiled at the base of the spine; one of the secondary types of life forces *(prana).*
Namakkal	A South Indian Town.
Nethi	A way of cleansing oneself of illusions or wrong identity.
Niyama	Lit. *Self-discipline.* The second of the eight limbs of yoga.
Nostradamus	French physician and astrologer who lived in the 16th century. Famous for his encrypted doomsday predictions of future events esp. that the world would come to an end during 2000 A.D.
Paramahamsa	Lit. *supreme swan,* a honorific term applied to an adept who enjoys liberation or enlightenment.
Paramparya	Lit. *from one to the other,* tradition.

Glossary

Pariharam	Relief.
Parikrama	Outer periphery of a temple.
Parivararjaka	A wandering monk, whose sadhana is to continuously travel by foot to various places of pilgrimage, living on alms and not remaining in the same place for more than a short duration
Pooja	Worship, appropriate procedure for invocation of the Divine.
Pournami	The full moon.
Prana	Fundamental life force; vital energy. Prana in the human body moves in the pranamaya kosha as five primary life currents known as *vayus* or vital airs: prana (outgoing breath), apana (incoming breath), vyana (retained breath), udana (ascending breath) and samana (equalizing breath).
Pranayama	The science of gaining control over one's energies. A powerful yogic practice that uses certain breathing techniques to generate and direct the flow of prana in the human body.
Pranic	Of prana.
Pratyahara	Lit. *withdrawal,* or sensory inhibition. The fourth of the eight limbs of yoga.
Preya	That which is plesant.
Rama	The hero of the epic Ramayana, believed to be an incarnation of Lord Vishnu.
Ramakrishna Paramahamsa	A mid-nineteenth century spiritual Master who lived mostly in Calcutta. A devotee of Goddess Kali, he frequently went into ecstatic states of samadhi. One of his best known disciples is Swami Vivekananda, who established and propagated the Ramakrishna Order which has a world wide following.

Ramana Maharshi	Early twentieth century spiritual Master who lived in the hills of Tiruvanamalai near Chennai, in South India. His teachings revolve around self inquiry. He is believed to have enlightened not only humans, but also a cow, a deer and a crow.
Rishi	Lit. *seer.* An enlightened being or mystic who sees beyond the limits of ordinary perception. In the Vedic age, rishis lived in forests and mountain retreats, either alone or with disciples.
Rudhraksha	Sacred beads, seeds of a tree found mostly in the Himalayas. Also known as the tears of Lord Shiva, the ascetic, rudhraksha is known to have many medicinal and transcendental qualities. A rudhraksha mala is one of the only few possessions of an Indian spiritual seeker.
Rupa	Lit. *form.*
Sadhana	Spiritual practices which are used as a means to realization.
Sadhu	A spiritual seeker.
Sahasranama	Ritualistic chanting of the various names of the lord. Here Sadhguru refers to abusing a person with many names.
Samadhi	State of equanimity, a merging of the subject and the object. The eigth of the eight limbs of yoga.
Sanyas	On the path of spirituality; the fourth of four stages of life as per the Varnashrama Dharma. The withdrawal from the world in search for Self Realization.
Sanyasi	An ascetic; a renunciate. The life, way and traditions of one who has irrevocably renounced worldy possessions and relationships to seek Divine awakening, Self Realization and spiritual upliftment

of humanity through the sharing of his wisdom, his peace, his devotion and his illumination.

Sampradaya	Tradition
Samyama	A confluence of the states of: dharana, dhyana and samadhi. Referring to the eight day meditation camp offered by Sadhguru where one is transported to explosive states of meditativeness. Held at Isha Yoga Center, this program is a possibility for those who are willing to shed lifetimes of karma and experience deep states of meditativeness, Samyama, and samadhi.
Sanathana	Timeless, eternal, everlasting
Sathsang	Lit. *in communion with Truth*, a congregation of seekers.
Savu	Lit. *death*.
Shankara	Lit. *the benevolent*, one of the many names of Shiva. Also refers to Adi Shankaracharya, the celebrated ninth century CE teacher of Advaita Vedanta, and the founder of four monastic orders. He lived only 32 years, travelling all over India and transformed the Hindu world in that time.
Shankaran Pillai	A common South Indian name. Refers to the hero in many of Sadhguru's jokes. He is usually a frail man who's wife is very large.
Shasthra	Lit. *teaching*. Sacred text.
Shishya	Lit *pupil or disciple*. One who has submitted himself to a teacher or a Guru.
Shiva	Lit. *that which is not*. The Great Lord. The destroyer in the trinity.
Shivarathri	Night of Shiva.

Shoonya Lit. *emptiness.* A unique form of meditation offered by Sadhguru in a live form in the Isha Yoga programs.

Shoonyaka Breath retention during yogic practice, especially in the practice of pranayama.

Shreya That which is good

Shri Short for Shrimath, a respectful way of address.

Shruthis Lit. *revelation.* Vedic litrature pertaining to unchanging, absolute reality.

Shuddhi Lit. *purification* A basic component of spiritual life.

Shudra Member of the fourth and lowest Hindu caste, that of menial laborers.

Sindhu A Region in North India and present Pakistan

Smruthis Remembered knowledge. Vedic scriptures pertaining to social situations, and code of conduct.

Spanda Hall A 64,000 sq. ft. meditation facility at Isha Yoga Center.

Spandana To resonate, empathic vibration.

Surya namaskar Lit. *Sun salutation.* Referring to a powerful practice that results in many benefits.

Tamil Nadu South Indian State.

Tantra The science of using mantra, the sound and yantra, the form. Refers to an esoteric Indian spiritual tradition.

Tantric Of tantra, a practitioner of tantra..

Tathwa Element, as in the five elements; principle or philosophy.

Thamasha Colloquial term in Hindi for fun, practical joke or prank. Also a certain theater form in North India.

Tirupur An industrial town in South India.

Udaya	Sunrise.
Vaasthu	Name of a mythical character, also the code of traditional architecture followed in India.
Vada	A popular South Indian savory made of ground lentils and deep fried.
Vanaprastha	Forest-dweller. The third of the four stages of life according to the *Varnashrama Dharma*.
Varnashrama Dharma	Referring to the texts describing the social structure of the four classes, the castes and the four stages of life.
Velliangiri Mountains	A tall peak in the Nilgiris Bio-sphere 30 kms from Coimbatore, Traditional pilgrimage spot. Also known to be the abode af many siddas and seers, rich in wildlife and medicinal plants. Isha Yoga Center is located at the foothills of these Mountains.
Visalakshi	Name of a Goddess or a woman
Vivekananda	The best known of the disciples of Ramakrishna, Vivekananda is often considered as a role model for Indian youth.
Yaga	A vedic ritual involving fire
Yagna	Sacrifice, one of the main pillars of the Vedic ritual system.
Yagnavalkya	Vedic scholar in the court of king Janaka.
Yama	The Lord of Death, the ruler of the nether world. Riding a buffalo, his vehicle, Yama visits a person at the time of death. Also means *moral observance*, one of the eight limbs of yoga.
Yantra	Lit. *form.*